CALORIE
COUNTER

This edition published 1994 by
Diamond Books
77–85 Fulham Palace Road
Hammersmith, London W6 8JB

First published 1984
Third edition 1991

© HarperCollins Publishers 1991

ISBN 0261 66324 0

Printed and bound in Great Britain by
BPCC Paperbacks Ltd

CONTENTS

PREFACE

This calorie counter reflects the changes that have occurred in the British diet over a surprisingly short period of time. More of the ethnic foods which have done so much to enliven our diet are now included, and many more of the products listed are designed to cater for an increasingly health-conscious age.

INTRODUCTION

Diets come and diets go, but still the most reliable way of losing weight—or of maintaining a sensible weight—is by counting Calories.

The energy the body needs to survive is generated from the nutrients—carbohydrates, fats, proteins and vitamins—in the food we eat. When we consume in this form more energy than our bodies use up in our daily life, then we put on weight. About half the energy used up by the body in a day is needed to enable it just to survive—this is the basal metabolic rate—while the other half is taken up by activity, by work or play. Generally speaking, people who do more need more and can consume more. A miner expends more energy than an office worker, a squash player more than a golfer. In the following pages there are tables which give the average energy used in a day doing certain jobs, and the energy used in an hour taking part in certain activities. But, for reasons still not perfectly understood by scientists, not everyone uses up the same amount of energy doing the same job or playing the same game; we each have to determine our own energy needs and decide for ourselves how much food energy we need to consume.

Also included among the tables are those for desirable weights according to height and frame. It has been calculated that one pound of body fat is equal to 3500 Calories, so for every pound required to be lost, 3500 Calories must come out of the diet—but not all at once! Anyone considering trying to lose a lot of weight should consult their doctor, and those just keen not to overdo it should remember that the best way to lose weight—or not to put it on—is to eat a sensible diet and to eat in moderation. Useful guidance on diets in general is given in the Collins **Gem Guide to Healthy Eating;** the Collins **Gem Guide to Food Additives** also provides very helpful information on food content.

The most convenient form of measurement of the energy value of foods for non-scientific use is the kilocalorie, or Calorie, which is what is given here. The foods are listed in *bold roman type* in alphabetical order in the left-hand column of each page; the name of the manufacturer (of branded foods) is given in the second column; and the energy values are given per 100 grams (3.5 ounces) in the third column. Where at all possible and available, in the last column Calorie values per portion or pack are given. If such information is not available, then the Calorie value per ounce has been given. Unbranded foods and Calorie values listed in **bold italic type** have been obtained with permission from *The Composition of Foods* (fourth edition), published by Her Majesty's Stationery Office. Further information on food composition is available in the fourth edition and in the supplements to it, which are being produced in a collaboration between the Ministry of Agriculture, Fisheries and Food and the Royal Society of Chemistry.

The publishers are grateful to all the manufacturers who gave information on their products. The list of foods included is as up to date as it was possible to make it, but it should be remembered that new food products are frequently put on the market and existing ones withdrawn, so it has not been possible to include everything. If you cannot find a particular food here, you can still, however, obtain a guideline figure by finding an equivalent product from a different manufacturer.

Weights and measures

Imperial to Metric

1 ounce (oz) = 28.35 grams (g)
1 pound (lb) = 453.60 grams (g)
1 fluid ounce (fl. oz) = 29.57 millilitres (ml)
1 pint = 0.568 litre

Metric to Imperial

100 grams (g) = 3.53 ounces (oz)
1 kilogram (kg) = 2.2 pounds (lb)
100 millilitres (ml) = 3.38 fluid ounces (fl. oz)
1 litre = 1.76 pints

Average daily Calorie expenditure, by occupation

Men		Women	
Sedentary			
Retired	2300	Elderly	
Office workers	2500	housewives	1980
Lab technicians	2850	Middle-aged	
Drivers, pilots,		housewives	2075
teachers, journalists,			
professional people,			
shop workers	2700		
Building workers	3000		
Moderately active			
University students	2950	Lab technicians	2125
Light industry,		Shop workers	2250
railway workers,		Univ. students	2300
postmen, joiners,		Factory workers	2320
farm workers	3000	Office workers	2200
Very active			
Steel workers	3250	Bakery workers, some	
Some farm workers	3450	factory workers	2500
Army cadets and			
recruits	3500		
Miners, forestry			
workers, dockers, some			
building workers	3600		

Average hourly Calorie requirement, by activity:

	Women	Men
Bowling	207	270
Cycling: moderate	192	256
hard	507	660
Dancing: ballroom	264	352
Domestic work	153	200
Driving	108	144
Eating	84	112
Gardening: active	276	368
Golf	144	192
Ironing	120	160
Office work: active	120	160
Rowing	600	800
Running: moderate	444	592
hard	692	900
Sewing and knitting	84	112
Sitting at rest	84	112
Skiing	461	600
Squash	461	600
Swimming: moderate	230	300
hard	480	640
Table tennis	300	400
Tennis	336	448
Typing	108	144
Walking: moderate	168	224

Desirable weights of adults

Small frame: men and women
Height without shoes

	Men						Women			
ft in	m	st lb	st lb	kgs		st lb	st lb	kgs		
4 8	1.42					6 8–	7 0	41.7–44.5		
4 9	1.45					6 10–	7 3	42.6–45.8		
4 10	1.47					6 12–	7 6	43.6–47.2		
4 11	1.50					7 1–	7 9	44.9–48.5		
5 0	1.52					7 4–	7 12	46.3–49.9		
5 1	1.55	8 0–	8 8	50.8–54.4		7 7–	8 1	47.6–51.3		
5 2	1.58	8 3–	8 12	52.2–56.3		7 10–	8 4	49 –52.6		
5 3	1.60	8 6–	9 0	53.5–57.2		7 13–	8 7	50.4–54		
5 4	1.63	8 9–	9 3	54.9–58.5		8 2–	8 11	51.7–55.8		
5 5	1.65	8 12–	9 7	56.3–60.3		8 6–	9 1	53.5–57.6		
5 6	1.68	9 2–	9 11	58.1–62.1		8 10–	9 5	55.3–59.4		
5 7	1.70	9 6–	10 1	59.9–64		9 0–	9 9	57.2–61.2		
5 8	1.73	9 10–	10 5	61.7–65.8		9 4–	10 0	59 –63.5		
5 9	1.75	10 0–	10 10	63.5–68		9 8–	10 4	60.8–65.3		
5 10	1.78	10 4–	11 0	65.3–69.9		9 12–	10 8	62.6–67.1		
5 11	1.80	10 8–	11 4	67.1–71.7						
6 0	1.83	10 12–	11 8	69 –73.5						
6 1	1.85	11 2–	11 13	70.8–75.8						
6 2	1.88	11 6–	12 3	72.6–77.6						
6 3	1.91	11 10–	12 7	74.4–79.4						

Desirable weights of adults

Medium frame: men and women
Height without shoes

ft	in	m	Men st lb	st lb	kgs	Women st lb	st lb	kgs
4	8	1.42				6 12–	7 9	43.6–48.5
4	9	1.45				7 0–	7 12	44.5–49.9
4	10	1.47				7 3–	8 1	45.8–51.3
4	11	1.50				7 6–	8 4	47.2–52.6
5	0	1.52				7 9–	8 7	48.5–54
5	1	1.55	8 6–	9 3	53.5–58.5	7 12–	8 10	49.9–55.3
5	2	1.58	8 9–	9 7	54.9–60.3	8 1–	9 0	51.3–57.2
5	3	1.60	8 12–	9 10	56.3–61.7	8 4–	9 4	52.6–59
5	4	1.63	9 1–	9 13	57.6–63.1	8 8–	9 9	54.4–61.2
5	5	1.65	9 4–	10 3	59 –64.9	8 12–	9 13	56.3–63.1
5	6	1.68	9 8–	10 7	60.8–66.8	9 2–	10 3	58.1–64.9
5	7	1.70	9 12–	10 12	62.6–69	9 6–	10 7	59.9–66.7
5	8	1.73	10 2–	11 2	64.4–70.8	9 10–	10 11	61.7–68.5
5	9	1.75	10 6–	11 6	66.2–72.6	10 0–	11 1	63.5–70.3
5	10	1.78	10 10–	11 11	68 –74.8	10 4–	11 5	65.3–72.1
5	11	1.80	11 0–	12 2	69.9–77.1			
6	0	1.83	11 4–	12 7	71.7–79.4			
6	1	1.85	11 8–	12 12	73.5–81.7			
6	2	1.88	11 13–	13 3	75.8–83.9			
6	3	1.91	12 4–	13 8	78 –86.2			

Desirable weights of adults

Large frame: men and women
Height without shoes

	Men				Women		
ft in	m	st lb	st lb	kgs	st lb	st lb	kgs
4 8	1.42				7 6–	8 7	47.2–54
4 9	1.45				7 8–	8 10	48.1–55.3
4 10	1.47				7 11–	8 13	49.4–56.7
4 11	1.50				8 0–	9 2	50.8–58.1
5 0	1.52				8 3–	9 5	52.2–59.4
5 1	1.55	9 0–	10 1	57.2–64	8 6–	9 8	53.5–60.8
5 2	1.58	9 3–	10 4	58.5–65.3	8 9–	9 12	54.9–62.6
5 3	1.60	9 6–	10 8	59.9–67.1	8 13–	10 2	56.7–64.4
5 4	1.63	9 9–	10 12	61.2–69	9 3–	10 6	58.5–66.2
5 5	1.65	9 12–	11 2	62.6–70.8	9 7–	10 10	60.3–68
5 6	1.68	10 2–	11 7	64.4–73	9 11–	11 0	62.1–69.9
5 7	1.70	10 7–	11 12	66.7–75.3	10 1–	11 4	64 –71.7
5 8	1.73	10 11–	12 2	68.5–77.1	10 5–	11 9	65.8–73.9
5 9	1.75	11 1–	12 6	70.3–78.9	10 9–	12 0	67.6–76.2
5 10	1.78	11 5–	12 11	72.1–81.2	10 13–	12 5	69.4–78.5
5 11	1.80	11 10–	13 2	74.4–83.5			
6 0	1.83	12 0–	13 7	76.2–85.7			
6 1	1.85	12 5–	13 12	78.5–88			
6 2	1.88	12 10–	14 3	80.7–90.3			
6 3	1.91	13 0–	14 8	82.6–92.5			

Daily Calories for maintenance of desirable weight

Calculated for a moderately active life. If you are very active add 50 Calories; if your life is sedentary take away 75 Calories.

| Weight | | | Age 18–35 | | Age 35–55 | | Age 55–75 | |
st	lb	kgs	Men	Women	Men	Women	Men	Women
7	1	44.9		1700		1500		1300
7	12	49.9	2200	1850	1950	1650	1650	1400
8	9	54.9	2400	2000	2150	1750	1850	1550
9	2	58.1		2100		1900		1600
9	6	59.9	2550	2150	2300	1950	1950	1650
10	3	64.9	2700	2300	2400	2050	2050	1800
11	0	69.9	2900	2400	2600	2150	2200	1850
11	11	74.8	3100	2550	2800	2300	2400	1950
12	8	79.8	3250		2950		2500	
13	5	84.8	3300		3100		2600	

A

Product	Brand	Calories per 100g/ 100ml	Calories per oz/ pack/ portion
Abalone, canned, drained		145	41
ABC letters	Bassett's	351	100
Ackee, canned		151	43
Aduki beans: *see Beans*			
Advocaat		65 per 1/6 gill	
Aero:			
milk chocolate medium	Rowntree Mackintosh	521	252 per bar
orange medium	Rowntree Mackintosh	527	255 per bar
peppermint medium	Rowntree Mackintosh	527	255 per bar
After Dinner mints	Co-op	460	35 per mint
After Eight mints	Rowntree Mackintosh	410	35 per mint
Agar, dried		312	88
All-bran		273	77
All-Bran	Kellogg's	249	71
All butter biscuits	St Michael Tesco	481 482	136 137
All butter cherry cake	Safeway	311	88
All butter cherry genoa cake	St Michael	327	93
All butter coconut cake	Safeway	382	107

All amounts given per 100g/100ml unless otherwise stated

Product	Brand	Kcal	Protein	CHO	Fat	Dietary Fibre
Blueberry Muffin	California Cake & Cookie	326	5.6	42.6	15.7	1.8
Caramel Wafer per biscuit	Tunnock's	454	4.6	68.0	20.1	
		120	1.2	18.0	5.3	
Cheese, Onion & Tomato Flan per flan	Menumaster	750	24	56.0	63.0	
Chocolate Swiss Roll	Lyons Cakes	370	4.5	53.9	16.6	1.2
Hibran bread per medium slice	Vibe	219	12.6	35.0	3.2	6.8
		72	4.2	11.6	1.1	0.1
per thick slice		96	5.5	15.4	1.4	0.2
Minestrone soup canned	Baxters	30	1.3	6.0	0.2	1.0
	Safeway	32	0.9	4.7	1.2	0.6
dried	Safeway	305	10.8	64.9	2.0	2.7
per 1pt/52g		150	5.4	33.0	1.0	1.4

All amounts given per 100g/100ml unless otherwise stated

Product	Brand	Kcal	Protein	CHO	Fat	Dietary Fibre
Blueberry Muffin	California Cake & Cookie	326	5.6	42.6	15.7	1.8
Caramel Wafer per biscuit	Tunnock's	454	4.6	68.0	20.1	
		120	1.2	18.0	5.3	
Cheese, Onion & Tomato Flan per flan	Menumaster	750	24	56.0	63.0	
Chocolate Swiss Roll	Lyons Cakes	370	4.5	53.9	16.6	1.2
Hibran bread per medium slice per thick slice	Vitbe	219	12.6	35.0	3.2	6.8
		72	4.2	11.6	1.1	0.1
		96	5.5	15.4	1.4	0.2
Minestrone soup canned	Baxters	30	1.3	6.0	0.2	1.0
	Safeway	32	0.9	4.7	1.2	0.6
dried	Safeway	305	10.8	64.9	2.0	2.7
per 1pt/52g		150	5.4	33.0	1.0	1.4

Product	Brand	Calories per 100g/ 100ml	Calories per oz/ pack/ portion
Amaranth: *see Chinese leaves*			
Ambrosia products: *see Rice, Sago, etc.*			
American brownies	California Cake & Cookie Company		115 per finger, 300 per square
American chocolate chip muffin	Tesco		265 each
American ginger ale	Hunts	36	11
	Safeway	36	11
	Schweppes	21	6
	Tesco	28	8
low calorie	Diet Hunts	1	
	Safeway	4	1
	Schweppes Slimline	1	
	Tesco	6	2
American mustard	Colman's	110	31
American potato and Leek chowder	Knorr		233 per packet
American Shoofly pie	California Cake & Cookie Company		160 per finger, 305 per square
American style deep pan pepper and mushroom pizza	St Michael		645 per pizza
American style mayonnaise	Safeway	690	193

Product	Brand	Calories per 100g/ 100ml	Calories per oz/ pack/ portion
American style double chocolate chip ripple ice cream	St Michael	243	68
malted cookie crunch	St Michael	264	74
toffee pecan crunch	St Michael	296	83
Anchor low fat spread	Anchor	389	109
Anchovies in oil, canned, fish only		280	79
Anchovy paste	Shippams	176	62 per 35g pack
Angel cake	Asda	396	
Angel layer slab cake	Tesco	384	115
Animal biscuits	Cadbury's	480	30 per biscuit
Anise seeds		337	96
Aniseed balls	Barratt	376	107
Applause	Mars		225 per bar
Apple and blackberry crumble	Safeway		935 per pack
	Tesco		1435 per pack
Apple and blackberry drink low calorie	Boots Shapers	6	2
Apple and blackberry dumplings	Ross	250	71
Apple and blackberry fruit filling	Morton		255 per 385g can
Apple and blackberry fruit pie filling	Tesco		260 per can

Product	Brand	Calories per 100g/ 100ml	Calories per oz/ pack/ portion
Apple and blackberry sponge pudding	Heinz		795 per can
Apple and blackcurrant juice	Robinsons	45	13
Apple and blackcurrant pie (frozen)	Tesco		1180 each
Apple and bran original crunchy bar	Jordans	394	132 per bar
Apple and cardamon sugar free bar	Holly Mill		170 per bar
Apple and celery salad	Asda	142	
Apple and hazelnut bar	Holly Mill		147 per bar
Apple and hazelnut cluster	Lyons	381	108
Apple and mango juice	St Michael	42	12
Apple and raspberry fruit filling	Morton		245 per 385g can
Apple and raspberry fruit pie filling	Tesco	66	19
Apple and raspberry juice	Robinsons	45	13
Apple and Sultana Salad	Safeway		450 per tub

Product	Brand	Calories per 100g/ 100ml	Calories per oz/ pack/ portion
Apple baked roll	Tesco	360	114
Apple 'C'	Libby	45	13
Apple chutney		193	55
Apple crumble		208	59
Apple crush, low calorie	Slimsta	4	7 per 180ml bottle
Apple drink, sparkling	Tango	36	11
Apple dumplings	Ross	250	71
Apple fruit filling	Morton	76	22
	Asda	76	
Apple fruit juice	Del Monte	44	13
Apple fruit pie filling	Tesco	64	18
Apple juice concentrated		30	11
		190	63
Apple, peach and nut salad	Safeway	241	605 per tub
	Sainsbury's	210	525 per tub
Apple pie	Littlewoods	352	100
	Lyons		200 each
	Asda	256	
Apple puffs	Tesco		250 each
Apple rings, dried	Tesco	254	72
Apple rice	Ambrosia	101	440 per 439g can
Apple sauce	Heinz	65	18

Product	Brand	Calories per 100g/ 100ml	Calories per oz/ pack/ portion
	O.K.	80	23
Apple sauce mix	Knorr	349	99
	Safeway	365	88 per 24g pack
Pour Over	Colman's	380	108
Apple slices	Asda	37	
Apple sparkle	St Michael	46	14
Apple sponge sandwich with fresh cream	St Michael		810 each
Apple super roll	Lyons		720 each
Apple yogurt	Eden Vale Munch Brunch	90	115 per pot
Apples, cooking			
baked (with skin)		31	9
baked without sugar		39	11
raw		37	10
stewed with sugar		66	19
stewed without sugar		32	9
Apples, eating		46	13
with skin and core		35	10
Appletise	Schweppes	43	13
Applewood smoked cheddar cheese	Ilchester	432	121
Apricot and chocolate chip cluster	Lyons	395	120
Apricot and guava yogurt	Gold Ski	114	171 per 150g pot
	St Michael	109	31

Product	Brand	Calories per 100g/ 100ml	Calories per oz/ pack/ portion
Apricot and mango yogurt	Raines	97	27
	Safeway	86	129 per 150g pot
Apricot and passionfruit yogurt	St Michael	100	28
Apricot and sultana stuffing mix	Knorr		295 per pack
Apricot bakewell tart	St Michael		165 each
Apricot brulee	Young's	280	79
Apricot chutney	Sharwood	148	42
	Tesco	147	42
Apricot conserve	Safeway	248	840 per 340g jar
	St Michael	240	68
	Tesco	268	76
Apricot date bar	Granose	283	85 per 30g bar
Apricot fromage frais slice	St Michael		350 each
Apricot fruit filling	Morton	64	18
Apricot Fruit For-All	Chivers	115	85 per portion
Apricot Fruit Softy	Eden Vale	129	37
Apricot halves in syrup	Del Monte	70	160 per can
Apricot jam	Robertson's	251	71
	Safeway	251	71
diabetic	Boots	236	67
	Dietade	233	66
no added sugar	Safeway	139	316 per 227g jar

Product	Brand	Calories per 100g/ 100ml	Calories per oz/ pack/ portion
reduced sugar	Boots	146	41
	Heinz Weight Watchers	124	35
Apricot lunchpack	Limmits		250 per pack
Apricot preserve	Baxters	241	819 per 340g jar
	Tesco	255	72
reduced sugar	Robertson's	150	43
Apricot pure fruit spread	Robertson's	120	34
Apricot rice	Ambrosia	101	440 per 439g can
Apricot yogurt	St Michael	39	11
French style	Littlewoods	102	153 per 150g pack
low fat	Littlewoods	83	125 per 150g pack
	Tesco	99	28
Apricots			
raw		28	8
raw (with stones)		25	7
stewed with sugar		60	17
stewed with sugar (with stones)		57	16
stewed without sugar		23	7
stewed without sugar (with stones)		21	6
Apricots, canned		106	30
Apricots, dried			
raw		182	52
stewed without sugar		66	19
stewed with sugar		81	23

Product	Brand	Calories per 100g/ 100ml	Calories per oz/ pack/ portion
Arctic circles			
double choc	Birds Eye		165 per piece
vanilla	Birds Eye		155 per piece
Arctic gateau			
choc 'n' cherry	Birds Eye		100 per 1/5 gateau
strawberry	Birds Eye		105 per 1/5 gateau
Arctic roll	Birds Eye		87 per 1/6 small roll
Areca nuts: *see Betel nuts*			
Aromat	Knorr	176	50
Arrowhead, raw		107	30
Arrowroot		355	101
Artichoke, globe			
raw		73	21
boiled		15	4
boiled (as served)		7	2
Artichoke, Jerusalem (boiled)		18	5
Arvi (colocasia) root, raw		85	24
Asafoetida (Hing)		297	84
Asparagus, boiled		18	5
boiled (as served)		9	3
Asparagus cream soup	Knorr 'No Simmer'	497	141
	Asda	458	
Asparagus soup	Heinz Weight Watchers	22	65 per 295g can

Product	Brand	Calories per 100g/ 100ml	Calories per oz/ pack/ portion
condensed	Campbell's	62	18
dried	Asda	461	
	Batchelors Cup-a-Soup	412	103 per 25g sachet as sold
	Safeway	373	106
	Tesco	365	103
Assorted Tools	Trebor Bassett	600	48 per sweet
Aubergine (brinjal, eggplant), raw			144
sliced, fried			60
Austrian cream of herb soup	Knorr		317 per pack
Austrian smoked cheese: *see Cheese*			
Autumn Gold cider			
bottle or can	Taunton	30	170 per pint
keg	Taunton	40	230 per pint
Avocado dressing	Duchesse	33	10
Avocado pear, fresh, raw		223	63

Product	Brand	Calories per 100g/ 100ml	Calories per oz/ pack/ portion
Baby Ribena juice			
apple and			
blackcurrant	Beecham	19	6
apple and cherry	Beecham	19	6
blackcurrant	Beecham	19	6
Baby Ribena juice drink, undiluted			
apple and honey	Beecham	316	94
blackcurrant	Beecham	316	94
blackcurrant and			
apple	Beecham	316	94
Bacardi			50 per 1/6 gill
Bacon			
collar joint, lean and fat, raw		319	90
collar joint, lean and fat, boiled		325	92
collar joint, lean only		191	54
dressed carcase, raw		352	100
fat, raw (average)		747	212
lean, raw (average)		147	42
rashers, lean only, fried (average)		332	94
rashers, lean only, grilled			
(average)		292	83
fat, cooked		692	196
cooked shoulder,			
sliced	Tesco	123	35
cured sweet Dutch	Littlewoods	230	65

Product	Brand	Calories per 100g/ 100ml	Calories per oz/ pack/ portion
half gammon, unsmoked, British	St Michael	350	99
joints	Littlewoods	120	34
loin	Littlewoods	160	45
shoulder joint, unsmoked, British	St Michael	390	111
steaks	Littlewoods	246	70
	Safeway	455	129
	Tesco	88	25
steaks, sweetcure	Tesco	246	70
Bacon, back			
rashers, raw		428	121
rashers, lean and fat, fried		465	132
rashers, lean and fat, grilled		405	115
Canadian style	St Michael	390	111
extra lean, British	St Michael	195	55
green	Littlewoods	246	70
green, Dutch	Littlewoods	226	64
rashers	Tesco	312	88
smoked, British	St Michael	390	111
smoked, Danish	St Michael	350	99
smoked, Dutch	Littlewoods	239	68
smoked, grilled	Bejam	314	89
unsmoked, Danish	St Michael	350	99
unsmoked, Dutch	St Michael	350	99
Bacon, gammon			
joint, lean and fat, raw		236	67
joint, lean and fat, boiled		269	76
joint, lean only		167	47

Product	Brand	Calories per 100g/ 100ml	Calories per oz/ pack/ portion
rashers, lean and fat, grilled		228	65
rashers, lean only		172	49
Bacon, middle			
rashers, raw		425	120
rashers, lean and fat, fried		477	135
rashers, lean and fat, grilled		416	118
green, Dutch	Littlewoods	217	62
rashers	Tesco	269	76
smoked	Littlewoods	420	119
smoked, Dutch	Littlewoods	230	65
Bacon, middle back, unsmoked, Ayrshire	St Michael	350	99
Bacon, streaky			
rashers, raw		414	117
rashers, lean and fat, fried		496	141
rashers, lean and fat, grilled		422	120
Canadian style	St Michael	390	111
green, Dutch	Littlewoods	281	80
rashers	Tesco	286	81
smoked, Dutch	Littlewoods	294	83
unsmoked, British	St Michael	375	106
Bacon sandwiches	St Michael	95	27
Bacon snacks	Waitrose	490	139
Bacon, egg and sausage flan	St Michael	320	115
Bacon, lettuce and tomato sandwiches	Safeway Tesco		560 per pack 485 per pack

Product	Brand	Calories per 100g/ 100ml	Calories per oz/ pack/ portion
Bacon, peppers and mushroom French bread pizza	Findus	192	54
Badam: *see Almonds*			
Bailey's Original Irish Cream			80 per 1/6 gill
Baked bean jackets	St Michael		170 each
Baked beans, in tomato sauce		64	18
Baked beans	Hartley's	65	275 per can
	Safeway	73	170 per can
in barbecue sauce	Heinz	72	160 per can
in tomato sauce	Crosse & Blackwell	73	160 per 220g can
	Heinz	72	20
in tomato sauce, no added sugar/starch	Whole Earth	70	310 per 440g can
low sugar and salt	Asda	59	
no added sugar	Heinz Weight Watchers	54	122 per 225g can
with burgerbites	Heinz	119	270 per 225g can
with chickbits	Heinz	113	255 per 225g can
with pork sausages in tomato sauce	Heinz	124	275 per 225g can
Baked potatoes, old		105	30
old (with skins)		85	24
Baked raspberry jam roll	Safeway	408	116

Product	Brand	Calories per 100g/ 100ml	Calories per oz/ pack/ portion
Bakewell slice	St Michael		205 each
Bakewell tart mix (as sold)	Green's	422	made up per portion 216
Baking powder		163	46
Balor (valor) beans			
fresh, raw		23	7
canned, drained		19	5
Bamboo shoots, canned			278
Banana blancmange	Brown and Polson	327	93
Banana cake	California Cake & Cookie Company		85 per finger, 210 per square
Banana chips, dried	Tesco	529	150
	Whitworths	517	147
Banana fruit bar	Prewetts		110 per bar
Banana in custard	St Michael	91	26
Banana madeira sandwich	St Michael	390	110
Banana munch bar	Holly Mill		140 per bar
Banana soya milk	Granose	60	300 per pack
Banana supershake	Eden Vale	75	146 per 194g pack
Banana supreme	Eden Vale	105	131 per 125g pack
Banana yogurt	Munch Bunch	99	124 per 125g pack
	Mr Men	96	27
	Safeway	95	143 per 150g pack

Product	Brand	Calories per 100g/ 100ml	Calories per oz/ pack/ portion
	Safeway Funtime	92	138 per 150g pack
	St Ivel Real	84	24
	St Ivel Shape	43	12
	Ski	83	125 per 150g pack
low fat	Littlewoods	96	144 per 150g pack
	Tesco	96	27
	Waitrose	90	135 per 150g pack
Bananas			
raw		79	22
raw (with skin)		47	13
Baps: see Bread rolls			
Bar six	Cadbury's	550	220 per bar
Barbecue beef and onion crisps	St Michael		400 per pack
Barbecue sauce		75	21
Coat and Cook	Homepride		175 per sachet
Cook In	Homepride		300 per can
Recipe Sauce	Knorr		260 per carton
Barbecue spare ribs	Tesco	178	710 per pack
	Safeway	187	750 per pack
	Sainsbury's	205	965 per pack
Barbican	Britvic	13	65 per can
Barcelona nuts		639	181
with shells		396	112
Barley			
boiled		120	34

Product	Brand	Calories per 100g/ 100ml	Calories per oz/ pack/ portion
whole grain, raw		327	93
Barley flakes	Holland and Barrett	313	89
Barley sugar	Littlewoods	365	103
	Trebor Bassett	365	23 per sweet
Barley, pearl, raw		360	102
boiled		120	34
Barlotti beans: see Beans			
Bassetti	Barratt	310	88
Bath Oliver biscuits	Fortts	375	45 per biscuit
Battenburg cake	Lyons	358	101
	St Michael	361	102
	Tesco	365	106
	Waitrose	362	103
Batter mix	Tesco	209	59
Complete	Green's	359	102
crispy	Green's	341	97
fish	Green's	341	97
pouch	Green's	348	99
quick	Whitworths	338	96
Bavarian ham, joints or slices	St Michael	161	46
Bavarian smoked cheese: see Cheese			
Bavarian style sandwich cake mix (as sold)	Green's	397	258 made up per portion

Product	Brand	Calories per 100g/ 100ml	Calories per oz/ pack/ portion
Bavarian vegetable soup	Knorr		139 per packet
Bean and mushroom stew	Granose	78	330 per can
Bean salad	Tesco	80	155 per pot
mixed	Asda	86	
Bean stew, Mexican	Granose	130	555 per can
Beanmilk	Itona	130	552 per 425g can
Beans			
Aduki, dried		328	92
boiled		143	40
Barlotti, canned		168	47
Black, dried		343	96
boiled		161	45
Black eye, dried		332	93
boiled		136	38
Broad, raw		121	34
boiled		107	30
Butter, dried		273	77
boiled		95	27
Canellini, canned		89	25
Flageolet, dried		350	98
boiled		114	32
French, boiled		7	2
frozen		36	10
Haricot, dried		271	77
boiled		93	26
Lima, dried		328	92

Product	Brand	Calories per 100g/ 100ml	Calories per oz/ pack/ portion
Mung, dried		328	92
boiled		118	33
Pinto, dried		353	99
boiled		146	41
Red kidney, dried		275	77
boiled		89	25
Runner, raw		25	7
boiled		18	5
Soya, dried		385	108
boiled		178	50
Beans, refried	Old El Paso	92	410 per 453g can
Beansprouts			
canned		9	3
mung (moong), fresh, raw		35	10
mung (moong), canned		9	3
Beatall lollies	Trebor Bassett	356	32 per lolly
Beef			
braising steak, raw		178	50
braising steak, lean, raw		125	35
brisket, lean and fat, raw		252	71
brisket lean and fat, boiled		326	92
fillet steak, grilled		147	42
mince, raw		221	63
mince, stewed		229	65
rump steak, lean and fat, raw		197	56
rump steak, lean and fat, fried		246	70
rump steak, lean and fat, grilled		218	62
rump steak, lean only, fried		246	70

Product	Brand	Calories per 100g/ 100ml	Calories per oz/ pack/ portion
rump steak, lean only, grilled		168	48
silverside, roast, lean and fat		285	80
silverside, roast, lean only		196	55
sirloin, lean and fat, raw		272	77
sirloin, lean and fat, roast		284	81
sirloin, lean only, roast		192	54
Stewing steak, lean and fat, raw		176	50
stewing steak, lean and fat, stewed		223	63
topside, lean and fat, raw		179	51
topside, lean and fat, roast		214	61
topside, lean only		156	44
Beef and ham paste	Gateway		85 per pot
Beef and kidney	Tyne Brand		455 per can
Beef and kidney pie	Tyne Brand		685 each
Beef and mushroom pasties	St Michael	258	73
Beef and mushroom pie	Tyne Brand		655 each
Beef and onion	Tyne Brand		470 per can
Beef and onion pasties	St Michael	262	74
Beef and onion sandwichmaker	Shippams	131	124 per 95g can
Beef and onion soup, low calorie	Knorr Quick Soup		35 per sachet
Beef and pickle sandwiches	Safeway		370 per pack

Product	Brand	Calories per 100g/ 100ml	Calories per oz/ pack/ portion
Beef and pork cannelloni	Findus Lean Cuisine		235 per pack
Beef and tomato soup, dried (as sold)	Batchelors Cup-a-Soup	333	75 per sachet
	Batchelors	307	178 per pint pack
instant	Safeway		65 per sachet
low calorie	Batchelors Slim-a-Soup		40 per sachet
with croutons	Batchelors Cup-a-Soup Special		100 per sachet
Beef and vegetable soup	Campbell's Main Course	55	240 per 425g can
	Heinz Big Soups	36	125 per 435g can
	St Michael	76	325 per 425g can
Beef 'n' vegetable soup with croutons (as sold)	Batchelors Snack-a-Soup		160 per sachet
Beef bourguignon cooking mix	Colman's		125 per pack
Beef bourguignon with rice	Bird's Eye Menu Master		445 per pack
Beef broth	Heinz Big Soups	29	155 per 435g can
Farmhouse condensed	Heinz	39	115 per 300g can
(undiluted)	Campbell's	67	205 per 295g can
Beef carbonnade	Sainsbury's		590 per pack

Product	Brand	Calories per 100g/ 100ml	Calories per oz/ pack/ portion
Beef casserole	Tyne Brand		340 per can
Beef consomme	Tesco		47 per 425g can
Beef consomme with sherry	Sainsbury's		106 per 425g can
Beef crisps	Tesco		130 per 25g packet
lower-fat	St Michael		310 per 65g packet
Beef cubes	Knorr	332	94
	Waitrose	296	84
Beef curry	Campbell's		435 per can
(frozen)	Tesco		440 per pack
and rice	Tyne Brand		455 per pack
with rice	Birds Eye		
	Menu Master		380 per pack
	Vesta		960 per pack
Beef drink	Oxo	100	28
Beef dripping		891	253
Beef enchiladas	St Michael		350 per pack
Beef goulash Cook in the Pot	Crosse & Blackwell		160 per pack
Beef goulash cooking mix	Colman's		130 per pack
Beef grillsteaks	Bird's Eye Steakhouse		175 each

Product	Brand	Calories per 100g/ 100ml	Calories per oz/ pack/ portion
Beef in barbecue sauce	Tesco		420 per pack
Beef in satay sauce	Findus Lean Cuisine		215 per pack
Beef japanaise	Findus Dinner Supreme		350 per pack
Beef julienne	Findus Lean Cuisine		235 per pack
Beef kheema		411	117
Beef koftas		350	99
Beef Lasagne	Heinz		264 per pack
Beef Madras	Safeway Trimrite Vesta		700 per pack 925 per pack
Beef oriental	Findus		310 per pack
Beef oriental with special egg rice	Heinz		280 per pack
Beef paste	Safeway Shippams Tesco	200	170 per pot 70 per pot 57
Beef provencale	Findus Lean Cuisine		270 per pack
Beef risotto	Tyne Brand Vesta		470 per pack 775 per pack
Beef roulade	St Michael		245 each grilled

Product	Brand	Calories per 100g/ 100ml	Calories per oz/ pack/ portion
Beef sausages			
fried		269	76
grilled		265	75
raw		299	85
Beef savoury rice (as sold)	Batchelors		435 per pack
Beef seasoning sauce mix	Colman's Cook In		115 per pack
	Colman's Pour Over		115 per pack
Beef slicing sausage	Asda	333	
Beef soup	Heinz		110 per 300g can
Beef steak pudding, cooked		223	63
Beef stew, cooked		119	34
Beef stew and dumplings	Campbell's		300 per can
	Birds Eye MenuMaster		240 per pack
	St Michael		500 per can
	Asda	136	
Beef stock cubes	Safeway	273	31 per cube
Beef stroganoff	St Michael		490 per pack
Beef stroganoff mix Cook in the Pot	Crosse & Blackwell		165 per packet

Product	Brand	Calories per 100g/ 100ml	Calories per oz/ pack/ portion
Beef stroganoff sauce	Homepride Cook In		295 per can
Beef strognoff cooking mix (as sold)	Colman's		125 per pack
Beef suet, shredded	Tesco	797	226
Beef teriyaki	Findus		335 per pack
Beef, tomato and coleslaw sandwiches	Waitrose		320 per pack
Beefburgers			
frozen, raw		265	75
fried		264	75
Beefburgers	Safeway	298	168 per beefburger
	St Michael	260	74
	Waitrose	246	140 per beefburger
	Asda	294	
in brown sauce (canned)	St Michael	102	29
low fat	Birds Eye Steakhouse		85 per burger, grilled
	Sainsbury's		75 per burger, grilled
90%	Findus	283	80
100%	Birds Eye Steakhouse		120 per burger, grilled

Product	Brand	Calories per 100g/ 100ml	Calories per oz/ pack/ portion
original	Birds Eye Steakhouse		130 per burger, grilled or fried
premium, grilled	Tesco	270	77
premium, raw	Tesco	290	82
quarter pounder, lean beef	Findus		175 per burger
top quality	St Michael	260	74
with onion	Gateway	262	78
Beef grills	Asda	303	
Beer			
bitter, canned		32	9
bitter, keg		31	9
bitter, draught		32	9
mild, draught		25	7
Beer shandy	Corona	25	7
Beetroot, raw		28	8
boiled		44	12
Beetroot	Tesco	44	12
baby	Safeway	26	85 per 327g pack
baby, sweet	Tesco	48	14
in redcurrant jelly	Baxters	162	494 per 305g jar
Beetroot, pickled			
all varieties	Haywards	40	11
baby	Waitrose	26	88 per 340g jar
	Safeway	26	85 per 327g jar
sliced or whole	Tesco	37	10
sliced	Littlewoods	37	126 per 340g pack
	St Michael	55	16

Product	Brand	Calories per 100g/ 100ml	Calories per oz/ pack/ portion	33
	Waitrose	37	126 per 340g jar	
sliced, in sweet vinegar	Waitrose	55	187 per 340g jar	
small whole	St Michael	55	16	
Belgian buns	Tesco	343	97	
Bel Paese: *see Cheese*				
Belle des champs cheese	Waitrose	300	85	
Bemax		347	98	
	Beecham	300	85	
crunchy	Beecham	310	88	
Benedictine			90 per 1/6 gill	
Bengal gram: *see Chickpeas*				
Bengal hot chutney	Sharwood	217	62	
Besan flour: *see Chickpeas*				
Betal (Areca) nuts		394	112	
Betal leaves (Pan)		61	17	
Bezique			45 per 1/6 gill	
Bierwurst: *see Sausages, delicatessen*				
Big Squeeze	Lyons Maid		115 each	
Bilberries, raw		56	16	
Biryani curry sauce mix	Sharwood		75 per sachet	
Biscuits home made		469	133	

Product	Brand	Calories per 100g/ 100ml	Calories per oz/ pack/ portion
sandwich		513	145
semi-sweet		457	130
short-sweet		469	133
Bitter lemon	Schweppes	33	10
	Waitrose	34	10
low calorie	Asda	50	
	Schweppes		
	Slimline	2	1
	Tesco	6	2
	Waitrose	3	1
Bitter lemon drink	Canada Dry	40	11
	Safeway	55	16
	Tesco	33	10
	Waitrose	34	10
	Hunts	34	10
low calorie	Canada Dry		
	Slim	2	1
	Safeway	5	1
	Diet Hunts	1	0.5 per 100ml
Bitter orange, sparkling	Schweppes	45	13
Bitter orange drink **low calorie**	Diet Hunts	3	1
Bitter sweet drink, low calorie, sparkling			
lemon/lime	Beecham	4	1
orange	Beecham	5	1
Black cherry cheesecake	Chambourcy		225 per carton

Product	Brand	Calories per 100g/ 100ml	Calories per oz/ pack/ portion
Black cherry conserve	Tesco	268	76
	Waitrose	250	71
Black cherry dessert	St Michael		160 per carton
Black cherry double decker	St Michael	124	35
Black cherry flavour jelly	Waitrose	272	77
Black cherry fruit filling	Morton	70	20
	Waitrose	70	20
Black cherry ice cream	Lyons Maid	180	'51
Black cherry jelly	Safeway	268	76
	Tesco	57	16
Black cherry preserve	Baxters	244	69
	Tesco	255	72
Black cherry ripple ice cream	Tesco	176	50
Black cherry yogurt	Mr Men	85	120 per pot
	Raines	96	140 per pot
	St Ivel Prize Fresh		115 per pot
	St Ivel Real		105 per pot
	Ski	82	123 per pot
low fat	Diet Ski	55	83 per pot
	St Ivel Shape	42	50 per pot
	St Michael	40	11
	Littlewoods	84	126 per pot
	Tesco	103	115 per pot

Product	Brand	Calories per 100g/ 100ml	Calories per oz/ pack/ portion
	Waitrose	95	143 per pot
whole milk	Waitrose	115	173 per pot
Black Forest Cornetto	Wall's		230 per super cone
Black Forest gateau	Co-op		89
	Gateway		91
	St Ivel		160 per carton
	St Michael	310	87
	Tesco	325	84
	Asda	291	
Black Forest Swiss roll	Tesco	333	93
Black Forest trifle	Eden Vale		150 per carton
Black gram (Urad dahl), raw		347	98
Black Jack chews	Trebor Bassett	385	15 per sweet
Black Magic Assortment			
brandy flavoured truffle	Rowntree Mackintosh		45 per sweet
butterscotch	Rowntree Mackintosh		30 per sweet
caramel	Rowntree Mackintosh		40 per sweet
chocolate Brazil	Rowntree Mackintosh		35 per sweet
coffee cream	Rowntree Mackintosh		30 per sweet
hazelnut cluster	Rowntree Mackintosh		45 per sweet
liquid cherry	Rowntree Mackintosh		30 per sweet

Product	Brand	Calories per 100g/ 100ml	Calories per oz/ pack/ portion
montelimar	Rowntree Mackintosh		45 per sweet
orange cream	Rowntree Mackintosh		45 per sweet
strawberry cup	Rowntree Mackintosh		45 per sweet
toffee and mallow	Rowntree Mackintosh		45 per sweet
truffle and nougat	Rowntree Mackintosh		50 per sweet
Black pudding, fried		305	86
Blackberries, raw		29	8
stewed without sugar		25	7
stewed with sugar		60	17
Blackberry and apple pie	St Michael	263	75
Blackberry and apple yogurt, low fat	Tesco Waitrose	97	27 145 per pot
Blackcurrant cheesecake	Mc Vities	321	90
Blackberry yogurt	Munch Bunch	95	130 per pot
Blackcurrant and aniseed twists	Trebor Bassett	356	26 per sweet
Blackcurrant and apple drink, low calorie	Boots Shapers		2 per 330ml bottle

Product	Brand	Calories per 100g/ 100ml	Calories per oz/ pack/ portion
Blackcurrant and apple juice	Appella	40	12
	Copella	50	15
Blackcurrant and apple juice drink	Ribena	56	17
concentrated	Ribena	278	82
undiluted	Baby Ribena	316	94
Blackcurrant and lime juice drink	Ribena	56	17
Blackcurrant and liquorice	Needlers	356	101
Blackcurrant baked slice	Asda	357	
Blackcurrant 'C'	Libby	42	12
Blackcurrant cheesecake	Eden Vale	207	59
	St Michael	263	75
	Young's	250	71
individual	Young's	245	69
Blackcurrant cheesecake mix (made up)	Lyons	234	66
Blackcurrant conserve	Safeway	248	70
	St Michael	240	68
	Tesco	268	76
	Waitrose	250	71
Blackcurrant delice	St Michael	240	68

Product	Brand	Calories per 100g/ 100ml	Calories per oz/ pack/ portion
Blackcurrant Devonshire cheesecake	St Ivel		225 per carton
Blackcurrant drink	Tesco	190	56
Blackcurrant flavour cordial concentrated		122	35
Blackcurrant flavour dessert mix, low calorie	Dietade	264	75
Blackcurrant fruit filling	Morton	78	22
	Waitrose	78	22
Blackcurrant fruit fool	St Michael		185 per carton
Blackcurrant Fruit For-All	Chivers	110	85 per portion
Blackcurrant fruit spread	Waitrose	124	35
Blackcurrant health drink	Lanes	130	37
Blackcurrant jam	Robertson's	251	71
	Safeway	251	71
	Waitrose	248	70
diabetic	Boots	236	67
no added sugar	Safeway	141	40
reduced sugar	Boots	156	44

Product	Brand	Calories per 100g/ 100ml	Calories per oz/ pack/ portion
	Heinz Weight Watchers	124	35
	Waitrose	124	35
Blackcurrant jelly	Safeway	268	76
	Tesco	57	16
	Waitrose	248	70
Blackcurrant juice	Baby Ribena	19	6
	Copella	50	14
	Hycal	243	72
concentrated	Western Isles	325	96
Blackcurrant juice drink	Ribena	59	17
sparkling	Ribena	53	16
concentrated	Ribena	293	87
	Baby Ribena	316	94
Blackcurrant preserve	Baxters	240	68
	Tesco	255	72
reduced sugar	Robertson's	150	43
Blackcurrant pure fruit spread	Robertson's	120	34
Blackcurrant sorbet	Tesco	127	33
Blackcurrant syrup	Boots	272	81
Blackcurrant vitamin C drink, undiluted	C-Vit	210	62
Blackcurrant yogurt	Safeway	93	140 per carton
low fat	Tesco	100	155 per carton
Blackcurrants, raw		28	8

Product	Brand	Calories per 100g/ 100ml	Calories per oz/ pack/ portion
stewed without sugar		24	7
stewed with sugar		59	17
Blackcurrants, canned	Hartley's		170 per can
Blackeye beans: *see Beans*			
Blackthorn cider	Taunton	34	200 per pint
Bloater, grilled		251	71
(with bones)		186	53
Bloater paste	Shippams	183	64 per pack
Blue Band margarine	Van den Berghs	740	1850 per 250g pack
Blueberries, raw/frozen			18
Blue cheese dressing	Kraft	482	143
	Safeway	260	74
Blue Riband	Rowntree Mackintosh	510	100 per biscuit
Blue ribbon vanilla ice cream	Wall's	90	105 per tub
cream of Cornish	Wall's	95	37
Blue ribbon vanilla ice cream bar	Wall's		85 per bar
Blue royale dressing	Hellmann's	318	90
Blue Stilton cheese: *see Cheese*			
Bobby beans, fresh, cooked	Tesco	35	10
Bockwurst: *see Sausages, delicatessen*			

Product	Brand	Calories per 100g/ 100ml	Calories per oz/ pack/ portion
Boeuf bourgignon	Baxters		440 per can
Boiled sweets		327	93
Bologna/Vegelinks	Granose	167	47
Bolognese Homestyle cooking sauce	Colman's		275 per carton
Bolognese mix (soya)	Protoveg Menu	275	78
Bolognese sauce, cooked		139	39
Bolognese sauce	Buitoni		145 per small can
	Napolina		285 per jar
	Safeway		165 per can
	Asda	80	
with bacon	Napolina		282 per jar
with mushrooms	Napolina		250 per jar
with peppers	Napolina		270 per jar
Bombay masala	Safeway Quorn Ready Meals		325 per pack
Bombay mix			140
Bon Bons, all flavours	Trebor Bassett	403	27 per sweet
Bone and vegetable broth		60	17
Boost	Cadbury's	485	255 per bar
Boston bean salad	Safeway	262	72
Bounty Bar		473	134
Bounty			
milk chocolate	Mars	483	137
plain chocolate	Mars	485	137

Product	Brand	Calories per 100g/ 100ml	Calories per oz/ pack/ portion
Bourbon biscuits	Peek Frean	468	60 per biscuit
	Waitrose	468	133
Bourbon creams			
	Asda	486	
	Safeway		70 per biscuit
	St Michael		65 per biscuit
	Tesco		65 per biscuit
Bournville digestive biscuits	Cadbury's	480	145 per biscuit
Bournville assorted biscuits	Cadbury's	500	60 per biscuit
Bournville chocolate bar, dark	Cadbury's	510	255 per 50g bar
Boursin: *see Cheese*			
Bovril		174	49
granules	Bovril	186	53
Brain			
calf, boiled		152	43
calf and lamb, raw		110	31
lamb, boiled		126	36
Braised beef	Tyne Brand		490 per can
Braised kidneys in gravy	Birds Eye MenuMaster		200 per pack
Braised steak	St Michael	100	28
Bramble jelly	Safeway	248	70
	Waitrose	248	70

Product	Brand	Calories per 100g/ 100ml	Calories per oz/ pack/ portion
Bramble jelly preserve	Tesco	255	72
Bramley apple pies	Safeway	338	957 per 283g pack
Bramley apple sauce	Pan Yan	121	34
	Tesco	92	26
Bramley apples, cooking (baked)	Tesco	31	9
Bran crunchy	Allinson	360	102
natural	Boots Second Nature	166	47
natural country	Jordans	167	47
toasted	Meadow Farm	360	102
Bran and apple original crunchy	Jordans	369	130 per bar
Bran bread: see Bread, brown			
Bran breakfast with apple and banana	Holly Mill	440	125
	Holly Mill	440	125
Bran Buds	Kellogg's	271	77
Bran crispbread Ideal	Holland and Barrett		20 per biscuit
Scan	Holland and Barrett		10 per biscuit
Bran Fare	Weetabix	228	65

Product	Brand	Calories per 100g/ 100ml	Calories per oz/ pack/ portion
Bran flakes	Asda	323	
	Kellogg's	302	86
	Tesco	325	92
	Waitrose	340	96
crunchy	St Michael	308	87
with sultana	Tesco	350	99
Bran muesli	Prewetts	320	91
	Waitrose	363	103
Bran oat crunch	Boots	335	95
Bran wheat		206	58
Brandy			50 per 1/6 gill
Brandy butter	Tesco	530	150
Brandy cream	Waitrose	443	131
Branston fruity sauce	Crosse & Blackwell	90	26
Branston spicy sauce	Crosse & Blackwell	112	32
Branston sweet pickle	Crosse & Blackwell	131	37
Brawn		153	43
	Waitrose	153	43
Hungarian style	Waitrose	224	64
Brazil nut chocolate bar	Cadbury's	550	156
Brazil nut toffees	Trebor Bassett	412	28 per sweet
Brazil nuts		619	175

Product	Brand	Calories per 100g/ 100ml	Calories per oz/ pack/ portion
with shells		277	79
Bread, bran		228	65
Bread, brown		223	63
Bread, currant		250	71
Bread, French		300	85
brown		264	75
wholemeal		248	70
Bread, garlic: see Garlic bread			
Bread, granary		248	70
Bread, malt		248	70
Bread, pitta			
white		251	71
wholemeal		232	66
Bread, soda		264	75
Bread, vogel			65
Bread, West Indian		284	81
Bread, wheatgerm		228	65
Bread, white		233	66
dried crumbs		354	100
fried		558	158
Bread, wholemeal (100%)		216	61
Bread and butter pudding		159	45
Breadcrumbs			
Wholemeal	Asda	343	

Product	Brand	Calories per 100g/ 100ml	Calories per oz/ pack/ portion
Bread rolls			
bagel			150 each
brioche			215 each
burger buns	Mothers Pride		140 each
	Safeway		140 each
croissant (40g)			170
croissant (50g)			220
Bread rolls, brown			
crusty		289	82
soft		282	80
bran baps	Safeway		130 each
granary baps	Tesco		185 each
Bread rolls, white			
crusty		290	82
soft		305	86
dinner roll		305	86
morning roll, Aberdeen			185
Bread rolls, wholemeal			
baps		290	83
rolls		245	70
Bread sauce		110	31
Bread sauce mix	Colman's Pour Over		140 per pack
	Knorr		145 per pack
	Safeway		95 per sachet
Breadfruit, canned, drained		64	18

Product	Brand	Calories per 100g/ 100ml	Calories per oz/ pack/ portion
Breadsticks (grissini)	Buitoni	360	102
Break-In chocolate biscuits	St Michael	590	167
Breakaway			
milk	Rowntree Mackintosh	500	105 each
plain	Rowntree Mackintosh	445	90 each
Breakfast biscuits	Gateway		65 each
Breakfast special	St Michael		108
Brie cheese: *see Cheese*			
Brinjal: *see Aubergine*			
Broad beans: *see Beans*			
Broccoli, raw		23	7
boiled		18	5
Broccoli and mushroom flan	Tesco		1145 per 450g flan
Broccoli in cream sauce	St Michael	112	32
Broccoli mornay	Tesco		560 per pack
Broccoli provencale	Sainsbury's		320 per pack
Broccoli quiche	St Michael	234	66
Brown ale, bottled		28	8
Brown bread: *see Bread, brown*			
Brown rice: *see also Rice, brown*			

Product	Brand	Calories per 100g/ 100ml	Calories per oz/ pack/ portion
Brown rice and vegetable salad	Tesco	105	265 per pot
Brown rice flakes	Holland and Barrett	203	58
Brown rice flour	Holland and Barrett	360	102
Brown sauce, bottled		99	28
Brown sugar: *see Sugar, brown*			
Brussels pate	Tesco	410	116
Brussels sprouts, raw		26	7
boiled		18	5
Brussels sprouts			
	Birds Eye	35	10
	Findus	26	7
	Ross	30	9
	Safeway	40	11
button	Waitrose	18	5
fresh	Littlewoods	26	7
Bubble and squeak	Ross	60	17
Bubble gum	Wrigley Hubba Bubba		15/24 per chunk
Buckwheat flour	Holland and Barrett	330	94
Buffet cornish pasty	Tesco		105 each
Buffet pork pie	Littlewoods	395	320 per pie

Product	Brand	Calories per 100g/ 100ml	Calories per oz/ pack/ portion
Bulgur wheat	Holland and Barrett	370	105
Bumper Harvest soups (Campbell's): *see flavours*			
Bunnytots	Rowntree Mackintosh	420	180 per 43g bag
Buns: *see flavours*			
Burfi, Asian		292	83
Burger bites	Hunters		135 per small bag
	St Michael		275 per 50g
Burger buns: *see Bread rolls*			
Burger mix	Granose	455	129
Burgundy wine sauce	Baxters Cooking-in	59	240 per can
Butter, salted		740	210
Butter, unsalted	St Ivel	750	213
	St Michael	740	210
Longboat	Dairy Crest	758	215
Welsh	Asda	725	
Butter beans: *see Beans*			
Butter biscuits	Littlewoods	495	43 per biscuit
	Waitrose	480	40 per biscuit
Butter cherry Genoa cake	Safeway	335	95
Butter crunch biscuits	St Michael	463	40 per biscuit
	Waitrose	456	35 per biscuit

Product	Brand	Calories per 100g/ 100ml	Calories per oz/ pack/ portion
Butter drops	Boots	448	148 per 33g stick
Butter Dundee cake	Safeway	382	108
Butter fruit biscuits	Littlewoods	485	42 per biscuit
Butter iced fruit bar	Safeway	371	105
Butter Madeira cake	Lyons	378	107
	St Michael	405	115
Butter mintoes	Waitrose	394	112
Butter puffs	St Michael	508	144
Butter sandwich cream biscuits	Sainsbury's		65 per biscuit
Butter truffles	St Michael	596	166
Butter walnut sandwich cake	St Michael	412	117
Buttered eclairs	Littlewoods	407	115
Buttered kipper fillets	Birds Eye	194	55
Butterfly crackers	St Michael	483	137
Butterkist popcorn	Tesco	390	111
Buttermilk	Raines	39	11
Buttermints	St Michael	440	125
Butterscotch dessert sauce	Lyons Maid	314	89
Butterscotch sensations	Needlers	435	123

Product	Brand	Calories per 100g/ 100ml	Calories per oz/ pack/ portion
Butterscotch sweets	Littlewoods	388	110
Buttons, chocolate	Cadbury's	530	175 per 33g standard pack

C

Product	Brand	Calories per 100g/ 100ml	Calories per oz/ pack/ portion
Cabana	Rowntree Mackintosh	440	235 each
Cabanos	Waitrose	387	110
sliced	Tesco	253	72
Cabaret biscuits, chocolate	Cadbury's	470	45 per biscuit
Cabbage			
Savoy, raw		26	7
spring, boiled		7	2
white, raw		22	6
Savoy, boiled		9	3
winter, boiled		15	4
winter, raw		22	6
Cabbage and mushroom bake	Tesco	125	435 per pack
Cabbage, red, raw		20	6
Caerphilly: *see Cheese*			
Cafe noir biscuits	Waitrose	391	25 per biscuit
Calabrese, fresh, boiled	Tesco	19	5
Californian corn chips	Phileas Fogg		225 per pack
Calypso beans (canned)	Batchelors	70	20
Cambozola: *see Cheese*			
Camembert: *see Cheese*			
Candy foams	Barratt	361	102

Product	Brand	Calories per 100g/ 100ml	Calories per oz/ pack/ portion
Canellini: *see Beans*			
Cannelloni	St Michael		385 per pack
canned	Buitoni		388 per can
frozen	Tesco		460 per pack
	Sainsbury's		410 per pack
Cantaloupe: *see Melon, musk*			
Cantonese sweet and sour Classic Chinese sauce	Homepride		450 per can
Capelletti (as sold)	Signor Rossi	280	79
Capellini	Waitrose	378	107
Capers			5
Captain's Pie	Birds Eye MenuMaster	116	335 per pack
Caramac	Rowntree Mackintosh	545	145 per bar
Caramel bar	Cadbury's	490	245 per bar
Caramel cake	St Michael	425	120
Caramel cookie rings	Tesco	481	136
Caramel delight dessert	St Michael		180 per carton
Caramel filled milk chocolate	Littlewoods	495	140
Caramel Granymels	Itona	390	111
Caramel log	Tunnock's	441	110 per log

Product	Brand	Calories per 100g/ 100ml	Calories per oz/ pack/ portion
Caramel ministicks	St Michael	473	134
Caramel sauce	Tesco	320	91
Caramel supreme	Eden Vale		160 per carton
Caramel toffee ice cream	Lyons Maid Gold Seal	210	60
Caramel wafers	Littlewoods	470	133
	Rowntree Mackintosh	395	75 per wafer
	Tesco	452	128
	Tunnock's	446	126
coated	Littlewood	490	139
Caraway seeds		333	94
Cardamom powder		311	88
Cariba	Schweppes		115 per can
low calorie	Schweppes Slimline		10 per can
Caribbean cocktail	Sooner	503	143
Caribbean crush	St Michael	47	14
Caribbean drink	St Michael	56	17
	Tesco	49	15
	Waitrose	85	25
Caribbean fruit juice	St Michael	55	16
Carmelle dessert mix (dry)	Green's	315	52 made up per portion
Carnival mix	Safeway	100	335

Product	Brand	Calories per 100g/ 100ml	Calories per oz/ pack/ portion
Carob bar (Newform, Sunwheel Kalibu): *see flavours*			
Carob biscuits	Prewetts		85 per biscuit
Carob chip bar	Holly Mill		60 per bar
Carob coated fruit bar	Granose	414	145 per 35g bar
Carob coated hazlenut bar	Granose		207 per bar
Carob coated lemon bar	Granose		162 per bar
Carob coated mixed fruit bar	Granose		169 per bar
Carob coated peanuts and raisins	Sunwheel Kalibu	503	143
Carob flour	Holland and Barrett	180	51
Carob powder	Sunwheel Kalibu	200	57
Carrot and apple juice	Copella	32	9
Carrot and nut salad	St Michael	253	72
Carrot and orange soup fresh	Safeway Sainsbury's		187 per can 390 per tub
Carrot cake	California Cake & Cookie Company		140 per finger, 320 per square
Carrots			
old raw		23	7
old boiled		19	5
raw		23	7

Product	Brand	Calories per 100g/ 100ml	Calories per oz/ pack/ portion
young boiled		20	6
young (canned)		19	5
Cartoons cake mix (dry)			
Disneys	Green's	408	64 per portion made up
My Little Pony	Green's	412	64 per portion made up
Snow White	Green's	414	64 per portion made up
Cashew nuts		561	159
Cassava, fresh, raw		135	38
frozen, raw		139	39
Cassoulet beans (canned)	Batchelors	65	18
Castaway bar, original	Holly Mill		197 per bar
Caster sugar, white	Tate and Lyle	394	112
Castle orange marmalade	Baxters	246	70
Catherine wheels	Barratt	300	85
centres	Tesco	372	105
liquorice	Tesco	334	95
Cauliflower, raw		13	4
boiled		9	3
Cauliflower bhajia		107	30
Cauliflower cheese		113	32
Cauliflower quiche	Safeway	246	975 each

Product	Brand	Calories per 100g/ 100ml	Calories per oz/ pack/ portion
Cayenne pepper	Safeway	402	114
Celeriac, boiled		14	4
Celery, raw		8	2
boiled		5	1
Celery and blue cheese cottage cheese	Eden Vale	92	26
Celery, apple and mandanin salad	Sainsbury's	130	325 per pot
Celery, corn and apple spread	Heinz	188	53
Celery, nut and sultana salad	Tesco		540 per tub
Celery soup, low calorie	Heinz Weight Watchers	21	60 per can
	Waitrose	20	60 per can
Cereals sandwich spread	Granose	225	64
Cervelat: *see Sausages, delicotossen*			
Ceylon tea, infused	Safeway	1	
Champs	Sooner		56 per packet
Channa dhal	Sharwoods		595 per can
Chapati, paratha and puri mix	Sharwood	345	98
Chapatis, made with fat		328	93
made without fat		202	57

Product	Brand	Calories per 100g/ 100ml	Calories per oz/ pack/ portion
Chapni kaddu: *see Gourd, bottle*			
Charcoal biscuits	Scott		40 per biscuit
Charlotte russe	St Michael	231	65
Chartreuse (green)			100 per 1/6 gill
Chayote: *see Cho cho*			
Cheddar and blue cheese spread	Kraft	273	77
Cheddar and onion cottage cheese	Eden Vale	121	34
	Safeway	127	36
	Tesco	121	34
	Waitrose	113	32
Cheddar cheese: *see Cheese*			
Cheddar cheese crispy pancakes	Findus		140 each
Cheddar cheese Pour Over sauce mix	Colman's		160 per pack
Cheddar cheese slices	Littlewoods	301	60 per slice
	St Michael	340	96
processed	Kraft	326	92
Cheddar cheese spread	Kraft	277	79
	Waitrose	260	74
with ham	Waitrose	260	74
with prawn	Waitrose	260	74
Cheddar spread	Sun-Pat	285	81

Product	Brand	Calories per 100g/ 100ml	Calories per oz/ pack/ portion
Cheese			
Austrian smoked		403	113
Bavarian smoked		285	80
Bel Paese		343	96
Boursin		414	116
Brie, Danish		339	95
Brie, French		314	88
Caerphilly		378	106
Cambozola		435	122
Camembert		300	84
Cheddar		418	117
Cheddar, Farmhouse		521	146
Cheddar-type, reduced fat		285	80
Cheshire		382	107
Cottage cheese		96	27
Curd cheese		192	54
Danbo		346	97
Danish blue		350	98
Derby		403	113
Dolcellata		357	100
Double Gloucester		411	115
Doux de Montagne		321	90
Edam		321	90
Emmental		385	108
Feta, Danish cows		261	73
Feta, Greek ewes		303	85
Goats milk soft cheese		200	56
Gorgonzola		400	112
Gouda		378	106

Product	Brand	Calories per 100g/ 100ml	Calories per oz/ pack/ portion
Gruyere		414	116
Jarlsberg		339	95
Lancashire		378	106
Leicester		407	114
Leicester, red		396	111
Lymeswold, blue/white		428	120
Maasdam		475	133
Mascapone		400	112
Melbury		325	91
Mozzarella, Danish		328	92
Mozzarella, Italian		310	87
Parmesan		457	128
Philadelphia		318	89
Port Salut		335	94
Quark skimmed milk cheese		71	20
Quark low-fat cheese		125	35
Quark medium-fat cheese		160	45
Ricotta		214	41
Roquefort		378	106
Sage Derby		407	114
Stilton, blue		417	117
Stilton, white		368	103
Wensleydale		382	107
Cheese and asparagus quiche	Tesco	228	800 per 350g flan
Cheese and bacon dip	Tesco		1055 per 227g pack

Product	Brand	Calories per 100g/ 100ml	Calories per oz/ pack/ portion
Cheese and broccoli quiche	Tesco	296	1055 per 356g flan
Cheese and celery sandwiches	Tesco		470 per pack
Cheese and chive flavour food snack	Boots Shapers	127	36
Cheese and ham bites	Tesco	486	138
Cheese and ham flavour food snack	Boots Shapers	127	36
Cheese and ham pancakes	Birds Eye		160 per pancake shallow-fried
	St Michael	221	63
Cheese and mushroom pizza	Tesco	228	65
Cheese and onion crisps	Christies	520	130 per 26g bag
	Hunters	520	130 per 26g bag
	Safeway	500	125 per 25g pack
	Tesco	520	147
	Waitrose	520	390 per 75g pack
lower-fat	St Michael	480	136
Cheese and onion flan	Tesco	326	92
Cheese and onion pizza (frozen)	Ross	210	60
	Safeway	233	66
	Tesco	229	65
(pack of 4)	Safeway	230	65

Product	Brand	Calories per 100g/ 100ml	Calories per oz/ pack/ portion
Cheese and onion puffs	Tesco	509	144
Cheese and onion quiche	Tesco	230	65
individual	Ross	260	74
Cheese and onion sandwich biscuits	Nabisco	522	47 per biscuit
Cheese and onion sandwiches	Tesco		520 per pack
Cheese and onion spread	Tesco	293	83
Cheese and pickle sandwiches	Safeway		420 per pack
Cheese and pineapple salad	Safeway	186	465 per tub
Cheese and salad poppy seeded bap	Waitrose	263	75
Cheese and tomato crisps, natural	Hedgehog	407	145 per 27g pack
Cheese and tomato crispy base pizza	Findus	208	59
Cheese and tomato pizza		234	66
Cheese and tomato pizza	Safeway	247	70
	Tesco	246	70
	Waitrose	222	63

Product	Brand	Calories per 100g/ 100ml	Calories per oz/ pack/ portion
French bread	Safeway	207	59
	Tesco	245	69
pack of 4	Safeway	230	65
Cheese and tomato sandwiches	Waitrose		480 per pack
Cheese, egg and bacon flan	Birds Eye Home Bake		1005 per flan
frozen	Safeway		(4 pack) 415 each
Cheese flavour food snack	Boots Shapers	128	36
Cheese flavoured savoury puffs	Waitrose	526	149
Cheese, gammon and salad granary bap	Waitrose		740
Cheese puffs	Tesco	537	152
Cheese sandwich biscuits	St Michael	520	45 per biscuit
	Tesco	418	40 per biscuit
	Waitrose	528	50 per biscuit
Cheese sauce		198	56
Cheese sauce mix (as sold)	Knorr		150 per packet
	Knorr Pour Over		180 per carton
	Safeway		125 per sachet
	Tesco		40 per packet
Cheese savouries	Asda	529	151
	Tesco	511	145

Product	Brand	Calories per 100g/ 100ml	Calories per oz/ pack/ portion
	Waitrose	517	147
Cheese singles	Kraft		60 each
Cheese snaps	St Michael	517	147
Cheese souffle		252	71
Cheese spread	Safeway		40 each
	Tesco		35 each
with chives	Co-op		79
with herbs	St Michael		99
with onion	Primula		71
with prawns	Co-op		81
with walnuts	St Michael		85
Cheese square	St Michael		164
Cheese Vege Burger	Realeat		135 each
Cheese waves	St Michael	512	143
Cheeseburger	Birds Eye Snack shots		370
with chips	McCain		470
Cheesecake: *see also flavours*			
Cheesecake		421	119
fresh cream	Tesco	275	78
New York style	St Michael	399	113
Cheesecake mix: *see also flavours*			
Cheesecake mix			
	Safeway		560 per pack
original	Green's	425	236 made up per portion

Product	Brand	Calories per 100g/ 100ml	Calories per oz/ pack/ portion
plain luxury recipe	Green's	430	236 made up per portion
Cheeselets	Peek Frean	345	3 per biscuit
Cheesy potato bake	Tesco		565 per pack
Chelsea buns	Tesco	320	91
Cherries, cooking			
raw		46	13
raw (with stones)		39	11
stewed with sugar		77	22
stewed with sugar (with stones)		67	19
stewed without sugar		39	11
stewed without sugar (with stones)			339
Cherries, cocktail, in syrup	Tesco	203	58
Cherries, glace	Safeway	218	62
	Waitrose	212	60
Cherry and walnut log	McVitie's		101
Cherry bakewell	Lyons		175 per small cake
Cherry brandy		255	72
Cherry cake, all butter	Safeway	311	88
Cherry flan filling	Armour	115	33
Cherry fruit pie filling	Tesco	105	30
Cherry Genoa cake	Waitrose	372	105
cut	Safeway	318	90

Product	Brand	Calories per 100g/ 100ml	Calories per oz/ pack/ portion
large	Safeway	318	90
Cherry Madeira cake	Tesco	350	99
cut	St Michael	403	114
Cherry Menthol	Boots	363	120 per 33g stick
Cherry truffles, diabetic	Boots	420	119
Cherry yogurt snack bar, carob coated	Sunwheel Kalibu	383	115 per 30g bar
Cherryade	Corona	25	7
	Safeway	28	8
	Tesco	23	7
	R. Whites	20	6
Cheshire cheese: *see Cheese*			
Chestnuts		170	48
with shells		140	40
Chevda (chevra, chewra), Asian		396	112
Chevra and chana chur, Asian		539	153
Chewing gum	Wrigley		
	Doublemint		9 per stick
	Fruit		9 per stick
Chews			
Apple	Trebor Bassett		13 per sweet
black jacks	Trebor Bassett		15 per sweet
Dinosaur 5	Trebor Bassett		16 per sweet
fruit salad	Trebor Bassett		15 per sweet
Moo Cheo	Trebor Bassett		17 per sweet

Product	Brand	Calories per 100g/ 100ml	Calories per oz/ pack/ portion
Postman Pat	Trebor Bassett		35 per sweet
Chickpea spread: *see Hummus*			
Chickpeas (Bengal gram), raw			32091
besan flour		326	92
Chick peas	Holland and Barrett	300	85
	Tesco	356	101
(cooked)	Tesco	154	44
canned	Boots	82	23
	Waitrose	75	21
Chicken			
dark meat, boiled		204	58
dark meat, raw		126	36
dark meat, roasted		155	44
light meat, boiled		163	46
light meat, raw		116	33
light meat, roasted		142	40
leg quarter (with bone)		92	26
meat and skin, raw		230	65
meat and skin, roasted		216	61
meat only, boiled		183	52
meat only, raw		121	34
meat only, roasted		148	42
Chicken			
boneless, stuffed	Tesco	206	57
casserole hen,			
meat only	Tesco	189	53

Product	Brand	Calories per 100g/ 100ml	Calories per oz/ pack/ portion
corn fed, meat and skin	Tesco	243	68
corn fed, meat only	Tesco	174	48
free range frozen, ready basted, meat and	Sainsbury's	215	60
skin	Tesco	242	67
poussin	Sainsbury's	215	60
quick cook with lemon and tarragon	Sainsbury's	215	60
roasting	Sainsbury's	215	60
whole, meat and skin	Tesco	212	59
whole, meat only	Tesco	166	46
whole, roast	Sainsbury's	225	63
Chicken breast			
grilled with skin		120	35
grilled and skin removed		86	25
boneless, baked	Sainsbury's	200	56
chargrilled	Tesco	210	59
en croute, baked escalope with bacon and mushroom	Sainsbury's	264	74
pizza topping	St Michael		255 each
fillet, skinless, raw	Tesco	148	41
in bread crumbs, baked	Sainsbury's	192	54

Product	Brand	Calories per 100g/ 100ml	Calories per oz/ pack/ portion
with mushroom filling	Tesco	189	53
Chicken drumsticks grilled with skin grilled without skin			90 65
Chicken legs baked, meat and skin	Sainsbury's	285	80
Chicken quarters meat and skin meat only roasted/grilled with skin	Tesco Tesco Sainsbury's	223 156 230	62 43 64
Chicken thighs meat and skin meat only boneless, baked roasted	Tesco Tesco Sainsbury's Tesco	252 203 285 265	70 56 80 74
Chicken wings	Waitrose	237	67
Chicken a l'orange	Findus Lean Cuisine		265 per pack
Chicken and bacon pancakes	Findus		100 each
Chicken and ham cacciatore with noodles	Heinz		250 per pack

Product	Brand	Calories per 100g/ 100ml	Calories per oz/ pack/ portion
Chicken and ham lasagne	Birds Eye Healthy Options		355 per pack
Chicken and ham paste	Princes		170 per pot
Chicken and ham pie	Safeway		355 per pie
Chicken and ham soup with croutons	Knorr Quick Soup		95 per sachet
Chicken and ham spread	Shippams	219	62
Chicken and leek soup, dried as sold	Batchelors Cup-a-Soup	408	98 per 24g sachet
	Knorr Quick Soup	414	95 per sachet
	Waitrose	376	165 per 44g pack
low calorie	Batchelors Slim-a-Soup	317	38 per sachet
Chicken and lemon soup, dried, low calorie	Knorr Quick Soup		30 per sachet
Chicken and lettuce sandwiches	Safeway		355 per pack
Chicken and mushroom casserole	Birds Eye MenuMaster		160 per pack
Chicken and mushroom pancakes	Birds Eye Snacks		150 per pancake shallow-fried
Chicken and mushroom pie	Fray Bentos		835 per pie

Product	Brand	Calories per 100g/ 100ml	Calories per oz/ pack/ portion
	Sainsbury's		405 per pie
Chicken and mushroom soup, dried	Knorr Quick Soup		85 per sachet
Chicken and oriental vegetables	Findus Lean Cuisine		260 per pack
Chicken and pasta bake	Tesco		485 per pack
Chicken and prawn Cantonese	Findus Lean Cuisine		245 per pack
Chicken and stuffing sandwichmaker	Shippams		135 per can
Chicken and sweetcorn savoury rice	Safeway		440 per pack
Chicken and sweetcorn soup	Safeway		281 per 425g can
	Campbell's		295 per 425g can
fresh	Sainsbury's		510 per tub
Chicken 'n' sweetcorn soup with croutons	Batchelors Snack-a-Soup	385	150 per sachet
Chicken and vegetable broth with rice	Campbell's Granny's soups		160 per 425g can
Chicken and vegetable pie	Tesco		1505 per 500g pie
	Tesco		440 per 145g pie

Product	Brand	Calories per 100g/ 100ml	Calories per oz/ pack/ portion
Chicken and vegetable soup	Campbell's Main Course		250 per 425g can
	Heinz Big Soups		185 per 435g can
	St Michael		245 per 425g can
low calorie	Heinz Weight Watchers	21	60 per 286g can
	Waitrose	14	41 per 295g can
dried, with croutons	Knorr Quick Soup		100 per sachet
instant, dried	Tesco		115 per sachet
Chicken and vegetable stewpot pie, individual	Ross		410 per pie
Chicken biryani	Sainsbury's		510 per pack
Chicken bites	St Michael		75
Chicken broth	Baxters		141 per 425g can
Chicken cacciatore	Sainsbury's		600 per pack
Chicken chasseur with rice	Tesco	106	540 per pack
	Birds Eye MenuMaster Healthy Option		390 per pack
Chicken chasseur Cook in Sauce	Homepride		185 per can
Chicken chasseur Cook in the Pot	Crosse & Blackwell		155 per packet

Product	Brand	Calories per 100g/ 100ml	Calories per oz/ pack/ portion
Chicken chasseur cooking mix	Colman's		115 per packet
	Tesco		145 per packet
Chicken chow mein	Sainsbury's		230 per pack
Chicken cordon bleu	St Michael	204	58
	Waitrose	206	58
Chicken cream soup	Knorr "No Simmer"		340 per pack
Chicken crisps	Christies	520	130 per 26g bag
Chicken croquettes	Safeway	260	74
Chicken curry	Co-op		400 per pack
	Boots Shapers Meals		295 per pack
canned	Campbells		485 per can
	Tesco		410 per can
	Tynebrand		330 per can
with rice	Birds Eye		400 per pack
	St Michael		340 per pack
Chicken curry pancakes	Findus		105 each
Chicken escalope with bacon, raw	Tesco	297	84
cooked	Tesco	278	79
Chicken fingers	St Michael		80 each
Chicken Goujons	St Michael		68
	Tesco		58
Chicken in Chinese sauce with rice	Heinz		288 per pack

Product	Brand	Calories per 100g/ 100ml	Calories per oz/ pack/ portion
Chicken Italienne	St Michael	174	49
Chicken Kiev	Sainsbury's		530 per serving
Chicken Korma	Findus		410 per pack
	Tesco		750 per pack
with rice	Birds Eye MenuMaster		550 per pack
	Safeway Microwave Ready meals		590 per pack
Chicken, Leek and sweetcorn pie	Safeway		505 per 198g pie
Chicken-like flavour protein food	Soyapro	242	69
Chicken liver pate	St Michael	224	64
Chicken livers	Waitrose	135	38
Chicken masala	Vesta	317	846 per pack for two
Chicken moghlai	Waitrose	201	64 per pack
Chicken nibbles	Tesco		79
Chicken noodle soup canned, low calorie	Heinz Weight Watchers	19	60 per 316g can
condensed	Campbell's		120 per can
dried	Batchelors		134 per pint pack as sold
low calorie	Boots Shapers soups		95 per sachet
Chicken nuggets	Tesco		93

Product	Brand	Calories per 100g/ 100ml	Calories per oz/ pack/ portion
Chicken pasties	Ross		240 each
Chicken pie			
family	Birds Eye		1075 per pie
	Tesco		1160 per pie
individual	Birds Eye		410 per pie
Shortcrust individual	St Michael		405 per pie
mini	St Michael		210 per pie
Chicken plate pie	Sainsbury's	430	1230
Chicken provencale Cook in Sauce	Homepride		140 per can
Chicken rice soup, condensed	Campbell's		170 per can
Chicken roll	Waitrose	136	39
cooked	Littlewoods	144	41
sliced	Tesco	130	37
Chicken salad meal	St Michael		340 per pack
Chicken salad sandwiches	Waitrose		275 per pack
Chicken samosa	Waitrose	226	64
Chicken savoury rice	Batchelors		440 per pack
Chicken seasoning sauce mix	Colman's Cook In		85 per pack
	Colman's Pour Over		85 per pack
Chicken slices	Soyapro	210	60
Chicken soup	Co-op		260 per can

Product	Brand	Calories per 100g/ 100ml	Calories per oz/ pack/ portion
low calorie	Sainsbury's Heinz Weight Watchers	22	280 per can 65 per 295g can
Chicken soup, dried	Batchelors Cup-a-Soup	428	107 per sachet
	Knorr Quick Soup		95 per sachet
	Waitrose	287	198 per pack
instant	Safeway	395	112
low calorie	Batchelors Slim-a-Soup	317	38 per sachet
Chicken spread	Littlewoods	205	72 per pack
	Shippams	219	77 per pack
Chicken spring roll	Waitrose	376	267 per average roll
Chicken steaks in breadcrumbs	Sainsbury's		205 each
Italian style, baked	Sainsbury's		69
Chicken stock cubes	Knorr	324	92
	Oxo	210	60
	Safeway	285	33 per cube
	Waitrose	322	91
Chicken stock powder	Knorr	198	56
Chicken Super Noodles	Batchelors		460 per pack as sold
Chicken supreme	Sainsbury's		560 per pack

Product	Brand	Calories per 100g/ 100ml	Calories per oz/ pack/ portion
	Tesco		325 per pack
Canned	Tesco		320 per can
with rice	Birds Eye		
	MenuMaster		460 per pack
	Findus		340 per pack
	Sainsbury's		450 per pack
low calorie	Boots shapers Meals		270 per pack
Chicken tikka masala	Safeway		565 per pack
	Sainsbury's		580 per pack
	Tesco		690 per pack
Chicken tikka sandwiches	Safeway		440 per pack
	Tesco		435 per pack
Chicory, raw		9	3
Children's pack			
boiled	Tesco	377	107
chews	Tesco	403	114
compressed	Tesco	365	103
Chilli bean and beef soup	Heinz		105 per 300g can
Chilli beans, canned	Batchelors		265 per can
Chilli Chinese pouring sauce, hot	Sharwood	138	39
sweet	Sharwood	186	53
Chilli con carne	Safeway		260 per pack
	Sainsbury's		490 per pack
	St Michael		285 per pack

Product	Brand	Calories per 100g/ 100ml	Calories per oz/ pack/ portion
canned	Campbells		610 per can
	Tynebrand		520 per can
with rice	Birds Eye Menu Master		375 per pack
Chilli con carne Cook in Sauce	Homepride		280 per can
Chilli con carne pizza, pan bake	Waitrose	222	777 per 350g pizza
Chilli con carne sauce mix	Colman's		145 per pack
Cook in the Pot	Crosse & Blackwell		160 per packet
Chilli powder		314	89
Chilli sauce		21	6
Chilli sauce mix	Knorr		160 per pack
Chillies			
dried			85
raw			6
Chillies in brine, whole green	Old El Paso		28 per can
Chinese barbecue sauce			
ginger and honey	Sharwood	140	40
Hoi Sin	Sharwood	161	46
orange and sherry	Sharwood	140	40
Chinese cakes and biscuits		415	118

Product	Brand	Calories per 100g/ 100ml	Calories per oz/ pack/ portion
Chinese chicken fried rice, special	Batchelors		615 per pack
Chinese fish balls, steamed		52	15
Chinese flaky pastries		392	111
Chinese glutinous rice flour cakes		290	82
Chinese herbs soup mixture: *see Ching bo leung*			
Chinese leaf and sweetcorn salad	Safeway	47	13
Chinese leaves (amaranth), raw		26	7
boiled	Tesco	6	2
Chinese meat buns (barbecued pork)		265	75
Chinese mixed vegetables	St Michael		165 per pack
Chinese mushroom, dried		284	81
Chinese pork luncheon meat		288	82
Chinese pouring sauce			
hot chilli	Sharwood	138	39
light soy	Sharwood	24	7
oyster	Sharwood	66	19
rich soy	Sharwood	60	17
sesame oil	Sharwood	900	255
sweet chilli	Sharwood	186	53
Chinese salted fish, steamed, bone removed		155	44
Chinese sauce mixes (Sharwood): *see flavours*			

Product	Brand	Calories per 100g/ 100ml	Calories per oz/ pack/ portion
Chinese style-chow mein	St Michael		355 per pack
Chinese-style hot and spicy pork	St Michael		505 per pack
Chinese noodles-style	St Michael	127	35
Chinese-style rice	St Michael	140	40
Chinese tofu	Granose	60	17
Ching bo leung (Chinese herbs soup mixture)		23	7
Chip Shop battered fillet, cod	Ross	190	54
haddock	Ross	180	51
Chip Shop chips	Ross	70	20
Chiplets, salt and vinegar	St Michael	487	138
Chips	Findus	109	31
	Safeway	122	35
American style fries	Sainsbury's	240	79
Chips, crinkle cut	Findus	120	33
	Littlewoods	137	622 per 454g pack
	Tesco	112	32
deep-fried	Birds Eye	247	70
shallow-fried	Birds Eye	229	65
Chips, oven	Mc Cain	140	41
	Safeway	150	688 per 454g pack
	Tesco	150	43

Product	Brand	Calories per 100g/ 100ml	Calories per oz/ pack/ portion
Cho cho (chayote, vegetable pear), raw		19	5
Choc and nut crunch	Lyon's Maid		170 each
Choc 'n' cherry Arctic gateau	Birds Eye		100 per 1/5 gateau
Choc 'n' nut cookies	Gateway		50 per biscuit
Choc 'n' nut Cornetto	Wall's		220 per cone
Choc 'n' nut ice cream	Wall's Gino Ginelli Tubs		57 per tub
Cup	Wall's Italiano		170 per cup
Choc 'n' nut Supermousse tub dessert	Birds Eye		150 per tub
Choc bars nutty choc	Wall's		190 per bar
Choc chip 'n' nut cookies	Huntley & Palmer	488	45 per biscuit
Choc ices	Safeway		130 per ice
caprice	Lyon's Maid		115 per ice
chunky dark	Wall's		160 per ice
dark and golden	Wall's		130 per ice
dark satin	Lyons Maid		128 per ice
nutcracker	Lyon's Maid		160 per ice
silky smooth	Lyons Maid		132 per ice

Product	Brand	Calories per 100g/ 100ml	Calories per oz/ pack/ portion
Chocolate and banana ice cream	Lyons Maid	181	51
Chocolate and blackcurrant gateau	Safeway	375	106
Chocolate and hazelnut spread	Tesco	533	151
Chocolate and mint mousse	Tesco		75 each
Chocolate and nut cookies	Waitrose		55 per biscuit
Chocolate and orange biscuits	Cadbury's		45 per biscuit
Chocolate and vanilla Swiss roll	Lyons	373	106
Chocolate biscuits, full-coated		524	149
Chocolate blancmange	Brown and Polson		135 per sachet
Chocolate Brazil	Rowntree Mackintosh Waitrose	574	35 per sweet 163
Chocolate Buttons	Cadbury's	530	175 per 33g standard pack
Chocolate cake, iced layer	Tesco St Michael	428 340	121 96
Chocolate cake mix diabetic	Safeway	315	662 per 210g pack as sold

Product	Brand	Calories per 100g/ 100ml	Calories per oz/ pack/ portion
	Boots	463	131
Chocolate cheesecake slice	St Michael		450 per portion
Chocolate chip and apricot chewy bar	Tesco		120 per bar
Chocolate chip and raisin cluster bar	Applefords		105 per bar
Chocolate chip and orange cookies	Waitrose		55 per biscuit
Chocolate chip cookies	St Michael		50 per biscuit
	Tesco		50 per biscuit
mini	Waitrose		15 per biscuit
Chocolate chip oat digestive	Tesco		75 per biscuit
Chocolate chip shortbread	Waitrose		100 per biscuit
Chocolate chip rich shortie	Tesco		55 per biscuit
Chocolate coated orange wafer	Boots Shapers Diet Chocolate		335 each
Chocolate coated wafer	Boots Shapers Diet Chocolate		340 each
Chocolate coated shortcake bar biscuits	Tesco	498	141

Product	Brand	Calories per 100g/ 100ml	Calories per oz/ pack/ portion
Chocolate coated Swiss roll	Tesco	406	115
Chocolate coated marshmallows	Tesco		75 each
Chocolate coated toffee rolls	Tesco	458	130
Chocolate covered mini roll	Safeway St Michael		115 each 145 each
Chocolate covered sponge roll	St Michael	412	117
Chocolate creams	Safeway		65 per biscuit
Chocolate cup cakes	Lyons		130 per cake
Chocolate dairy toffees	Trebor Bassett	468	45 per toffee
Chocolate delight dessert	St Michael	139	39
Chocolate dessert Lovely	St Michael Waitrose Birds Eye		145 per carton 311 per 72g pack 235 per tub
Chocolate dessert sauce	Lyons Maid	283	80
Chocolate digestives: *see Digestive biscuits*			
Chocolate drink diabetic semi-skimmed	Boots St Michael	341 66	97 19
Chocolate, drinking	Cadbury's	385	20 per portion

Product	Brand	Calories per 100g/ 100ml	Calories per oz/ pack/ portion
Chocolate drop teacake mix	Green's	419	61 made up per portion
Chocolate eclairs	Trebor Bassett	470	39 per sweet
Chocolate fancies	Lyons		120 each
Chocolate fingers	Lyons	414	117
Chocolate flavour dessert mix	Dietade		30 per pack
Chocolate flavour limes	Littlewoods	406	115
Chocolate fruit roll	Trebor	382	16 per sweet
Chocolate fudge	Trebor	457	43 per sweet
Chocolate fudge brownie mix, American style	Green's	453	79 per portion made up
Chocolate fudge mousse	Tesco		80 each
Chocolate ginger crunch biscuits	Waitrose		30 per biscuit
Chocolate ice cream	Waitrose	185	55
dairy	Bertorelli	211	60
non-dairy	Lyons Maid	180	51
soft scoop	Safeway	167	49
Chocolate King Cone	Lyons Maid		219 per cone
Chocolate log and buttercream cake	Safeway	428	121

Product	Brand	Calories per 100g/ 100ml	Calories per oz/ pack/ portion
Chocolate malted food drink, low fat instant	Horlicks	393	111
Chocolate menthe dairy ice cream	Bertorelli	233	66
Chocolate milkshake	St Michael	86	24
	Waitrose	73	22
Chocolate mint creams	Trebor Bassett	380	38 per sweet
Chocolate mints	Trebor Bassett		24 per sweet
	Birds Eye		110 per tub
	Safeway		60 per tub
	Sainsbury's		120 per tub
	St Michael		145 per tub
Chocolate mud pie	St Michael	416	116
Chocolate Munch Bunch	Eden Vale	108	135 per 125g pack
Chocolate nut cookies	Safeway	500	142
Chocolate Oliver biscuits	Fortts		90 per biscuit
Chocolate orange crunch mix, dry	Tesco	419	119
made up	Tesco	270	77
Chocolate orange marble cake	St Michael	416	116

Product	Brand	Calories per 100g/ 100ml	Calories per oz/ pack/ portion
Chocolate orange roll	Tesco		120 each
Chocolate Pavlova cake	Waitrose	300	85
Chocolate peanuts and raisins	Tesco	489	139
Chocolate peppermint creams	St Michael	400	127
Chocolate popcorn	Tesco	414	117
Chocolate rice	Ambrosia		450 per 439g can
Chocolate ripple ice cream	Lyons Maid	181	51
Chocolate roll	Lyons		120 each
jam and vanilla	Lyons		115 each
mini	Safeway		115 each
Chocolate sandwich cake	Waitrose	460	130
	Lyons	378	107
Chocolate sauce	Tesco	331	94
Chocolate soft scoop ice cream	Safeway	168	47
Chocolate sponge and sauce pudding mix	Green's	402	323 per portion made up
Chocolate sponge cake mix Luxury (dry)	Tesco	416	118

Product	Brand	Calories per 100g/ 100ml	Calories per oz/ pack/ portion
(made up) traditional recipe	Tesco	370	105
	Green's	344	91 per portion made up
Chocolate sponge pudding	Heinz	296	84
Chocolate sponge roll with buttercream	St Michael	403	114
Chocolate sponge slice cake	Littlewoods	363	103
Chocolate spread hazelnut	Cadbury's	315	45 per portion
	Cadbury's	570	85 per portion
	Sun-Pat	520	147
Chocolate sundae cups	Lyons Maid		160 each
Chocolate supreme	Eden Vale	134	168 per 125g pack
Chocolate swirl ice cream	Lyons Maid Gold Seal	192	54
Chocolate Swiss roll with buttercream	St Michael	377	107
Chocolate teacakes	Littlewoods	427	121
Chocolate yogurt low fat	Sainsbury's Mr Men		110 per carton
	Tesco		125 per carton
Chomp bar	Cadbury's		115 each
Chopped cured pork slices	St Michael	194	55
Chopped ham and pork, canned		270	77

Product	Brand	Calories per 100g/ 100ml	Calories per oz/ pack/ portion
Chorizo: *see Sausages, delicatessen*			
Chorley cakes	St Michael		290 each
	Waitrose		285 each
Choux buns	St Michael		235 each
Choux pastry, raw		214	61
cooked		330	94
Choux ring dessert	St Michael	424	120
Chow mein	Vesta	361	679 per pack for two as served
low calorie	Batchelors Slim-a-Meal	301	242 per 80.5g pack
Chow mein style pot meal	Boots Shapers		205 per pot
Christmas pudding		304	86
Chuckles roll	Trebor Bassett	363	11 per sweet
Chump chops: *see lamb, pork, etc*			
Chunky chicken (canned)	St Michael		310 per can
country style	Shippams		350 per can
Indian style	Shippams		250 per can
Spanish style	Shippams		315 per can
supreme	Shippams		330 per can
Chunky chicken with bacon and ham pie	Waitrose	302	86

Product	Brand	Calories per 100g/ 100ml	Calories per oz/ pack/ portion
Chunky curried beef (canned)	St Michael	99	28
Chunky steak in rich gravy (canned)	St Michael	100	28
Chunky steak with kidney pie	Waitrose	288	82
Chutney: *see flavours*			
Cider, dry		36	10
sweet		42	12
vintage		101	29
Cider	Autumn Gold	30	170 per pint bottled or canned
	Blackthorn	34	200 per pint
	Diamond White	54	310 per pint
	Special Vat	44	250 per pint
	Strongbow	36	210 per pint
low alcohol	Strongbow		45 per 275ml bottle
	Tesco		75 per 330ml bottle
Cider apple and herbs stuffing mix	Knorr		360 per pack
Cinnamon powder		261	74
Citric acid	Boots	247	70
Citrus fruit drink, carbonated	Boots Shapers		3 per 330ml bottle

Product	Brand	Calories per 100g/ 100ml	Calories per oz/ pack/ portion
Clam chowder	Waitrose	43	12
Clams, seasoned, canned		112	32
with shells, raw		54	15
without shells, raw		88	25
Classic Chinese sauces (Homepride): *see flavours*			
Classic curry sauces (Homepride): *see flavours*			
Clear fruits	Waitrose	356	101
Clear soup with croutons, low calorie, dried			
beef	Batchelors Slim-a-Soup	371	40 per sachet
chicken	Batchelors Slim-a-Soup	390	40 per sachet
Cloudy lemonade	Boots Shapers	1	3 per 330ml bottle
Clover dairy spread	Dairy Crest		193
Clover light			101
Club biscuits			
coffee	Jacobs	503	113 per biscuit
fruit	Jacobs	471	113 per biscuit
milk	Jacobs	510	117 per biscuit
mint	Jacobs	495	113 per biscuit
orange	Jacobs	497	113 per biscuit
plain	Jacobs	494	112 per biscuit
wafer	Jacobs	517	100 per biscuit
Cluster beans: *see Guare*			
Coat and cook sauces (Homepride): *see flavours*			
Cob or hazelnuts		380	108

Product	Brand	Calories per 100g/ 100ml	Calories per oz/ pack/ portion
with shells		137	39
Coca-cola		39	11
Cock-a-Leekie soup	Baxters	24	102 per 425g can
	Heinz Special Recipie	20	90 per 425g can
Cockles, boiled		48	14
Cocktail sausage rolls	St Michael		55 each
Coco Pops	Kellogg's	358	101
Coco Ready Brek	Lyons	388	110
Cocoa		312	88
Coconut			
creamed		600	170
desiccated		604	171
fresh		351	100
kernel only		351	100
Coconut milk		21	6
Coconut oil		883	250
Coconut and honey original crunchy bar	Jordans	416	138 per bar
Coconut biscuits	Huntley & Palmer	511	51 per biscuit
Coconut cake, all butter	Safeway	417	118
	Waitrose	375	106
with buttercream	St Michael	415	118

Product	Brand	Calories per 100g/ 100ml	Calories per oz/ pack/ portion
Coconut Coasters	Cadbury's	485	45 per biscuit
Coconut cookies	Burton's		50 per biscuit
	Huntley & Palmer		80 per biscuit
Coconut crumble creams	Waitrose		65 per biscuit
Coconut crunch bar	Boots Second Nature		150 per bar
Coconut crunch cake	Lyons		135 each
Coconut macaroons	Tesco		142 each
Coconut mallows	Peek Frean	384	46 per biscuit
Coconut Nice creams, assorted	Safeway		80 per biscuit
Coconut rings	Safeway		40 per biscuit
Coconut sponge sandwich	Tesco	225	113
Coconut sponge with buttercream	Safeway	430	122
Coconut toppers	Cadbury's		65 each
Coconut yoghurt	Safeway	119	179 per 150g pack
	Tesco	96	27
Cod			
baked		96	27
baked (with bones and skin)		82	23
cooked		138	39

Product	Brand	Calories per 100g/ 100ml	Calories per oz/ pack/ portion
fried in batter		199	56
grilled		95	27
poached		94	27
smoked, poached		101	29
poached (with bones and skin)		82	23
smoked, raw		79	22
steamed		83	24
steamed (with bones and skin)		67	19
Cod bites, battered	Tesco		30 each
Cod, dried			
salted, boiled		138	39
salted, raw		130	37
Cod fillets			
fresh, raw		76	22
battered	Waitrose	245	69
battered Chip Shop	Ross	185	56
breaded, in natural crumb	Ross	170	48
breaded, in wholemeal crumb	Ross	170	48
breaded	Waitrose	110	31
chilled	Young's	75	21
frozen	Ross	80	23
	Safeway	80	23
	Waitrose	80	23
in breadcrumbs	St Michael	118	33
in breadcrumbs (frozen)	Safeway	140	40
ovencrisp	St Michael	250	71

Product	Brand	Calories per 100g/ 100ml	Calories per oz/ pack/ portion
prime, poached	Young's	78	22
	Waitrose	101	29
skinless	Asda	76	
Cod fillet fish fingers	Birds Eye		50 per finger grilled, fried 60
Cod fish cakes	Ross		60 each
Cod fish fingers	Co-op		55 each grilled
	Findus		60 each
	Safeway		60 each
			70 each baked/grilled, shallow-fried 80
oven crispy	Birds Eye		
Cod in butter sauce	Birds Eye		
	MenuMaster		155 per pack
	Safeway	90	135 per 150g
	Tesco		175 per pack
Cod in cheese sauce	Birds Eye		
	MenuMaster		175 per pack
Cod in cream sauce	Birds Eye		
	MenuMaster		125 per pack
Cod in mushroom sauce	Birds Eye		
	MenuMaster		180 per pack
Cod in parsley sauce	Birds Eye		
	MenuMaster		140 per pack
	Safeway	80	120 per 150g pack
	St Michael		150 per pack

Product	Brand	Calories per 100g/ 100ml	Calories per oz/ pack/ portion
Cod roe			
hard, raw		113	32
fried		202	57
Cod, smoked	Asda	79	
Cod steak			
in butter sauce	Findus		175 per pack
	Ross		140 per pack
in cheese sauce	Findus		160 per pack
	Ross		170 per pack
in parsley sauce	Findus		155 per pack
	Ross		130 per pack
in sweetcorn sauce	Ross		130 per pack
Cod steaks			
frozen, raw		68	19
	Birds Eye		80 per steak
	Waitrose	70	100 per 142g steak
battered	Findus		215 each
breaded, in			
wholemeal crumb	Ross		180 each
crispy	Birds Eye		190 each shallow -fried, deep-fried 215
in breadcrumbs	Findus		245 each
in wafer light batter	Birds Eye		195 each baked/ grilled, shallow-fried 220
in wholemeal crumb	Birds Eye		195 each grilled /baked, shallow-fried 220

Product	Brand	Calories per 100g/ 100ml	Calories per oz/ pack/ portion
oven crispy	Birds Eye		215 per steak baked or grilled
Cod and broccoli pie, frozen	Sainsbury's		365 per 350g pie
Cod and cauliflower au gratin	St Michael		645 per 454g pack
crumble	Littlewoods	117	468 per 400g pack
Cod and prawn pie	Tesco	195	55
	Young's	195	55
individual	St Michael	150	43
Cod crumble	Ross	195	55
Cod florentine	St Michael		305 per 340g pack
Cod liver oil		899	255
Cod mornay	Birds Eye MenuMaster		420 per pack
Coffee, ground, roasted		287	81
infusion, 5 minutes		2	1
instant		100	28
Coffee and chicory essence		218	62
Coffee Break	Safeway	50	14
Coffee cake mix, Austrian style	Green's	388	292 made up per portion
Coffee Choice	Safeway	330	94
Coffee Club biscuits	Jacobs	503	113 per biscuit

Product	Brand	Calories per 100g/ 100ml	Calories per oz/ pack/ portion
Coffee Compliment	Cadbury's	540	10 per portion
Coffee cream	Rowntree Mackintosh		30 per sweet
Coffee creams	Peek Frean	480	56 per biscuit
	St Michael	534	151
	Tesco	464	132
	Waitrose	476	135
Coffee cup	Rowntree Mackintosh		40 per sweet
Coffee ice cream, dairy	Bertorelli	196	56
Coffee mondarin gateau	Ross		4430 each
Coffee-mate	Carnation		10 per tsp
Cola	Canada Dry	34	10
	Safeway	40	12
	St Michael	46	14
bottled	Tesco	30	9
canned	Tesco	32	9
diabetic	Boots	1	
Diet	Canada Dry Safeway		0.3 per 175ml pack
low calorie	Tesco	4	1
	Waitrose	4	1
Cola refresher	Trebor Bassett		7 per sweet
Cola sherbets	Trebor Bassett	359	23 per sweet

Product	Brand	Calories per 100g/ 100ml	Calories per oz/ pack/ portion
Cole, dried, boiled		12	3
Coleslaw	St Ivel	125	35
	St Michael	172	49
	Safeway	198	56
	Tesco	104	29
	Waitrose	128	36
apple	Tesco	157	45
apple and sultana	Safeway	202	57
canned	Heinz	126	36
classic	Eden Vale	127	36
coarse cut	Eden Vale	124	35
curried	Tesco	204	58
diet	Eden Vale	55	16
fruity	Eden Vale	207	59
reduced calorie dressing, other recipes	Tesco	52	15
in vinaigrette	Tesco	60	17
in vinaigrette, other recipes	Tesco	40	11
low calorie	St Ivel Shape	38	11
	Safeway	52	15
	Waitrose	62	18
mild	Eden Vale	200	57
other recipes	Tesco	124	35
premier	St Ivel	230	65
	Tesco	189	54
other recipes	Tesco	168	48

Product	Brand	Calories per 100g/ 100ml	Calories per oz/ pack/ portion
reduced calorie dressing	Littlewoods	54	15
	Tesco	44	12
spicy	Eden Vale	201	57
with cheese and chives	St Michael	286	81
Coleslaw dressing	Kraft	449	133
Coley fillet, raw		75	21
steamed		100	28
Colocasia: *see Arvi*			
Comforters	Barratt	333	94
Complete batter mix (as sold)	Green's	359	102
Compound cooking fat		894	253
Condensed milk			
sweetened, skimmed		267	76
sweetened, whole		322	91
Consomme			
condensed	Campbell's	8	2
specialty soup	Crosse & Blackwell	22	6
Continental mixed vegetables	Safeway	57	226 per 397g pack
Continental stir fry vegetables (as sold)	Birds Eye	42	12
fried	Birds Eye	53	15

Product	Brand	Calories per 100g/ 100ml	Calories per oz/ pack/ portion
Continental vegetable mix	Tesco	313	89
Cook In sauce (Colman's): *see flavours*			
Cook in Sauces (Homepride): *see flavours*			
Cook in the Pot (Crosse & Blackwell): *see flavours*			
Cookeen cooking fat	Van den Berghs	900	255
Cookie crunch biscuits	Tesco	452	128
Cookies	Tesco	304	86
Cooking chocolate			
milk	Tesco	532	151
plain	Tesco	540	153
white	Tesco	526	149
Cooking fat	Cookeen	900	255
compound		894	253
Cooking-in Sauces (Baxters): *see flavours*			
Cooking margarine	Safeway	726	206
Cooking mixes (Colman's): *see flavours*			
Cooking oil, blended	Tesco	875	248
Coolmints	Trebor Bassett	382	6 per sweet
Coriander leaves, dried		279	79
seeds		298	84
Corn chips	Phileas Fogg		225 per 40g pack
Californian	St Michael		430 per 75g pack
Corn cobs: *see Corn on the cob*			

Product	Brand	Calories per 100g/ 100ml	Calories per oz/ pack/ portion
Corn oil	Boots	899	255
	Mazola	900	255
	Safeway	900	255
	Sunwheel	900	255
	Tesco	875	248
	Waitrose	900	266
Corn on the cob			120 per average 200g cob
Corn, popping	Holland and Barrett	375	106
Corn relish	Safeway	118	33
Corned beef		217	62
Corned beef and pickle sandwiches with salad	Tesco		320 per pack
	St Michael		280 per pack
Cornetto			
Black Forest	Wall's		230 per super cone
choc & nut	Wall's		220 per cone
choco rico	Wall's		250 per super cone
mint choc chip	Wall's		235 per cone
strawberry	Wall's		205 per cone
tutti frutti	Wall's		240 per super cone
Cornflakes		368	104
	Kellogg's	350	99
	Safeway	354	100
	Tesco	354	100
	Waitrose	345	98

Product	Brand	Calories per 100g/ 100ml	Calories per oz/ pack/ portion
Crunchy Nut	Kellogg's	378	107
Cornflour		354	100
Cornish dairy bar	Lyons Maid		90 each
Cornish ice cream			
dairy	Lyons Maid	202	57
vanilla	Safeway	169	50
	Tesco	181	51
Cornish pastie		332	94
	Ross		240 each
Cornish puff pastry pasties	St Michael	239	68
Cornish wafers	Jacobs	514	43 per biscuit
	Safeway	514	45 per biscuit
Cornmeal, sifted, raw		368	104
unsifted, raw		353	100
Cottage cheese: *see also flavours*			
Cottage cheese	Holland and Barrett	110	31
	Littlewoods	96	218 per 227g pack
	Safeway	104	116 per 113g pack
	St Michael	97	27
	Waitrose	94	108 per 113g pack
creamy, natural	St Michael	133	38
creamy, with prawn	St Michael	175	50
crunchy	Eden Vale	114	32
diet, natural	Eden Vale	83	24
diet, onion and			

Product	Brand	Calories per 100g/ 100ml	Calories per oz/ pack/ portion
chive	Eden Vale	81	23
diet, pineapple	Eden Vale	90	26
natural	Eden Vale	97	27
	Raines	100	28
	St Ivel	94	27
	St Ivel Shape	79	22
with apple, celery and nut	St Michael	157	45
with beef and horseradish	St Michael	147	42
with cheddar and onion	Raines	120	34
with chives	Raines	100	28
	Safeway	104	232 per 227g pack
with pineapple	Raines	95	27
	St Michael	107	30
with prawns	St Michael	167	47
with tuna, sweetcorn and pepper	St Michael	149	42
Cottage pie	Littlewoods	186	263 per pie
	Tesco	198	56
	Waitrose	136	585 per 425g pie
fresh potato, family	St Michael	168	48
large	St Michael	155	44
small	St Michael	144	41
Cough candy twists	Trebor Bassett	356	26 per sweet
Country cake	St Michael	405	115

Product	Brand	Calories per 100g/ 100ml	Calories per oz/ pack/ portion
Country cereal mix, vegetarian	Boots	367	104
Country chicken and leek soup	Crosse & Blackwell Pot Soup		62 made up per sachet
Country crunch biscuits	Peek Frean	445	36 per biscuit
Country herb stuffing mix	Tesco	383	109
	Waitrose	320	91
Country Maid instant milk	Wander	355	101
Country mix vegetables	Findus	55	16
	Ross	30	9
Country muesli	Jordans	345	98
Country recipe sausages	Wall's Light and Lean	198	99 per sausage
Country stir fry vegetables (as sold)	Birds Eye	28	8
fried	Birds Eye	35	10
Country Store	Kellogg's	346	98
Country strawberry dairy ice cream	Safeway	223	66
Country style mixed fruit cake	St Michael	360	102

Product	Brand	Calories per 100g/ 100ml	Calories per oz/ pack/ portion
Country vegetable soup			
Homestyle	Heinz	43	125 per 300g can
low calorie	Heinz Weight Watchers		60 per 286g can
with croutons	Knorr Quick Soup		90 per sachet
Courgettes (zucchini, squash), raw			257
Couscous		227	64
Cow peas: *see Blackeye beans under Beans*			
Cox's apples	Tesco	46	13
Crab			
boiled (with shell)		25	7
canned		81	23
boiled		127	36
Crab bisque	Campbell's		220 per 295g can
	Sainsbury's		190 per 425g can
	Tesco		175 per 425g can
Crabmeat in brine	Armour	80	136 per 170g can
Crab paste	Shippams	183	137 per 75g pack
	Safeway	205	154 per 75g pack
Crab pate	St Michael	226	64
Cracked wheat	Holland and Barrett	311	88
Cracker barrel Cheddar cheese	Kraft	406	115

Product	Brand	Calories per 100g/ 100ml	Calories per oz/ pack/ portion
Crackers			
Hovis	Tesco	484	137
wholemeal	St Michael	459	130
Cracknels	Rowntree Mackintosh		40 per sweet
Cranberries, raw		15	4
Cranberry sauce	Safeway	137	39
	Tesco	148	42
and wine	Colman	215	61
jellied	Baxters	258	73
whole fruit	Baxters	143	41
Cream			
aerosol spray		340	95
clotted		590	166
double		445	125
extra thick		465	130
half		160	42
imitation		304	85
non-dairy		285	80
single		200	56
soured		207	58
sterilized, canned		242	68
whipping		375	105
Cream cheese			
and chives	Waitrose	435	123
soft	St Ivel	460	130
Cream crackers		440	125

Product	Brand	Calories per 100g/ 100ml	Calories per oz/ pack/ portion
Cream dessert, chocolate	Young's	250	71
raspberry	Young's	200	57
Cream doughnuts	St Michael	365	103
Cream fruit trifle, individual	St Michael	158	45
Cream of asparagus soup	Baxters		285 per 425g can
	Heinz Special Recipie		180 per 425g can
dried, with croutons	Batchelors Cup-a-Soup Special		130 per sachet
	Knorr Quick Soup	467	132
Cream of celery soup	Heinz		130 per 300g can
	Tesco		185 per 425g can
condensed	Campbell's		270 per 295g can
Cream of chicken and sweetcorn soup with croutons	Batchelors Cup-a-Soup Special		120 per sachet
Cream of chicken and vegetable soup with croutons	Batchelors Cup-a-Soup Special		120 per sachet
Cream of chicken soup, canned		58	16
condensed		98	28
condensed, as served		49	14
Cream of chicken soup	Baxters		280 per 425g can

Product	Brand	Calories per 100g/ 100ml	Calories per oz/ pack/ portion
	Crosse & Blackwell		180 per 283g can
	Heinz		140 per 300g can
	Safeway		260 per 425g can
condensed	Campbell's		300 per 295g can
dried, with croutons	Knorr Quick Soup	466	132
Cream of chicken with white wine soup	Heinz Special Recipie		210 per 425g can
Cream of Cornish ice cream	Wall's	90	32
Cream of leek soup	Baxters		220 per 425g can
Cream of mushroom soup, canned		53	15
Cream of mushroom soup	Baxters		230 per 425g can
	Crosse & Blackwell		170 per 283g can
	Heinz		130 per 300g can
	Safeway		215 per 425g can
	Tesco		230 per can
condensed	Campbell's		270 per 425g can
dried	Batchelors Cup-a-Soup Special		120 per sachet
Cream of pheasant soup	Baxters		260 per 425g can
Cream of scampi soup	Baxters		240 per 425g can

Product	Brand	Calories per 100g/ 100ml	Calories per oz/ pack/ portion
Cream of smoked trout soup	Baxters		240 per 425g can
Cream of tomato and vegetable soup, dried	Batchelors		350 per pint pack
Cream of tomato soup, canned, ready to serve		55	16
condensed		123	35
condensed, as served		62	18
Cream of tomato soup	Baxters		300 per 425g can
	Heinz		180 per 300g can
	Safeway		255 per 425g can
	St Michael		235 per 425g can
condensed	Campbell's		365 per 295g can
dried, with croutons	Knorr Quick Soup	458	130
Cream of vegetable soup, dried	Batchelors		305 per pint pack
with croutons	Batchelors Cup-a-Soup Special		135 per sachet
	Knorr Quick Soup	465	132
Cream scones	St Michael		300 each
Cream soda	Whites	20	6
Cream wafers, assorted	Safeway	505	143
Creamed coconut	Sharwood	600	170
Creamed garlic sauce	Burgess	435	122

Product	Brand	Calories per 100g/ 100ml	Calories per oz/ pack/ portion
Creamed macaroni	Ambrosia		405 per 439g can
Creamed rice	Ambrosia		395 per 439g can
	Libby		390 per 439g can
	Safeway		385 per 439g can
low fat	Ambrosia	75	330 per can
traditional	Safeway		460 per 439g can
Creamed sago	Ambrosia	81	355 per 439g can
Creamed semolina	Ambrosia	83	365 per 439g can
Creamed spinach	Findus	60	17
	Safeway	40	11
Creamed tapioca	Ambrosia	83	365 per 439g can
Creamed tomato soup	Crosse & Blackwell	71	220 per can
Creamola foam crystals	Creamola	323	92
Creme caramel	Eden Vale		140 per carton
	Ross		155 each
	Safeway		140 each
	St Ivel		130 per carton
Creme de menthe			80 per 1/6 gill
Creme eggs	Cadbury's		175 each
Crinkle cut chips: *see Chips, crinkle cut*			
Crisp 'n' Dry			
solid cooking oil	Spry	900	255
vegetable oil	Spry	900	255
Crisp bake pork pies	St Michael	349	99

Product	Brand	Calories per 100g/ 100ml	Calories per oz/ pack/ portion
individual	St Michael	339	96
Crispbread, rye		321	91
wheat, starch reduced		388	110
Crispbread			
brown rye	Safeway		35 per slice
light	Gateway		20 per slice
light whole meal	Gateway		15 per slice
rye light	St Michael		15 per slice
Crisps: *see also flavours*			
Crisps	Golden Wonder	530	140
	Sooner	533	144 per 27g pack
crinkle cut	Tesco	568	161
	Waitrose	520	147
crinkle cut, ready			
salted	Safeway	543	407 per 75g pack
jacket	Safeway		120 per 25g pack
	Smiths		150 per 25g pack
ready salted	Christies	520	130 per 26g pack
	Safeway	500	125 per 25g pack
	St Michael	545	155
	Tesco	547	155
	Waitrose	520	390 per 75g pack
ready salted lower-fat	St Michael	485	137
wholewheat	Nature's Snack	550	110 per 20g pack
wholewheat cheese	Nature's Snack	550	130 per 20g pack
Crispy batter mix	Green's	341	97
Crispy cod, haddock, etc: *see Cod, Haddock, etc*			

Product	Brand	Calories per 100g/ 100ml	Calories per oz/ pack/ portion
Crispy thins	Waitrose	484	137
Crofters' thick vegetable soup	Knorr		240 per 1 1/2 pint pack
Croissants	St Michael	383	109
Croquette potatoes baked or grilled	Birds Eye		50 each
Croutons	St Michael	558	158
Crumble mix	Granny Smiths	454	1022 per 225g pack made up
(as sold)	Tesco	673	191
(made up)	Tesco	459	130
	Whitworths	466	132
Crumpets	Sunblest	182	80 per crumpet
	Tesco	168	80 per crumpet
Scottish	Tesco	260	95 per crumpet
Crunch bar	St Michael	450	128
Crunch bar mix, apple apple and	Green's	355	224 per portion made up
blackcurrant	Green's	408	220 per portion made up
Crunch creams	Peek Frean	482	58 per biscuit
Crunch mixes: see flavours			
Crunchie bar	Cadbury's	465	110 per small 24g bar, standard 195
Crunchy Bemax	Beecham	310	88

Product	Brand	Calories per 100g/ 100ml	Calories per oz/ pack/ portion
Crunchy bran	Allinson	360	102
Crunchy cereal	Safeway	438	118
Crunchy coated peanuts	Sooner	490	196 per 40g pack
Crunchy cottage cheese	Eden Vale	114	32
Crunchy creams	Waitrose	506	65 per biscuit
Crunchy crumble mix	Tesco	460	130
Crunchy nut cereal	Granose	493	140
Crunchy Nut Corn Flakes	Kellogg's	378	107
Crunchy oat cereal	Sainsbury's	417	117
Crunchy oat mvesli	St Michael	440	123
Crunchy sticks, ready salted	Safeway	481	361 per 75g pack
salt and vinegar	Safeway	487	365 per 75g pack
Crystals	Trebor Bassett	357	5 per sweet
Cub Lion bar	Rowntree Mackintosh	495	80 per bar
Cube sugar, white	Tate and Lyle	394	112
Cucumber (khira, kakdi), raw			103
pickled, sliced	Safeway	28	8
Cucumber dressing	Heinz All Seasons	276	78
Cucumber relish	Safeway	118	33

Product	Brand	Calories per 100g/ 100ml	Calories per oz/ pack/ portion
Cucumber sandwich spread	Heinz	183	52
Cumin seeds		375	106
Cup-a-Soup (Batchelors): *see flavours*			
Cup-a-Soup Special (Batchelors): *see flavours*			
Cup cakes, chocolate	Lyons	338	96
orange and lemon	Lyons	361	102
Curacao		311	88
Curd cheese: *see Cheese*			
Curly wurly	Cadbury's	470	135 per 29g bar
Currant bun mix (as sold)	Tesco	410	116
made up	Tesco	347	98
Currant buns		302	86
Currants, dried		243	69
Curried beans	Safeway	75	165 per 227g can
with sultanas	Heinz	88	200 per 255g can
Curried chicken, canned	St Michael	120	510 per can
Curried chicken Toast Topper	Heinz	73	21
Curried fruit chutney	Pan Yan	144	41
	Sharwood	141	40
	Tesco	141	40
Curry leaves, raw		88	25

Product	Brand	Calories per 100g/ 100ml	Calories per oz/ pack/ portion
Curry powder		325	92
	Safeway	535	152
	Tesco	353	100
Curry rice, mild, cooked	Uncle Ben's	136	36
Curry sauce	Colman's Pour Over/Cook In	350	125 per pack
	Homepride Cook In	112	421 per pack
chilled	Tesco	85	24
Curry savoury rice	Safeway	342	435 per pack
Curry style pot meal	Boots Shapers	327	245 per pot
Custard powder		354	100
Custard pudding, egg		118	33
powder, made up		118	33
Custard			
Devon, canned	Ambrosia	100	440 per 439g can
instant mix	Brown and Polson	404	115
	Rowntree	416	118
	Safeway	428	121
low fat	Ambrosia	74	315 per 425g can
ready to eat	St Michael	120	600 per carton
Custard apple, raw		92	26
Custard creams	Peek Frean	483	53 per biscuit
	Safeway	507	65 per biscuit
	Tesco	464	60 per biscuit

Product	Brand	Calories per 100g/ 100ml	Calories per oz/ pack/ portion
diabetic	Boots	555	157
Custard tart		287	81
Cuttlefish, raw		81	23

D

Product	Brand	Calories per 100g/ 100ml	Calories per oz/ pack/ portion	123
Dairy Cassata Bombe	Bertorelli	215	61	
Dairy cheese, soft	Tesco	271	77	
with chives	Tesco	290	82	
with pineapple	Tesco	358	101	
Dairy cream and chocolate sponge	Birds Eye		110 per 1/6 sponge	
Dairy cream choux buns	Birds Eye		130 per bun	
Dairy cream doughnuts	Birds Eye		170 per doughnut	
Dairy cream eclairs	Birds Eye		145 per eclair	
	Safeway	388	120 per eclair	
Dairy cream sponge	Asda	281		
	Birds Eye		130 per 1/6 sponge	
	Ross	270	77	
	Tesco	313	89	
Dairy fudge	Trebor	457	43 per sweet	
Dairy ice cream		167	47	
Dairy Milk chocolate bar	Cadbury's	530	105 per 20g bar	
Dairy milk ices	Lyons Maid	124	35	
Dairy Milk miniatures	Cadbury's	530	30 per miniature	
Dairy spread				
Clover	Dairy Crest	682	193	
Clover light		390	111	

Product	Brand	Calories per 100g/ 100ml	Calories per oz/ pack/ portion
Delight	Van den Berghs	398	113
Delight extra low very low fat	Van den Berghs	228	64
low fat	Outline	370	105
	Tesco	393	111
Dairy spread processed cheese	St Michael	300	85
Dairy toffees	Rowntree Mackintosh		30 per sweet
	Trebor Bassett	456	30 per sweet
Dairy topping low fat	Asda	107	
Dairylea cheese spread	Kraft	273	232 per 85g pack
Damson jam	Waitrose	248	70
Damson preserve	Tesco	255	72
Damsons			
raw		38	11
raw (with stones)		34	10
stewed without sugar		32	9
stewed without sugar (with stones)		29	8
stewed with sugar		69	20
stewed with sugar (with stones)		63	18
Danbo cheese: *see Cheese*			
Dandelion and burdock	Corona	20	6
	Whites	25	7

Product	Brand	Calories per 100g/ 100ml	Calories per oz/ pack/ portion
Dandelion coffee	Symingtons	320	91
Dandex coffee	Lanes	385	109
Danish blue cheese: *see Cheese*			
Danish salami	Waitrose	520	588 per 113g pack
Dansak Classic curry sauce	Homepride	103	394 per 383g pack
Darjeeling tea, infused	Safeway	1	
Dark and aromatic Chinese sauce mix	Sharwood	270	185 per sachet
Dark and golden choc ice	Wall's		130 per ice
Dark Bournville chocolate bar	Cadbury's	510	255 per 50g bar
Dark choc ice	Waitrose	290	180 per 62ml ice
Dark satin choc ice	Lyons Maid		128 per ice
Date and apple dessert bar	Prewetts Fruit Bars	238	100 per 42g bar
Date and apricot bar	Granose	340	85 per 25g bar
Date and fig dessert bar	Prewetts	262	110 per 42g bar
Date and muesli bar	Boots	324	145 per bar
Date and walnut cake	Waitrose	406	115
Date and walnut cottage cheese	Safeway	119	34

Product	Brand	Calories per 100g/ 100ml	Calories per oz/ pack/ portion
Date bar	Granose	352	88 per 25g bar
Dates			
raw		144	41
Dates, dried			
raw		248	70
(with stones)		213	60
chopped	Whitworths	273	77
dessert	Whitworths	213	60
stoned	Holland and Barrett	240	68
	Whitworths	248	70
sugar rolled	Tesco	279	79
Decaffeinated coffee			
beans	Waitrose	194	55
filter fine	Waitrose	287	81
freeze-dried	Safeway	330	94
instant (freeze-dried)	Waitrose	100	28
Delight, sugar free, strawberry	Asda	443	
Delight dairy spread	Van den Berghs	398	113
Deltas	St Michael	515	146
De luxe bean mix (dried)	Holland and Barrett	265	75
Deluxe muesli	Prewetts	360	102
	Sunwheel	390	111
	Sunwheel	392	111

Product	Brand	Calories per 100g/ 100ml	Calories per oz/ pack/ portion
Demerara sugar		394	112
Derby cheese: *see Cheese*			
Desiccated coconut		604	171
Dessert bars (Prewetts): *see flavours*			
Dessert logs, Sonata	Wall's		130 per 1/6 log
Viennetta	Wall's		135 per 1/6 log
Dessert mixes (Dietade): *see flavours*			
Dessert pies, apple	Lyons	349	99
Dessert sauces (Lyons Maid): *see flavours*			
Dessert topping, dry	Tesco	512	145
made up	Tesco	181	51
Dessert white sauce	Ambrosia	97	27
Devon butter	Safeway	731	207
Devon creams	Peek Frean	487	58 per biscuit
Devon custard	Ambrosia	100	440 per 439g can
Devon sponge cake mix (dry)			223 made up per portion
	Green's	396	
Devon toffees	Littlewoods	416	118
	Waitrose	430	122
Devonshire cheesecake			
blackcurrant	St Ivel	250	225 per carton
strawberry	St Ivel	250	225 per carton
Devonshire trifles, individual	Ross	160	180 each

Product	Brand	Calories per 100g/ 100ml	Calories per oz/ pack/ portion
Dextrosol tablets, all varieties	Dextrosol	347	98
Diabetic bourbon creams	Boots	467	132
Diabetic cake mix (dry)			
chocolate	Boots	463	131
plain	Boots	459	130
Diabetic cherry truffles	Boots	420	119
Diabetic chocolate coated wafers	Boots	560	159
orange	Boots	555	157
Diabetic chocolate drink	Boots	341	97
Diabetic Cola	Boots	1	
Diabetic continental chocolate assortment	Boots	519	147
Diabetic custard creams	Boots	555	157
Diabetic dressing	Boots	155	44
Diabetic drinks (Boots): see flavours			
Diabetic fruit cocktail	Boots	24	7
Diabetic fruit flavour drops	Boots	367	104
Diabetic ginger creams	Boots	468	133

Product	Brand	Calories per 100g/ 100ml	Calories per oz/ pack/ portion
Diabetic hazelnut biscuits	Boots	428	121
Diabetic honey spread	Boots	256	73
Diabetic jams (Boots, Dietade): *see flavours*			
Diabetic jelly crystals (Boots): *see flavours*			
Diabetic Lincoln biscuits	Boots	402	114
Diabetic marmalade	Dietade	230	65
fine cut	Boots	239	68
thick cut	Boots	239	68
Diabetic marzipan bars	Boots	465	132
Diabetic milk chocolate	Boots	512	145
coffee cream	Boots	574	163
hazelnut	Boots	518	147
strawberry cream	Boots	552	156
yogurt cream	Boots	556	158
Diabetic milk chocolate drops	Boots	512	145
Diabetic milk chocolate wafers			
caramel	Boots	523	148
Diabetic mint imperials	Boots	371	105
Diabetic muesli biscuits	Boots	437	124

Product	Brand	Calories per 100g/ 100ml	Calories per oz/ pack/ portion
Diabetic pastilles			
fruit flavours	Boots	100	28
peppermint	Boots	99	28
Diabetic peach slices	Boots	20	6
Diabetic pear quarters	Boots	21	6
Diabetic plain chocolate	Boots	500	142
Diabetic praline truffles	Boots	582	165
Diabetic preserves	Thursday Cottage	140	40
Diabetic sweetener (powder)	Boots	360	102
Diamond White cider	Taunton	54	310 per pint
Diet cola	Safeway	0	0
Diet cottage cheese			
natural	Eden Vale	83	24
onion and chive	Eden Vale	81	23
pineapple	Eden Vale	90	26
Diet drinks: *see flavours*			
Diet lemonade	Safeway	0	0
Diet Ski yogurt (Eden Vale): *see flavours*			
Dietade (Appleford): see products			
Digestive bars, chocolate coated	Tesco	504	95 each

Product	Brand	Calories per 100g/ 100ml	Calories per oz/ pack/ portion
Digestive biscuits			
chocolate		493	140
plain		471	134
	Asda	488	
	Boots	457	30 per biscuit
	Huntley & Palmer	463	63 per biscuit
	Mitchellhill		60 per biscuit
	Safeway	493	70 per biscuit
	St Michael	499	75 per biscuit
	Tesco	496	75 per biscuit
Bourneville	Cadbury's	480	45 per biscuit
for cheese, small	Safeway	490	10 per biscuit
fruit	Huntley & Palmer	451	50 per biscuit
Hovis	Nabisco	486	57 per biscuit
	Tesco	481	136
milk chocolate	Cadbury's	490	50 per biscuit
	Safeway	505	65 per biscuit
	Waitrose	499	141
milk half coated	Huntley & Palmer	502	65 per biscuit
plain chocolate	Safeway	500	142
	St Michael	505	143
	Tesco	508	144
	Waitrose	505	143
plain half coated	Huntley & Palmer	496	65 per biscuit
small	Peek Frean	490	48 per biscuit

Product	Brand	Calories per 100g/ 100ml	Calories per oz/ pack/ portion
sweetmeal	Tesco	470	133
Digestive creams	Boots	497	60 per biscuit
Dijon mustard	Colman's	170	48
Dill cucumber, pickled	Tesco	14	4
Dill seeds		305	86
Dill, sliced	Tesco	17	5
Dinner balls	Granose	145	41
Disneys Cartoons cake mix			64 per portion made up
	Green's	408	
Dixie crackers	Safeway	431	20 per biscuit
Dogfish			
fried in batter		265	75
fried (with waste)		244	69
Dolcelatte cheese: *see Cheese*			
Dolly mixtures	Bassett's	366	104
	Tesco	377	107
Dolmio (as sold)			
original	Dolmio	41	11
with mushrooms	Dolmio	39	11
with peppers	Dolmio	40	11
Double choc Arctic circles	Birds Eye		165 per piece
Double Decker	Cadbury's	465	235 per 51g bar

Product	Brand	Calories per 100g/ 100ml	Calories per oz/ pack/ portion
Double Gloucester cheese: *see Cheese*			
Double Top dessert topping (canned)	Nestle	178	50
Doublemint chewing gum	Wrigley		9 per stick
Doughnut mix	Granny Smiths	425	1664 per 392g pack made up
Doughnuts		349	99
	St Michael	365	260 per doughnut
dairy cream	Birds Eye		170 per doughnut
Doux de Montagne cheese: *see Cheese*			
Dover sole			
fillet, raw		82	23
fillet, fried		215	60
fillet, poached		92	26
with bones, poached		65	18
Dried mixed fruit	Asda	248	
Drifter	Rowntree Mackintosh	460	130 per biscuit
Drinking chocolate		366	104
	Asda	387	
	Cadbury's	385	20 per portion
	Ovaltine	387	110
	Safeway	358	101
	Tesco	390	111
	Waitrose	395	112

Product	Brand	Calories per 100g/ 100ml	Calories per oz/ pack/ portion
fat reduced	Boots	345	98
granules	St Michael	366	104
instant	Ovaltine	400	113
Dripping			
beef		891	253
Driver's			
gin and tonic	Britvic	31	55 per 180ml pack
whisky and			
American ginger ale	Britvic	31	57 per 180ml pack
white rum and cola	Britvic	37	66 per 180ml pack
Drumstick: *see Horseradish*			
Dry ginger	Tesco	19	6
low calorie	Tesco	6	2
Dry ginger ale	Hunts	16	5
	Safeway	24	7
	Schweppes	15	4
	Waitrose	22	7
low calorie	Safeway	5	1
Dry roasted peanuts	Safeway	570	570 per 100g pack
	Sooner	602	301 per 50g pack
	Waitrose	625	1406 per 225g pack
Duchesse dessert	St Michael	224	64
Duck			
meat only, raw		122	35
meat only, roast		189	54
meat, fat and skin, raw		430	122
meat, fat and skin, roast		339	96

Product	Brand	Calories per 100g/ 100ml	Calories per oz/ pack/ portion
Duck liver pate	Tesco	256	73
Duckling			
fresh	Waitrose	400	113
frozen	Waitrose	400	113
Dumplings		211	60
Dundee cake	Safeway	312	88
	Tesco	336	95
butter	Safeway	382	108
large	Safeway	312	88
Dutch cheese: *see Edam, Gouda, under Cheese*			
Dutch shortcake biscuits	Huntley & Palmer	539	40 per biscuit

E

Product	Brand	Calories per 100g/ 100ml	Calories per oz/ pack/ portion
Earl Grey tea, infused	Safeway	1	1 per 125g pack
Easy cook rice	Safeway	364	103
	Waitrose	360	102
American	Waitrose	360	102
cooked	Tesco	120	34
raw	Tesco	353	100
Eccles cakes, all butter	Waitrose	390	111
Echo margarine	Van den Berghs	740	210
Eclairs		376	107
	Waitrose	410	116
chocolate	Young's	440	125
dairy cream	Birds Eye		145 per eclair
milk chocolate	Cadbury's	450	20 each pocket pack standard pack 40
Economy burgers	Birds Eye Steakhouse		100 per burger grilled, fried 110
	Safeway	264	75
Edam cheese: *see Cheese*			
Eddoes, fresh, cooked	Tesco	181	51
Eel			
raw		168	48
raw, flesh only		168	48
stewed		201	57
Egg and bacon sandwiches	St Michael	325	420 per pack

Product	Brand	Calories per 100g/ 100ml	Calories per oz/ pack/ portion
Egg and cress sandwiches	St Michael	204	295 per pack
Egg and mayonnaise sandwiches	Waitrose		620 per pack
Egg, cheese and bacon flan	Sainsbury's		420 per 602g flan
Egg custard dessert mix, no bake (as sold)	Green's	380	148 made up per portion
Egg custard tarts	St Michael	267	76
Egg, ham, cheese and tomato quiche	Tesco	247	70
Egg lasagne: *see Lasagne*			
Eggnog and raisin dairy ice cream	Safeway	224	66
Eggplant: *see Aubergine*			
Eggs			
boiled		147	42
dried		564	160
fried		232	66
omelette		190	54
poached		155	44
raw, white only		36	10
raw, whole		147	42
raw, yolk only		339	96
scrambled		246	70
all sizes	Waitrose	147	42
brown fresh	St Michael	147	42

Product	Brand	*Calories per 100g/ 100ml*	*Calories per oz/ pack/ portion*
brown size 3	St Michael	147	42
free range	St Michael	147	42
size 2	Safeway	96	27
size 3	Safeway	88	25
size 4	Safeway	81	23
Eggs, ducks'			
raw, whole		188	53
salted whole, boiled, without shell		198	56
"Eight" fruit muesli	Granose	408	116
8 varieties; biscuits for cheese	Waitrose	452	128
Elderberry and cherry yoghurt	Safeway	86	129 per 150g pack
11 + fruit drink, long life	Safeway	46	13
Elmlea cream alternative			
single	Van den Berghs	195	55
whipping	Van den Berghs	330	94
Emmental cheese: *see Cheese*			
Endive, raw		11	3
English apple juice: *see Apple juice*			
English butter	Safeway	731	207
English Cheddar: *see Cheese*			
English mustard	Safeway	95	90 per 95g pack
as sold	Colman's	480	136
made up	Colman's	180	51

Product	Brand	Calories per 100g/ 100ml	Calories per oz/ pack/ portion
English recipe **sausages**	Wall's Light and Lean	190	95 per sausage
chipolata	Wall's Light and Lean	190	108 per two chipolatas
Evaporated milk *unsweetened, whole*		158	45
	Asda	159	
	Carnation	160	45
	Libby	158	45
	Safeway	159	45
	Tesco	183	52
	Waitrose	159	270 per 170g can
full cream	Nestle Ideal	160	45
Everton mints	Trebor Bassett	365	23 per sweet
Exotic fruit and nut mix			
dried	Tesco	269	76
tub	Tesco	467	132
Exotic fruit and nuts	Waitrose	445	126
Exotic juice	St Ivel Real	47	14
Extra hot chicken **curry**	Tesco		420 per can
Extra Jam, all flavours	Chivers	255	40 per portion
Extra strong mints	Needlers	364	411 per 113g pack
roll	Trebor Bassett	378	10 per mint

Product	Brand	Calories per 100g/ 100ml	Calories per oz/ pack/ portion	145
Fab	Lyons Maid	133	69 each	
Faggots		268	76	
in rich sauce	Tesco	172	635 per pack	
Family Favourites processed cheese (average)	Saint Ivel	280	79	
Fancies, chocolate	Lyons	449	127	
Fancy iced cakes		407	115	
Farmhouse biscuits	Jacobs	488	39 per biscuit	
Farmhouse Bran				
apple and apricot	Weetabix	326	92	
honey and nut	Weetabix	335	95	
toasted	Weetabix	300	85	
Farmhouse cake	Waitrose	359	102	
Farmhouse chicken and leek soup	Knorr	338	225 per 1 1/2 pint pack	
Farmhouse crackers	Safeway	488	8 per biscuit	
Farmhouse fruitcake mix	Granny Smiths	388	1704 per 439g pack made up	
Farmhouse lentil mix, vegetarian	Boots	349	99	
Farmhouse pate	St Michael	238	67	
Farmhouse potato and vegetable soup	Crosse & Blackwell Pot Soup		64 per sachet made up	

Product	Brand	Calories per 100g/ 100ml	Calories per oz/ pack/ portion
Farmhouse vegetable soup			
dried	Batchelors	283	147 per pint pack as sold
	Hera	376	470 per pack
Feast	Wall's		260 each
Fennel, fresh, cooked	Tesco	22	6
Ferguzade	Beecham	94	28
Feta cheese: *see Cheese*			
Fibre bran	Safeway	248	99 per 40g pack
Fiesta fruit jellies	Needlers	304	380 per 125g pack
'55' Juice			
'55' Apple	Britvic	43	12
'55' Grapefruit	Britvic	50	14
'55' Orange	Britvic	51	14
'55' Pineapple	Britvic	51	14
Fig and orange biscuits, hand-baked	Boots	484	137
Fig and raisin bar	Granose	340	85 per 25g bar
Fig bar biscuits	Tesco	362	103
Fig biscuits	Prewetts		79 per biscuit
Fig rolls	Asda	334	
	Jacobs	355	54 per biscuit
	Littlewoods	348	58 per biscuit
	Safeway	350	99
Figs *fresh, raw*		41	12

Product	Brand	Calories per 100g/ 100ml	Calories per oz/ pack/ portion
dried, raw		213	60
dried, stewed without sugar		118	33
dried, stewed with sugar		136	39
green, raw		41	12
Fine beans, fresh, cooked	Tesco	34	10
Fine cut marmalade: *see Marmalade*			
Finger biscuits	Cadbury's	495	25 per biscuit
Finger sandwich	Waitrose	155	44
Finnan haddock			
frozen, raw	Tesco	89	25
frozen, steamed	Tesco	101	29
Fish 'n' chips, oven crispy	Birds Eye		470 per pack baked
Fish 'n' Chips candy	Trebor Bassett	540	54 per sweet
Fish batter mix (as sold)	Green's	341	97
Fish cakes: *see also Cod, Haddock, etc*			
Fish cakes			
frozen		112	32
fried		188	53
	Findus	118	33
	Safeway	121	34
	Waitrose	112	56 per fish cake
	Birds Eye		each grilled 90, fried 140
cod, chilled	Young's	213	60

Product	Brand	Calories per 100g/ 100ml	Calories per oz/ pack/ portion
raw	Tesco	112	32
salmon	Birds Eye		100 each grilled fried 160
traditional	Ross	120	34
Fish fingers: *see also Cod, Haddock, etc.*			
Fish fingers			
frozen		178	50
fried		233	66
Fish paste		169	48
Fish pie		128	36
traditional	St Michael	112	32
Fish steaks			
battered	Findus	217	215 each
in butter sauce	Ross	90	140 per pack
Fisherman's Choice	Birds Eye MenuMaster		320 per pack
Fisherman's pie	St Michael	136	39
Five Centre bar	Cadbury's	425	215 per bar
Five fruit juice	Waitrose	52	15
Five spice powder			0
Fivepints milk powder			
dry	St Ivel		133
made up	St Ivel		270 per pint
Flageolet beans: *see Beans*			
Flake			
Flake	Cadbury's	530	180 per 34g bar

Product	Brand	Calories per 100g/ 100ml	Calories per oz/ pack/ portion
Flake 99	Cadbury's	530	65 per 13g bar
Flake and fruit	Asda	356	
Flaky pastries, Chinese		392	111
Flaky pastry mix (as sold)	Tesco	558	158
Flan case	Lyons	320	91
all sizes	Tesco	323	92
Flan fillings (Armour): *see flavours*			
Flans: *see flavours*			
Flapjack biscuits	Tesco	442	125
Flash fry steak	St Michael	128	36
Flora			
cooking fat, white sunflower	Van den Berghs	900	255
margarine	Van den Berghs	740	210
sunflower oil	Van den Berghs	900	255
Florentines chocolate biscuits	St Michael	545	155
Florida cocktail yogurt, low calorie	Diet Ski	54	81 per 150g pack
Florida orange mini juice	Wall's		30 per portion
Florida salad	Asda	243	
	Littlewoods	125	284 per 227g pack
	St Michael	205	58

Product	Brand	Calories per 100g/ 100ml	Calories per oz/ pack/ portion
	Tesco	102	29
	Waitrose	163	370 per 227g pack
Florida spring vegetable soup, dried	Knorr	280	79
Flour			
brown (85%)		327	93
chapati, brown, coarse		331	94
chapati, white, plain		332	94
millet		354	100
patent (40%)		347	98
rice		366	104
white (72%) household, plain		350	99
white (72%) self-raising		339	96
white breadmaking (72%)		337	96
wholemeal (100%)		318	90
brown	Tesco	333	94
buckwheat	Holland and Barrett	330	94
carob	Holland and Barrett	180	51
maize	Holland and Barrett	370	105
plain	Safeway	327	93
	Tesco	321	91
	Whitworths	350	99
plain, traditional	Waitrose	341	97
plain, superfine	Waitrose	340	96
rice, brown	Holland and Barrett	360	102

Product	Brand	Calories per 100g/ 100ml	Calories per oz/ pack/ portion
rye	Holland and Barrett	335	95
self-raising	Safeway	327	93
	Tesco	310	88
	Whitworths	339	96
self-raising, traditional	Waitrose	341	97
self-raising superfine	Waitrose	340	96
soya, low fat	Holland and Barrett	350	99
wheatmeal, strong brown	Safeway	327	93
white, strong plain	Waitrose	342	97
white, strong plain	Safeway	337	96
white	Tesco	333	94
wholemeal	Boots Second Nature	306	87
wholemeal 100%	Holland and Barrett	320	91
wholemeal 85%	Holland and Barrett	330	94
wholewheat, strong 100%	Safeway	318	90
wholewheat	Tesco	338	96
	Waitrose	318	90
wholewheat 100%	Jordans	300	85
Foam crystals, all flavours	Creamola	323	92

Product	Brand	Calories per 100g/ 100ml	Calories per oz/ pack/ portion
Fondant fancies	Littlewoods	373	106
	St Michael	339	96
Food, wholemeal	Boots Second Nature	306	87
Foo-juk: *see Soya thread*			
Forest fruit juice drink	Ribena	52	15
Forest fruits yogurt	Gold Ski	115	172 per 150g pack
	Ski (Eden Vale)	85	128 150g pack
Four fruit cocktail drink, long-life	Waitrose	54	per 200ml pack 108
Four fruits in water	Dietade	21	6
Fox's Glacier Fruits	Rowntree	380	
	Mackintosh		12 per sweet, stick pack
	Rowntree Mackintosh	380	20 per sweet, bag
Fox's Glacier Mints	Rowntree Mackintosh	380	12 per sweet, stickpack
	Rowntree Mackintosh	380	20 per sweet, bag
Frankfurters		274	78
	Asda	378	
	St Michael	295	84
sliced	Tesco	302	86
Freedent chewing gum peppermint	Wrigley		9 per stick

Product	Brand	Calories per 100g/ 100ml	Calories per oz/ pack/ portion 153
spearmint	Wrigley		9 per stick
French beans, boiled		7	2
French bread pizza			
bacon, peppers and mushrooms	Findus		325 per pizza
cheese and tomato	Birds Eye		295 per pizza
chilli beef, sweetcorn and peppers	Findus		365 per pizza
red Leicester, edam and mozzarella	Findus		400 per pizza
sausage	Birds Eye		315 per pizza
French Brie cheese: *see Cheese*			
French dressing		658	187
	Heinz	511	145
classic	Kraft	496	147
oil-free	Waistline	13	4
Shake and serve	St Michael	640	179
French fries:			
crinkle cut	McCain	117	33
straight cut	McCains	121	34
French mustard	Colman's	115	33
	Safeway	75	21
French mustard and honey roast ham	Waitrose	173	49
French oil dressing	Safeway	480	142
French onion quiche	St Michael	260	74
French onion soup	Baxters	24	102 per 425g can

Product	Brand	Calories per 100g/ 100ml	Calories per oz/ pack/ portion
	Waitrose	15	44 per 295g can
dried	Waitrose	315	85 per 27g pack
dried instant special	Safeway	38	75 per pint pack
dried, with croutons	Batchelors Cup-		54 per 16g pack
	a-Soup Special	338	as sold
instant	Tesco	328	50 per sachet
French sandwich cake	Lyons	369	105
jam	Waitrose	399	113

French style yogurt: *see also flavours*

French style yogurt, all varieties	Eden Vale	87	109 per 125g pack
Fresh cream fruit cocktail	Safeway	141	40
Fresh cream fruit trifle	St Michael	165	47
Fresh cream meringues	St Michael	338	96
Fresh cream rum baba cake	Tesco	256	73
Fresh cream trifle	Tesco	176	50
Fresh fruit marmalade	St Michael	240	68
Fresh mints	Boots Cadbury's	363	454 per 125g pack 25 per mint
Fresh orange marmalade, thick cut	Waitrose	248	70

Product	Brand	Calories per 100g/ 100ml	Calories per oz/ pack/ portion
Fresh vegetable dip	St Michael	718	204
Fresh vegetable flan	St Michael	228	65
Freshly squeezed orange juice	Tesco	42	12
Fromage frais			
natural		114	32
0% fat		0	0
apricot fruited	St Michael		125 per pot
strawberry	Asda	156	
fruits of the forest	Eden Vale		130 per pot
	St Michael		125 per pot
strawberry	Eden Vale		135 per pot
Frosties	Kellogg's	355	101
Frosties	Trebor Bassett	365	23 per sweet
Fructose	Holland and Barrett	400	113
Fruit and bran bar	Prewetts	202	85 per 42g bar
Fruit and bran biscuits	Boots Second Nature	418	119
Fruit'n Fibre	Kellogg's	338	96
Fruit and fibre muesli	Waitrose	293	83
Fruit and nut bar	Cadbury's	470	270 per 57g bar
Fruit and nut bar, chocolate coated	Tesco	502	142

Product	Brand	Calories per 100g/ 100ml	Calories per oz/ pack/ portion
Fruit and nut bar with honey	Boots	447	127
Fruit and nut biscuits	Holland and Barrett		60 per biscuit
carob coated	Holland and Barrett		70 per biscuit
Fruit and nut carob bar			
no added sugar	Sunwheel Kalibu	483	290 per 60g bar
with raw sugar	Sunwheel Kalibu	503	302 per 60g bar
Fruit and nut cereal bar	St Michael	444	95 per bar
Fruit and nut chocolate	Nestle	475	135
Fruit and nut chunky bar	Cadbury's		245 per bar
Fruit and nut cookies	Barbara's		210 per biscuit
	Cadbury's	450	45 per biscuit
Fruit and nut dessert bar	Prewetts	310	130 per 42g bar
Fruit and nut loaf mix, wholemeal (as sold)	Green's	370	150 per portion made up
Fruit and nut muesli	Waitrose	354	100
35%	Safeway	326	92
Fruit BonBons	Cadbury's	380	20 each

Product	Brand	Calories per 100g/ 100ml	Calories per oz/ pack/ portion
Fruit buns	Tesco	300	85
Fruit cake			
plain		354	100
rich		332	94
rich, iced		352	100
all butter			
wholemeal	Safeway	348	99
iced	Waitrose	375	106
Fruit chews	St Michael	370	105
Fruit chutney, curried	Tesco	141	40
Fruit Club biscuits	Jacobs	471	113 per biscuit
Fruit cocktail	Libby	79	22
	Safeway	95	170 per 114g can
diabetic	Boots	24	7
fresh cream	Safeway	141	560 per 397g pack
in apple juice	Waitrose	50	14
in fruit juice	Asda	46	
	Del Monte	47	13
in natural juice	Tesco	48	14
in syrup	Del Monte	67	19
	Tesco	74	21
	Waitrose	95	390 per 411g can
low calorie	Boots Shapers	22	6
Fruit cocktail trifle	Waitrose	134	536 per 400g pack
Fruit creams	Trebor Bassett	333	31 per sweet
Fruit digestive biscuits	Huntley & Palmer	451	50 per biscuit

Product	Brand	Calories per 100g/ 100ml	Calories per oz/ pack/ portion
Fruit fillings (Morton): *see flavours*			
Fruit flavour drops	Boots	363	103
	Littlewoods	357	101
diabetic	Boots	367	104
Fruit flavour pastilles			
diabetic	Boots	100	28
Fruit flavoured jellies	Littlewoods	296	84
Fruit flavoured toffees	Trebor Bassett	456	31 per sweet
Fruit fool	Asda	158	
Fruit For-All (Chivers): *see flavours*			
Fruit gums		172	49
	Rowntree Mackintosh	265	5 per gum tube, carton 6
Mr Men	Bassett's	308	87
real	Bassett's	293	83
	St Michael	340	96
soft	Wilkinson	319	90
Fruit harvest ice cream (Lyons Maid): *see flavours*			
Fruit jellies	Tesco	367	104
	Waitrose	296	84
Fruit loaf, sliced	Tesco	310	88
Fruit malt loaf	Littlewoods	262	74
Fruit mixture, dried	Whitworths	245	69
Fruit muesli bar	Boots	377	170 per bar
Fruit, nuts and seeds	Waitrose	470	133

Product	Brand	Calories per 100g/ 100ml	Calories per oz/ pack/ portion
Fruit of the forest low fat yogurt	Tesco	106	30
Fruit pastilles	Needlers	322	91
	Rowntree		11 each, tube
	Mackintosh	350	carton 14
	Tesco	322	91
	Waitrose	322	91
Fruit pie			
individual, pastry top and bottom		369	105
pastry top		180	51
Fruit pie filling, canned		95	27
Fruit pie fillings (Tesco): *see flavours*			
Fruit pies (Lyons): *see flavours*			
Fruit salad			
canned		95	27
dried	Holland and Barrett	192	54
	Whitworths	159	45
in syrup	Waitrose	91	387 per 425g can
Fruit salad chews	Trebor Bassett	385	15 per sweet
Fruit sauce	Tesco	67	19
	Waitrose	120	34
Fruit scones	Tesco	286	81
Fruit sensations	Needlers	334	95
Fruit shortcake	Tesco	460	39 per biscuit

Product	Brand	Calories per 100g/ 100ml	Calories per oz/ pack/ portion
Fruit shortcake biscuits	Peek Frean	443	36 per biscuit
	Safeway	477	40 per biscuit
	St Michael	476	35 per biscuit
Fruit shorties biscuits	Boots	452	30 per biscuit
Fruit snack bar, carob coated	Sunwheel Kalibu	340	102 per 30g bar
Fruit sponge pudding mix (as sold)	Green's	386	292 per portion made up
Fruit spread			
pear 'n' apple	Sunwheel	239	68
pear 'n' apricot	Sunwheel	264	75
pear 'n' black cherry	Sunwheel	258	73
pear 'n' strawberry	Sunwheel	242	69
Fruit sugar	Dietade	394	112
Fruitcake mix, farmhouse (as sold)	Granny Smiths	388	1704 per 439g pack made up
Fruited hardy cake	Sainsbury's	450	126
Fruited malt loaf	Waitrose	243	69
Fruited treacle crumpets	St Michael	280	79
Fruits of the forest yoghurt creamy	Waitrose	143	179 per 125g pack
Fruits of the forest yogurt	St Ivel	81	23
low calorie	St Ivel	41	12
Fruity sauce	Branston	90	26

Product	Brand	Calories per 100g/ 100ml	Calories per oz/ pack/ portion
	O.K.	90	26
	Safeway	98	28
Fruity sherbets	Needlers	345	98
Fruities (Birds Eye): *see flavours*			
Fudge	Cadbury's	435	130 per 30g bar
	Littlewoods	398	113
	Rowntree Mackintosh		45 per sweet
	Tesco	413	117
bars	St Michael	447	127
Fudge cake	Lyons		160 each
Fudge milk shake	Waitrose		195 per carton
Fudge yogurt	Mister Men	100	28
	Munch Bunch	92	115 per 125g pack
Funtime	Safeway	95	143 per 150g pack
Fudge yule log	Asda	406	
Funtime yoghurts (Safeway): *see flavours*			
Fusille bianche	Waitrose	222	63

G

Product	Brand	Calories per 100g/ 100ml	Calories per oz/ pack/ portion	165
Gala slice	Tesco	241	68	
Galaxy	Mars	547	155	
Galliano			75 per 1/6 gill	
Gambit	Cadbury's	520	210 per 40g bar	
Game consomme	Baxters	9	36 per 425g can	
Game pie	Waitrose	221	63	
Gammon				
joint, raw, lean and fat		239	67	
joint boiled, lean and fat		271	76	
joint boiled, lean		167	47	
raw, lean		82	23	
roast, lean		214	60	
steaks	Tesco	179	51	
Gammon flavour grills	Asda	231		
Garden mint sauce	Safeway	10	3	
Gari, raw		351	100	
Garibaldi biscuits	Peek Frean	358	32 per biscuit	
	Tesco	373	40 per biscuit	
	Waitrose	370	35 per biscuit	
Garlic, raw		117	33	
Garlic and herbs stuffing mix	Knorr	411	117	
Garlic bread	Safeway		600 per 170g baguette	

Product	Brand	Calories per 100g/ 100ml	Calories per oz/ pack/ portion
	Sainsbury's		605 per 170g baguette
Garlic butter	Safeway	695	197
Garlic dressing Italian	Duchesse	33	10
	Kraft	426	126
	Tesco	450	128
Italian style	St Michael	138	39
Garlic mayonnaise	Hellmanns	720	204
	Safeway	745	211
	Waitrose	734	208
Garlic oil dressing	Safeway	440	130
Garlic pate	Tesco	397	113
Garlic prawns	Young's	75	21
Garlic sauce mix	Knorr	435	123
Garlic sausage: *see Sausages, delicatessen*			
Gateau roule, various fillings	Waitrose	354	100
Gelatin		338	96
Genoa cake	Tesco	362	103
decorated	Littlewoods	323	92
Georgia pecan pie ice cream	Safeway	246	73
German salami	Waitrose	427	121
German sausage, Extrawurst	Waitrose	350	99

Product	Brand	Calories per 100g/ 100ml	Calories per oz/ pack/ portion
Ghee			
butter		898	255
palm		897	254
vegetable		898	255
Gherkins			
raw		11	3
Gin			50 per 1/6 gill
Ginger			
roots, raw		46	13
Ginger ale	Canada Dry	38	11
low calorie	Canada Dry Slim	1	1 per 113ml pack
American	Hunts	36	11
	Schweppes	21	6
	Tesco	28	8
American, low calorie	Diet Hunts	1	
	Tesco	6	2
dry	Hunts	16	5
dry	Schweppes	15	4
Ginger and bran biscuits, carob coated	Holland and Barrett	—	70 per biscuit
Ginger and honey Chinese barbecue sauce	Sharwood	140	40
Ginger and lemon biscuits, hand-baked	Boots	514	146

Product	Brand	Calories per 100g/ 100ml	Calories per oz/ pack/ portion
Ginger and pear bar	Boots	344	98
Ginger bar	Shepherd Boy Bars		162 per bar
Ginger beer	Asda	30	
	Corona	29	9
	Idris Old English	35	10
	Safeway	49	15
	Schweppes	34	10
	St Michael	47	14
	Tesco	48	14
	Whites	29	8
with lemonade	Idris Old English	37	11
Ginger biscuits, plain chocolate	St Michael	490	45 per biscuit
Ginger creams	Waitrose	488	65 per biscuit
diabetic	Boots	468	133
Ginger extra jam	Waitrose	248	70
Ginger fingers	Boots	439	124
Ginger fudge snack bar, carob coated	Sunwheel Kalibu	403	121 per 30g bar
Ginger nuts		456	129
	Peek Frean	431	36 per biscuit
	Safeway	426	45 per biscuit
Ginger pear bar	Granose	366	110 per 30g bar

Product	Brand	Calories per 100g/ 100ml	Calories per oz/ pack/ portion
Ginger preserve	Safeway	256	73
Ginger preserve marmalade	Tesco	275	78
Ginger snaps	St Michael	423	35 per biscuit
Gingerbread		373	106
Glace cherries		212	60
	Safeway	218	62
	Tesco	341	97
	Waitrose	212	60
	Whitworths	212	60
Glace fruit drops	Needlers	375	106
Glacier Fruits, Fox's	Rowntree Mackintosh	380	12 each, stick pack, bag 20
Glacier Mints, Fox's	Rowntree Mackintosh	380	12 each, stick pack, bag 20
Glazed chicken	Findus Lean Cuisine	110	31
Glitter fruits mints	Trebor Bassett Trebor Bassett	349 349	22 per sweet 22 per sweet
Globe artichoke: *see Artichoke, globe*			
Glucose drink, sparkling	Boots	77	.23
Glucose energy tablets	Lucozade	339	96
Glucose health drink	Safeway	80	24
Glucose liquid, BP		318	90

Product	Brand	Calories per 100g/ 100ml	Calories per oz/ pack/ portion
Glucose powder	Boots	340	96
with vitamin C	Boots	340	96
Glycerin soft pastilles			
honey and lemon	Boots	318	90
honey and orange	Boots	318	90
Goan Vindaloo curry sauce	Sharwood	79	225 per can
Goats milk cheese: *see Cheese*			
Gold margarine	St Ivel	390	111
very low fat	St Ivel	275	77
Gold Seal ice cream (Lyons Maid): *see flavours*			
Gold Ski yogurts (Eden Vale): *see flavours*			
Gold Spinner processed cheese	St Ivel	280	79
Gold coffee, dry	Safeway	330	94
Golden breadcrumbs	Tesco	371	105
Golden chicken and mushroom soup	Heinz	42	125 per 300g can
Golden churn	Kraft	680	193
Golden cooking crumbs	Waitrose	340	96
Golden cup	Rowntree Mackintosh	450	100 per small cup
Golden cutlets	St Michael	83	24

Product	Brand	Calories per 100g/ 100ml	Calories per oz/ pack/ portion
Golden Delicious apples	Tesco	46	13
Golden marzipan	Waitrose	408	116
Golden mints	Boots	363	103
Golden plums	Waitrose	58	329 per 568g pack
Golden Ready Brek	Lyons	391	111
Golden savoury rice	Batchelors	328	439 per 134g sachet as sold
Golden Shred marmalade	Robertson's	251	71
Golden spread	St Michael	710	201
Golden sweetcorn, no salt added	Del Monte	101	29
Golden syrup		298	84
	Tate and Lyle	298	84
Golden syrup preserve	Tesco	303	86
Golden toffee	Rowntree Mackintosh	460	30 per sweet
Golden vegetable rice (frozen), cooked	Uncle Ben's	105	30
Golden vegetable savoury rice	Safeway	336	420 per 125g pack
Golden vegetable soup	Heinz Big Soups	37	155 per 435g can
	Heinz	41	125 per 300g can

Product	Brand	Calories per 100g/ 100ml	Calories per oz/ pack/ portion
	Knorr Quick Soup	427	85 per sachet
condensed	Campbell's	47	140 per 295g can
dried	Batchelors	360	234 per 65g pint pack as sold
	Batchelors Cup-a-Soup	357	75 per 21g sachet as sold
dried, instant (as sold)	Safeway	363	103
dried, low calorie	Batchelors Slim-a-Soup	300	39 per 13g sachet
dried, with croutons	Batchelors		157 per 43g sachet as sold
	Snack-a-Soup	365	
Goose, roast		319	90
Gooseberries			
green, raw		17	5
green, stewed without sugar		14	4
green, stewed with sugar		50	14
ripe, raw		37	10
	Hartley's	70	80 per 114g can
Gooseberry cream	Rowntree Mackintosh		40 per sweet
Gooseberry crumble	Waitrose	160	45
Gooseberry flan filling	Armour	89	25
Gooseberry fruit fool	St Michael	160	45

Product	Brand	Calories per 100g/ 100ml	Calories per oz/ pack/ portion
Gooseberry fruit pie filling	Tesco	95	27
Gooseberry slice	St Michael	318	90
Gooseberry yoghurt	Safeway	91	137 per 150g pack
	Waitrose	90	135 per 150g pack
Gorgonzola cheese: *see Cheese*			
Gouda cheese: *see Cheese*			
Goulash	Granose	54	230 per can
Goulash mix (dry)	Tesco	310	88
Goulash sauce mix	Knorr	380	108
Goulash soup	Waitrose	67	285 per 425g can
Gourd			
bitter (karela), fresh, raw		9	3
bitter (karela), canned, drained		7	2
bottle (chapni kaddu), raw		16	5
ridge (turia), raw		16	5
round (tinda)		21	6
Granny Smith apples	Tesco	46	13
Granulated sugar	Tate and Lyle	394	112
Granulated sweetener	Asda	376	
Granules	Bovril	186	53
Granymels			
caramel	Itona	390	111
liquorice	Itona	395	112
mint	Itona	370	105

Product	Brand	Calories per 100g/ 100ml	Calories per oz/ pack/ portion
treacle	Itona	400	113
Grape and blackcurrant juice	Waitrose	71	21
Grape juice			
red	Prewetts	66	20
red long life	Safeway	55	16
red sparkling long life	Safeway	47	14
red	Schloer	49	15
red sparkling	Schloer	49	15
red	Volonte	60	18
red, 700ml pack	Waitrose	70	21
red, litre pack	Waitrose	55	16
white long life	Safeway	55	16
white sparkling long life	Safeway	47	14
white	Schloer	48	14
white sparkling	Schloer	49	15
white, 700ml pack	Waitrose	70	21
white, litre pack	Waitrose	59	17
Grapefruit			
raw		22	6
canned		60	17
whole fruit, raw		11	3
Grapefruit, pink			
flesh and skin		7	2
flesh only		28	8
juice		35	10

Product	Brand	Calories per 100g/ 100ml	Calories per oz/ pack/ portion
Grapefruit and pineapple drink	Britvic	40	11
Grapefruit 'C'			
reduced calories	Libby	32	9
sweetened	Libby	58	16
Grapefruit drink	Waitrose	92	27
dilutable	Boots Shapers	8	2
sparkling	Tango	42	12
with pineapple juice	Corona	99	29
Grapefruit fruit juice	Del Monte	38	11
sweetened (canned)	Heinz	64	19
Grapefruit juice			
sweetened canned		38	11
unsweetened canned		31	9
	Boots	31	9
	Britvic	54	15
	Prewetts	31	9
	Schweppes	46	14
	St Ivel Mr Juicy	31	9
	St Ivel Real	31	9
chilled	Tesco	42	12
concentrated			
(frozen)	Tesco	136	39
freshly squeezed	Safeway	38	11
	Waitrose	40	12
long life	Tesco	42	12
	Waitrose	36	11
pure, chilled	Waitrose	30	9

Product	Brand	Calories per 100g/ 100ml	Calories per oz/ pack/ portion
pure, long life	Safeway	35	10
sweetened	Hunts	62	18
	Libby	38	11
unsweetened	Libby	31	9
Grapefruit			
marmalade	Baxters	249	846 per 340g jar
medium cut	Waitrose	248	70
Grapefruit segments			
in juice	Libby	30	9
	St Michael	41	12
	Waitrose	36	10
in natural juice	Tesco	34	10
in syrup	Tesco	63	18
	Waitrose	62	18
Grapefruit squash			
diluted	Quosh	43	13
real, undiluted	Quosh	123	36
Grapefruit whole fruit			
drink	Robinsons	95	28
Grapenuts		355	101
Grapes			
black		61	17
white		63	18
Gravy			
cubes	Knorr	348	99
granules (as sold)	Safeway	438	124
granules (made up)	Safeway	35	10
granules	Tesco	490	139

Product	Brand	Calories per 100g/ 100ml	Calories per oz/ pack/ portion
	Waitrose	507	144
mix	Tesco	265	75
powder	Waitrose	263	75

Green banana: *see Plantain*

Green beans
canned	Tesco	14	4
cut (canned)	Del Monte	19	5
cut	Waitrose	19	75 per 397g pack
dried	Batchelors		43 per 33g sachet
	Surprise	130	as sold
sliced (frozen)	Birds Eye	28	8
sliced (canned)	Safeway	19	54 per 284g can
whole (frozen)	Birds Eye	35	10
whole (canned)	Safeway	40	159 per 397g can

Green Label mango chutney
	Sharwood	217	62

Green peppers, fresh
	Littlewoods	15	4
	Tesco	24	7

Greengages
raw		47	13
raw (with stones)		45	13
stewed without sugar		40	11
stewed without sugar (with stones)			3811
stewed with sugar		75	21
stewed with sugar (with stones)			7220

Grillsteaks
beef	Birds Eye		185 each grilled
	Steakhouse		or fried

Product	Brand	Calories per 100g/ 100ml	Calories per oz/ pack/ portion
beef	Findus	233	66
	St Michael	279	79
beef, low fat	Birds Eye Steakhouse		155 each grilled or baked
lamb			
	Birds Eye Steakhouse		190 each grilled or fried
value	Birds Eye Steakhouse		175 each grilled, fried 190
Grissini (breadsticks)	Buitoni	360	450 per 125g pack
Grizzly bars, all varieties	Grizzly Bars		100 per bar
Groundnut oil	Boots	899	255
	Waitrose	900	266
Grouse, roast		173	49
(with bone)		114	32
Gruyere cheese: *see Cheese*			
Guare (cluster beans)		23	7
Guava and apple juice Copella		36	11
Guavas			
fresh, raw		62	18
in syrup, canned		60	17
Gulab jamen (jambu)		357	101
home made		348	99

Product	Brand	Calories per 100g/ 100ml	Calories per oz/ pack/ portion
Haddock			
fresh, raw		73	21
fresh, fried		174	49
fresh, fried (with bones)		160	45
fresh, steamed		98	28
fresh, steamed (with bones and skin)		75	21
battercrisp	St Michael		255 each
breaded	Gateway	235	66
frozen	Safeway	65	19
in light crispy batter	Sainsbury's	135	38
in natural crispy crumbs	Sainsbury's	135	38
Haddock fillets			
battered, Chip Shop	Ross	189	53
breaded	Co-op	182	51
in crispy batter	Sainsbury's	135	38
in oven crisp bread crumbs	St Michael		505 per 283g pack
with butter	Macrae		170 per 170g pack
Haddock goujons	Tesco	192	54
Haddock nuggets, breaded		Tesco	65 each
Haddock steaks			
battered	Asda	186	
	Findus		215 each
in breadcrumbs	Safeway		225 each
in butter sauce	Ross		165 per 170g pack

Product	Brand	Calories per 100g/ 100ml	Calories per oz/ pack/ portion
in light crispy crumb	Findus		245 each
in oven crisp batter	Tesco		260 per portion
Haddock, smoked			
steamed		101	29
steamed (with bones and skin)		66	19
buttered	Birds Eye	85	24
	Asda	114	
cutlets	Ross	114	32
fillets with butter	Co-op		335 per 170g pack
	Ross		165 per 170g pack
Haddock and cod pie	St Michael	111	430 per pack
Haddock and courgette bake	St Michael	91	260 per pack
Haddock and prawn crumble	Ross		515 per pack
Haddock and prawn gratinee	Sainsbury's	163	650 per pack
Haddock bake	Ross		370 per pack
	Asda	90	
Haddock cordon blev	Tesco	200	260 each
Haddock fillet fish fingers	Birds Eye		50 each grilled, shallow fried 55
Haddock fish fingers crumb crisp	Findus	191	54
Haddock mornay	St Michael	125	500 per pack

Product	Brand	Calories per 100g/ 100ml	Calories per oz/ pack/ portion
Haggis, boiled		310	88
Hake			
fillet, raw		71	20
fillet, steamed		107	30
on bone, raw		35	10
Halibut			
raw		92	26
steamed		131	37
steamed (with bones and skin)		99	28
Halva, Greek		615	174
Halwa, Asian		381	108
Ham			
canned		120	34
	Armour	122	554 per 454g can
	Tesco	94	27
	Waitrose	108	31
Beechwood smoked	Asda	193	
Bavarian slices	St Michael	160	45
Blackforest	Waitrose	371	105
Brunswick	Waitrose	176	50
Buckingham	Waitrose	121	34
Danish, slices	St Michael	130	37
French mustard and honey roast	Waitrose	173	49
honey roast double loin, cooked	Littlewoods	151	43
honey roast thin sliced	St Michael	124	35

Product	Brand	Calories per 100g/ 100ml	Calories per oz/ pack/ portion
honey roast, continental	Waitrose	199	56
honey roast, sliced	Tesco	134	38
Italian dry cured sliced	St Michael	300	85
joints, Bavarian	St Michael	161	46
Maryland	Waitrose	156	44
mild cure, cooked	Littlewoods	130	37
mild cure, sliced	Tesco	103	29
oak smoked, English	Waitrose	163	46
Old English Virginia	Waitrose	163	46
peppered	Asda	207	
	Waitrose	173	49
premier smoked, sliced	Tesco	162	46
premier, sliced	Tesco	168	48
roast, cooked	Littlewoods	132	37
shoulder	Waitrose	121	34
shoulder, cured (cooked)	Waitrose	256	73
smoked	Waitrose	121	34
smoked spiced sliced	St Michael	220	62
traditional matured wafer thin sliced	Asda	95	
York	Waitrose	176	50

Product	Brand	Calories per 100g/ 100ml	Calories per oz/ pack/ portion
Ham and bacon sandwichmaker	Shippams	134	127 per 95g can
Ham and beef paste	Shippams	198	69 per 35g pack
Ham and beef roll, canned	Crosse & Blackwell	226	64
Ham and cheese quiche	Waitrose	211	60
Ham and cheese savoury toasts	Findus	220	62
Ham and cheese Toast Topper	Heinz	141	40
Ham and chicken roll, canned	Crosse & Blackwell	220	62
Ham and mushroom lasague	Boots Shapers Ready Meals	107	290 per pack
Ham and mushroom quiche	Sainsbury's	260	73
Ham and mushroom pizza	Asda	220	
	Birds Eye Home Bake	242	640 per 265g pizza
(frozen) pack of 4	Marietta		210 per pizza
(frozen) pack of 4	Safeway		220 per pizza
five inch	Tesco		235 per 100g pizza
wedge, pack of 4	Marietta		365 each
Ham and pepper pasta break	Eden Vale		260 per carton

Product	Brand	Calories per 100g/ 100ml	Calories per oz/ pack/ portion
Ham and Swiss cheese quiche	Waitrose	213	840 per 397g quiche
Ham and tongue roll	Crosse & Blackwell	270	77
Ham, cheese and pineapple sandwiches	Tesco		265 per pack
Ham, cheese and salad sandwiches	Waitrose		520 per pack
Ham, chicken and lettuce sandwiches with mayonnaise	Boots		390 per pack
Ham cubes	Knorr	251	71
Ham salad roll	Tesco		325 per roll
Ham salad wholemeal bap	Waitrose	203	58
Ham sandwich	Waitrose	211	60
Ham sausage· *see Sausages, delicatessen*			
Ham spread	Shippams	173	61 per 35g pack
	St Michael	193	55
Hard gums			
American	Trebor Bassett	327	93
	Littlewoods	325	92
	Tesco	377	107
fruit salad	Trebor Bassett	277	79
Hare			
stewed		192	54

Product	Brand	Calories per 100g/ 100ml	Calories per oz/ pack/ portion
stewed (with bones)		139	39
Haricot beans: *see Beans*			
Haricot verts	Findus	67	19
	Waitrose	25	7
Harlequin dessert			
chocolate	Wall's		110 per 1/5 pack
strawberry	Wall's		110 per 1/5 pack
Harvest brown	St Michael		70 per slice
Harvest crisp bread	Kavli		40 per slice
Harvest nut mix, vegetarian	Boots	410	116
Harvest thick vegetable soup	Crosse & Blackwell Healthy Balance	40	170 per can
Hash browns	Tesco		70 each
Haslet	Waitrose	153	43
Haunted House spaghetti shapes in tomato sauce	Heinz	72	150 per can
Havarti cheese	Waitrose	344	98
Hawaiian drink	Safeway	43	13
Hazelnut and almond muesli bar	Granose	460	115 per 25g bar
Hazelnut and herbs stuffing mix	Knorr	428	385 per pack
Hazelnut bar	Granose	476	238 per 50g bar

Product	Brand	Calories per 100g/ 100ml	Calories per oz/ pack/ portion
Hazelnut biscuits	Boots Second Nature	448	127
diabetic	Boots	428	121
Hazelnut carob bar	Kalibu	507	380 per 75g bar
Hazelnut chocolate bar	Boots Shapers	542	154
Hazelnut chocolate spread	Asda	526	
	Cadbury's	570	85 per portion
	Sun-Pat	520	147
	Waitrose	530	150
Hazelnut cluster	Rowntree Mackintosh		45 per sweet
Hazelnut confectionery bar, no added sugar	Sunwheel Kalibu	533	224 per 42g bar
Hazelnut cookies	Waitrose	493	85 per biscuit
Hazelnut muesli bar	Granose	476	119 per 25g bar
Hazelnut oil	Sainsbury's	884	247
	Tesco	900	252
Hazelnut roll	Tesco	384	109
Hazelnut yoghurt	Safeway	98	147 per 150g pack
	Waitrose	98	147 per 150g pack
Hazelnuts	Holland and Barrett	380	108
	Tesco	625	177
	Whitworths	639	181

Product	Brand	Calories per 100g/ 100ml	Calories per oz/ pack/ portion
kernels	Littlewoods	380	108
Healthy Balance ketchup	Crosse & Blackwell	89	25
Heart			
lamb, raw		119	34
ox, raw		108	31
ox, stewed		179	51
pig, raw		93	26
sheep, roast		237	67
Hedgehog crisps, natural	Hedgehog	407	110 per 27g pack
Herb and garlic dressing	Heinz All Seasons	302	86
	Safeway	229	65
Herb and vegetable vegeburger	Real Eats	200	140 per 70g burger
Herb butter, Welsh	Safeway	704	200
Herb cream dressing	Waitrose	224	64
Herb crisps, natural	Hedgehog	407	145 per 27g pack
Herb salad dressing	St Michael	105	30
Herb thins	St Michael	522	148
Herb vegebanger	Real Eats	828	60 each
Herbs and garlic spreading cheese	Medley	319	90

Product	Brand	Calories per 100g/ 100ml	Calories per oz/ pack/ portion
Herbs sandwich spread	Granose	263	75
Herring			
raw		234	66
fried		234	66
fried (with bones)		206	58
grilled		199	56
grilled (with bones)		135	38
roe, fried		244	69
roe, soft, raw		80	23
Hibran bread			
medium sliced	Vitbe	201	66 per slice
thick sliced	Vitbe	201	80 per slice
Hickory smoked peanuts	Planters	610	170
Hi-fi biscuits	Itona		90 per biscuit
High bake water biscuits	Jacobs	394	31 per biscuit
	Tesco	402	114
	Waitrose	393	111
High fibre muesli	Holland and Barrett	340	96
High fibre porridge	Boots Second Nature	335	95
Highland lentil soup	Knorr	314	300 per 1 1/2 pint pack
Highland shorties	Waitrose	495	50 per biscuit

Product	Brand	Calories per 100g/ 100ml	Calories per oz/ pack/ portion
Highlander's broth	Baxters	43	185 per can
Hi-Juice 66	Schweppes	51	15
Hilo biscuits	Rakusen	307	15 per biscuit
Hing: *see Asafoetida*			
Hob nobs	McVitie		135 per biscuit
Hob nob bar	McVitie		70 each
Hoi Sin Chinese barbecue sauce	Sharwood	161	46
Hoi Sin spare ribs	Waitrose	165	47
Hoi sin stir fry sauce	Knorr		235 per carton
Homestyle country vegetable soup	Heinz	41	125 per can
Hominy (maize grits), raw		362	103
Honey			
comb		281	80
in jars		288	82
	Holland and Barrett	280	79
Acacia	Waitrose	304	86
Australian	Waitrose	304	86
Australian, clear	Waitrose	304	86
Canadian	Waitrose	304	86
Canadian clover	St Michael	290	82
Canadian, set	Safeway	300	85
clear	Gales	310	88

Product	Brand	Calories per 100g/ 100ml	Calories per oz/ pack/ portion
clear	Safeway	300	85
comb	Holland and Barrett	280	79
cut comb	Waitrose	304	86
English	Waitrose	304	86
Greek	Waitrose	304	86
Mexican	Waitrose	304	86
Mexican, set	Safeway	300	85
pure, clear	Waitrose	304	86
pure, set	Waitrose	304	86
set	Gales	310	88
set	Safeway	300	85
several varieties	Boots	288	82
Tasmanian	Waitrose	304	86
whole range	Tesco	289	82
wild flower	St Michael	290	82
Honey, almond and raisins original crunch	Jordans	396	112
Honey and almond original crunchy bar	Jordans	412	135 per bar
Honey and blackcurrant Glycerin pastilles	Boots	322	91
Honey and lemon Glycerin soft pastilles	Boots	318	90
Honey and malt soya milk	Provamel	50	15

Product	Brand	Calories per 100g/ 100ml	Calories per oz/ pack/ portion
Honey 'n' nut cornflakes	Tesco	379	107
Honey and nut farmhouse bran	Weetabix	335	95
Honey and oatmeal cookies	Waitrose	479	80 per biscuit
Honey and orange Glycerin soft pastilles	Boots	318	90
Honey crunch bar	Boots	432	140 each
Honey menthol	Boots	363	120 per 33g stick pack
Honey muesli	Boots Second Nature	417	118
Honey Smacks	Kellogg's	346	98
Honey spread, diabetic	Boots	256	73
Honeycomb crunch bar	St Michael	450	128
Horlicks		396	112
Horlicks food drink malted	Beecham	386	114
malted chocolate, low fat, instant	Beecham	393	111
malted, low fat, instant	Beecham	382	113

Product	Brand	Calories per 100g/ 100ml	Calories per oz/ pack/ portion
Horlicks hot chocolate drink, low fat, instant	Beecham	402	119
Horlicks maltlets	Beecham	386	109
Horseradish (drumstick)			
raw		59	17
leaves		72	20
pods		42	12
Horseradish mustard	Colman's	140	40
Horseradish relish	O.K.	100	28
Horseradish sauce	Safeway	90	26
	Tesco	125	35
	Waitrose	80	23
cream	Tesco	187	53
creamed	O.K.	200	57
	Safeway	185	52
	Waitrose	190	54
Hostess ice cream	Lyons Maid	223	63
Hot and sour stir fry sauce	Knorr		167 per carton
Hot brunch	Allinson	357	250 per 70g pack
Hot chocolate drink	Carnation	379	107
instant	Waitrose	385	109
low fat, instant	Horlicks	402	119
sugar-free	Carnation	360	65 per 17.5g sachet
Hot dogs	Asda	181	

Product	Brand	Calories per 100g/ 100ml	Calories per oz/ pack/ portion
Hot oat cereal	Safeway	384	109
Hot pot			
cooked		114	32
frozen	Safeway	120	485 per pack
Houmous: *see Hummus*			
Hovis bread		228	65
Hovis crackers	Nabisco	468	29 per biscuit
	Safeway	470	30 per biscuit
Hovis digestive biscuits	Nabisco	486	57 per biscuit
	Safeway	481	55 per biscuit
Hubba Bubba Bubble Gum, all flavours	Wrigley		15/24 per chunk
Humbugs	Tesco	407	115
Hummus (chickpea spread)		185	52
100s and 1000s	Tesco	375	106
Hycal juice, ready to drink			
blackcurrant	Beecham	243	72
lemon	Beecham	243	72
orange	Beecham	243	72
raspberry	Beecham	243	72

I

Product	Brand	Calories per 100g/ 100ml	Calories per oz/ pack/ portion
Ice cream: *see also flavours*			
Vanilla, dairy		196	55
Vanilla, non-dairy		178	50
Ice cream dessert vanilla	Asda	236	
Ice cream bar			
blue ribbon vanilla	Wall's		85 per bar
Ice cream roll	Birds Eye		55 per 1/6 of roll
	Safeway	178	50
Iced bun cluster	Tesco	316	90
Iced chocolate cake	Tesco	428	121
Iced fruit cake	Asda	348	
	Waitrose	375	106
Iced gem biscuits	Peek Frean	380	5 per biscuit
Iced Madeira sandwich cake	Waitrose	423	120
Iced marzipan sponge	Tesco	413	117
Iced ring doughnuts	Tesco	420	119
Iced rings	Safeway	443	126
	Waitrose	443	126
Iced sports biscuits	Tesco	443	126
Iced tarts	Lyons	417	118
Icing			
fondant		392	110
royal		303	85

Product	Brand	Calories per 100g/ 100ml	Calories per oz/ pack/ portion
Icing sugar	Tate and Lyle	392	111
Ideal sauce	Heinz Ploughman's	106	30
Imperial mints	Trebor Bassett	376	18 each, giant roll, small roll 10
Indian tea		108	31
Indian chicken stir fry meal	Ross	86	295 per pack
Indian fried special savoury rice	Batchelors	465	660 per pack
Indian rice	Sharwoods	135	38
Indian stir fry	Asda	32	
Indian tonic water	Britvic	32	47 per 150ml can
	Canada Dry	24	27 per 113ml pack
	Hunts	24	7
	Tesco	25	7
low calorie	Canada Dry Slim	1	1 per 113ml pack
	Diet Hunts	1	0.5 per 100ml pack
	Tesco	6	2
Indian vegetable curry accompaniment	Sharwood	27	8
Indonesian pork satay and rice	Sharwoods Eastern Light Meals	101	345 per meal
Instant coffee: *see Coffee, instant*			

Product	Brand	Calories per 100g/ 100ml	Calories per oz/ pack/ portion
Instant custard: *see Custard*			
Instant mashed	Cadbury's		
potatoes	Smash	265	55 per portion
(as sold)	Safeway	265	188 per 71g pack
(made up)	Safeway	60	17
dried, made up with full cream milk	Yeoman	52	15
dried, made up with water	Yeoman	49	14
dried, made up, complete mix	Yeoman	52	15
with chopped onion, made up	Yeoman	53	15
without added salt, made up	Yeoman	49	14
Instant milk: *see Milk, brands*			
Instant potatoes			
made up		70	20
powder		318	90
Instant soups: *see flavours*			
Irish stew			
cooked		124	35
cooked (with bones)	Birds Eye	114	32
canned	Menu Master		295 per pack
	Tesco	94	370 per can
	Tyne Brand	96	375 per can
Irn bru	Barr	39	100 per 250ml can
low calorie	Barr	4	14 per 330ml can

Product	Brand	Calories per 100g/ 100ml	Calories per oz/ pack/ portion
Island Fruits	Schweppes	38	11
Italian beef bolognese stir fry	Ross	85	290 per pack
Italian dressing, low calorie	Boots Shapers	92	26
Italian garlic dressing	Kraft	426	126
	Tesco	450	128
Italian ham and onion pizza	St Michael	265	74
Italian oil dressing	Safeway	440	130
Italian salami thin sliced	Waitrose	411	117
	St Michael	491	139
Italian sauce	Whole Earth	60	17
Italian style chicken breast supreme	St Michael	148	295 per pack
Italian style garlic dressing	St Michael	138	39
Ivory Coast tuna skipjack steak in oil	Armour	289	578 per 200g can

Product	Brand	Calories per 100g/ 100ml	Calories per oz/ pack/ portion
Jack Daniels			60 per 1/6 gill
Jacket crisps all flavours	St Michael	500	375 per 75g packet
	Smiths	580	145 per 25g packet
Jacket potatoes			
with baked beans	Tesco		310 each
with cheese	Tesco		410 each
with chilli	Tesco		370 each
with corned beef hash	Tesco		390 each
Jackfruit, canned, drained		101	29
Jaffa cakes	McVitie		50 per biscuit
	St Michael		45 per biscuit
Jaffa orange drink	St Michael	110	33
colour free	St Michael	110	33
long life	Waitrose	37	11
Jaffa orange yoghurt	Safeway	96	144 per 150g pack
	Raines	89	135 per 150g pot
Jaggery		367	104
Jalapeno bean dip	Old El Paso	106	315 per 297g can
Jalapenos, pickled	Old El Paso	32	91 per 283g can
Jam			
fruit with edible seeds		261	74
stone fruit		261	74
all flavours	Moorhouse	255	40 per portion
all varieties	Robertson's	251	71

Product	Brand	Calories per 100g/ 100ml	Calories per oz/ pack/ portion
no sugar	Whole Earth	120	34
Jam and vanilla chocolate roll	Lyons	385	109
Jam baked slice	Asda	369	
Jam creams	Waitrose	479	70 per biscuit
Jam roly poly	Ross	370	105
Jam sandwich creams	Safeway	470	133
	St Michael	475	135
Jam sponge pudding	Safeway	359	102
	Tesco	333	94
Jam Swiss roll	St Michael	312	88
Jam tarts		384	109
	Lyons	414	117
Jambon de Bayonne, sliced	St Michael	230	65
Jamboree mallows	Peek Frean	382	77 per biscuit
Japanese medlar: see Loquats			
Jarlsberg cheese: see Cheese			
Jellabi, Asian		309	88
Jelly			
cubes		259	73
made with milk		86	24
made with water		59	17
	Rowntree's	268	76
Jelly animals	Waitrose	311	88

Product	Brand	Calories per 100g/ 100ml	Calories per oz/ pack/ portion
Jelly babies	Trebor Bassett	321	91
	Littlewoods	341	97
	St Michael	323	92
	Tesco	372	105
	Waitrose	311	88
Jelly beans	Trebor Bassett	335	95
	Littlewoods	362	103
	Tesco	340	96
Jelly-Creams			
chocolate	Chivers	365	160 per portion
other flavours	Chivers	370	160 per portion
Jelly crystals			
all flavours	Dietade		40 per pack
Jelly diamond cake decorations	Tesco	305	86
Jelly jam, Pure Fruit, all flavours	Hartley's	260	40 per portion
Jelly, fruit juice all all flavours	Chivers	290	285 per tablet
Jersey creams	Peek Frean	482	per biscuit 58
Jersey potatoes	Waitrose	80	300g/10oz pack
	Waitrose	80	23
Jersey Royal potatoes, canned	Safeway	53	150 per 283g can
Juicy Fruit chewing gum	Wrigley		9 per stick

Product	Brand	Calories per 100g/ 100ml	Calories per oz/ pack/ portion
Jumbo grills vegetarian	Protoveg Menu	251	71
Junior Drifter	Rowntree Mackintosh	460	75 per biscuit
Junior rolls with jam filling	Waitrose	290	82
Just mints	Tesco	406	115

Product	Brand	Calories per 100g/ 100ml	Calories per oz/ pack/ portion
Kabanos: *see Sausages, delicatessen*			
Kaisar: *see Saffron*			
Kakdi: *see Cucumber*			
Kale, fresh, boiled	Tesco	33	9
Kantola			
fresh, raw		19	5
canned, drained		18	5
Karela: *see Gourd, bitter*			
Kashmir dressing	Hellmann's	319	90
Kashmir mild curry sauce mix	Sharwood		80 per sachet
Kashmiri Korma	Tesco	113	384 per pack
Kedgeree		151	43
Kennett syrup biscuits	Huntley & Palmer	500	63 per biscuit
Kenya coffee			
fine filter, infused	Safeway	2	1
ground, infused	Safeway	2	1
Khira: *see Cucumber*			
Kia-Ora drinks: *see also flavours*			
Kia-Ora low sugar drink, concentrated	Schweppes	26	8
Kidney			
all types, raw		89	25
lamb, fried		155	44

Product	Brand	Calories per 100g/ 100ml	Calories per oz/ pack/ portion
Kidney beans: *see Beans*			
King Cone (Lyons Maid): *see flavours*			
Kipper fillets	Ross	210	60
	Waitrose	190	54
buttered	Birds Eye	194	55
with butter	Findus	191	54
	Ross	200	57
	St Michael	307	87
Kippered mackerel			
chilled	Young's	323	92
fillets	Ross	210	60
Kippers			
baked		205	58
baked (with bones)		111	31
boil in bag	Asda	234	
boned	Waitrose	190	54
frozen, raw	Tesco	237	67
Loch Fyne	St Michael	368	104
whole	Waitrose	152	43
Kiri sparkling apple juice	Bulmer	38	109 per half pint
Kirsch			50 per 1/6 gill
Kit Kat	Rowntree Mackintosh	505	4-finger bar 250, 2-finger bar 110
Kiwi fruit, fresh		63	18
Kiwi fruit yoghurt	Safeway	92	138 per 150g pack

Product	Brand	Calories per 100g/ 100ml	Calories per oz/ pack/ portion
Knickerbocker glory	Tesco		210 each
Kofta	Asda	240	
Kola Kubes	Trebor Bassett	354	17 per sweet
Kop Kop roll	Trebor Bassett	338	16 per sweet
Korma Classic curry sauce	Homepride	83	305 per can
Korma curry sauce	Sharwood		540 per 283g can
Korma mild curry cooking mix	Colman's	335	110 per pack
Kracka wheat	McVitie		37 per biscuit
Krakowska: see Sausages, delicatessen			
Krona margarine	Van den Berghs	740	210
Silver	Van den Berghs	740	210
Krunchy carob bar, no added sugar	Sunwheel Kalibu	432	259 per 60g bar
Kumquats			
fresh		64	18
canned		138	39

Product	Brand	Calories per 100g/ 100ml	Calories per oz/ pack/ portion
Lady's fingers: *see Okra*			
Lager, bottled		29	8
Lager shandy	Corona	24	7
Lamb			
breast, lean and fat, raw		378	107
breast, lean and fat, roast		410	116
breast, lean only, roast		252	71
chump steaks, boneless, lean and fat, raw			65
chump steaks, boneless, lean and fat, grilled			61
dressed carcase, raw		333	94
fat, cooked		616	175
fat, raw (average)		671	190
lean, raw (average)		162	46
leg, lean and fat, raw		240	68
leg, lean and fat, roast		266	75
leg, lean only, roast		191	54
minced, lean, raw			60
minced, fried			75
scrag and neck, lean and fat, raw		316	90
scrag and neck, lean and fat, stewed		292	83
scrag and neck, lean only, stewed		253	72
scrag and neck, lean only, stewed (with fat)		128	36
shoulder, lean and fat, raw		314	89
shoulder, lean and fat, roast		316	90

Product	Brand	Calories per 100g/ 100ml	Calories per oz/ pack/ portion
shoulder, lean only, roast		196	56
Lamb chops			
loin, lean and fat, raw		377	107
loin, lean and fat, grilled		355	101
loin, lean and fat, grilled (with bone)		277	79
loin, lean only, grilled		222	63
loin, lean only, grilled (with bone)		122	35
Lamb cubes	Knorr	318	90
Lamb cutlets			
best end neck, on the bone, lean and fat, grilled		303	85
lean and fat, raw		386	109
lean and fat, grilled		370	105
lean and fat, grilled (with bone)		244	69
lean only, grilled		222	63
lean only (grilled with fat and bone)		97	27
Lamb grills	Asda	272	
Lamb grillsteak			
	Birds Eye Steakhouse		190 each, grilled or fried
Lamb hotpot	St Michael	103	760 per pack
Lamb kheema		310	88
Lamb kofta	St Michael	162	600 per pack
Lamb mixed grills	Waitrose	211	60

Product	Brand	Calories per 100g/ 100ml	Calories per oz/ pack/ portion
Lamb ragout Cook in the Pot	Crosse & Blackwell	389	160 per packet
Lamb rogan josh	Asda	183	
	Waitrose	136	435 per 320g pack
Lamb samosa	Waitrose	376	214 per 57g pack
Lamb Tikka Masala	Findus	112	260 per pack
Lancashire cheese: *see Cheese*			
Lancashire hot pot	Asda	96	
Lard		891	253
Lasagne	Batchelors Microchef Meals		390 per pack
	Birds Eye Menu Master		435 per pack
	Findus	120	360 per pack
	Safeway Microwave Ready Meals	151	455 per pack
as sold	Signor Rossi	272	77
dry	Buitoni	350	99
	Buitoni Country Harvest	318	90
egg	Safeway	346	98
egg, Quick-Cook, cooked	Tesco	135	38
egg, Quick-Cook, raw	Tesco	343	97
egg, verdi	Safeway	346	98
fresh	St Michael	144	410 per pack

Product	Brand	Calories per 100g/ 100ml	Calories per oz/ pack/ portion
vegetarian	Prewetts Ready		
	Meals	98	295 per pack
	Safeway	111	335 per pack
verdi			
as sold	Signor Rossi	309	88
dry	Buitoni	340	96
egg, Quick-Cook, raw	Tesco	343	97
Lasagne pescatore	Sainsbury's	150	450 per pack
Lasagne pomodoro	Sainsbury's	121	425 per pack
Lasagne vegetali	Sainsbury's	105	315 per pack
Lattice sausage rolls	St Michael	396	112
Laverbread		52	15
Lean roast beef and gravy	Birds Eye MenuMaster	84	310 per 113g pack
Leek and potato bake	Tesco	113	384 per pack
Leek and potato crumble	Sainsbury's		470 per pack
Leeks			
raw		31	9
boiled		24	7
Leicester cheese: *see Cheese*			
Lemon and barley drink, undiluted	Tesco	107	32

Product	Brand	Calories per 100g/ 100ml	Calories per oz/ pack/ portion
Lemon and honey drink	Lanes	95	28
Lemon and honey health drink	Lanes	75	21
Lemon and lime drink	Littlewoods	34	10
	Quosh	28	8
diabetic	Boots	5	2
low calorie,			
diluted	Quosh	2	1
undiluted	Quosh	90	27
	Safeway	99	29
	Tesco	89	26
	Waitrose	85	25
Lemon/lime drink, concentrated			
	Kia-Ora	99	29
Lemon and lime drops	Boots	363	120 per 33g stick pack
Lemon and lime marmalade	Rose's	260	74
Lemon and lime whole fruit drink	Robinsons	95	28
Lemon and lime-flavoured concentrate	Safeway	220	65
Lemon and Sultana Devonshire cheese cake	St Ivel		250 per carton
Lemon bar	Granose	368	184 per 50g bar

Product	Brand	Calories per 100g/ 100ml	Calories per oz/ pack/ portion
Lemon barley crush, ready to drink	Lucozade	72	21
Lemon barley drink	Boots	120	36
	Robinsons	30	9
diabetic	Boots	10	3
dilutable	Boots Shapers	10	3
undiluted	Quosh	94	28
Lemon barley water	Corona	91	27
	Robinsons	105	31
	Safeway	95	28
real, undiluted	Quosh	160	47
Lemon Bon Bons	Trebor Bassett	403	27 per sweet
Lemon bubble gum	Wrigley Hubba Bubba		15/24 per chunk
Lemon cheese	Moorhouse	295	45 per portion
	Waitrose	329	93
Pure Fruit	Hartley's	295	45 per portion
Lemon cheesecake, baked	St Michael	248	70
Lemon Chinese sauce mix, sweet and sour	Sharwood	296	225 per sachet
Lemon cream flan	St Michael	365	103
Lemon curd			
home made		290	82
starch base		283	80
	Asda	290	
	Gales	280	79

Product	Brand	Calories per 100g/ 100ml	Calories per oz/ pack/ portion
	Moorhouse	285	45 per portion
	Robertson's	291	82
	Safeway	294	83
	Tesco	331	94
	Waitrose	276	78
Lemon curd tart	Lyons		150 each
Lemon drink, diet	Asda	6	
Lemon drink low calorie	Britvic	37	10
	Safeway	14	4
	Sunfresh	17	5
Lemon and honey health drink	Lanes	75	21
Lemon and lime drink	Quosh		45 per carton
	Safeway	100	28
Lemon barley low calorie	Robinsons	30	8
	Boots Shapers	10	3
Lemon flavour dessert mix	Dietade		45 per 14g pack as sold
Lemon flavour jelly crystals	Waitrose	272	77
	Dietade		40 per pack as sold
Lemon, honey and ginger drink	Boots	140	40

Product	Brand	Calories per 100g/ 100ml	Calories per oz/ pack/ portion
Lemon iced Madeira cake	St Michael	415	118
Lemon jelly	Littlewoods	260	74
	Safeway	268	76
	Tesco	57	16
diabetic crystals	Boots	365	103
Lemon jelly marmalade, fine-cut	Waitrose	248	70
Lemon juice	Hycal	243	72
	Jif	15	4
	Safeway	7	2
	Tesco	8	2
	Waitrose	13	4
less sharp, dilutable	Boots Shapers	8	2
less sharp, undiluted	PLJ	25	7
longlife	Tesco	48	14
original sharp, undiluted	PLJ	25	7
sharp, dilutable	Boots Shapers	8	2
Lemon Madeira cake mix	Granny Smiths	326	1190 per 365g pack made up
Lemon marmalade, fine shred	Baxters	253	853 per 340g jar
Lemon mayonnaise	Hellmanns	720	204
	Safeway	745	211
	Waitrose	734	208

Product	Brand	Calories per 100g/ 100ml	Calories per oz/ pack/ portion
Lemon meringue crunch mix (as sold)			1968 per 780g pack made up
	Granny Smiths	252	
	Tesco	410	116
Lemon meringue pie		323	92
Lemon meringue pie mix	Green's	416	192 per portion made up
Lemon meringues	Lyons	382	108
Lemon mousse	St Michael	237	67
Lemon Pavlova	Young's	295	84
Lemon pie filling mix	Green's	353	55 per portion made up
	Royal	147	552 per 375g pack made up
Lemon puffs	Huntley & Palmer	521	80 per biscuit
	Sainsbury's		75 per biscuit
	Tesco		85 per biscuit
Lemon shred marmalade	Safeway	251	71
	Tesco	286	81
Lemon slice cake, fresh cream	Tesco	406	115
Lemon sole			
raw		81	23
fried		216	61

Product	Brand	Calories per 100g/ 100ml	Calories per oz/ pack/ portion
fried (with bones)		171	48
steamed		91	26
steamed (with bones and skin)		64	18
fillets	Waitrose	80	23
golden	Young's	103	29
whole	Waitrose	80	23
whole breaded	St Michael	132	37
Lemon sole bonne femme	Young's	85	24
Lemon sorbet	Waitrose	114	34
Lemon sorbet ice cream	Tesco	107	30
	Wall's Gino Ginelli Tubs	121	34
Lemon squash	St Michael	172	51
diabetic	Roses	5	1.5
diluted	Britvic	19	5
diluted	Britvic High Juice	26	7
low calorie	Dietade	2	1
undiluted	Britvic	97	27
	Britvic High Juice	129	37
Lemon Surprise	Bertorelli	225	158 per 70g pack
Lemon tops cake mix	Granny Smiths	355	1104 per 311g pack made up
Lemon torte	St Michael	311	187
Lemon yoghurt	Safeway	92	138 per 150g pack

Product	Brand	Calories per 100g/ 100ml	Calories per oz/ pack/ portion	227
French style	Littlewoods	102	153 per 150g pack	
	St Michael	103	29	
Lemonade, bottled		21	6	
Lemonade	Corona	24	7	
	Safeway	26	8	
	Safeway	23	76 per 330ml can	
	Schweppes	23	7	
	St Michael	44	13	
	Tesco	22	6	
	Waitrose	28	8	
diabetic	Boots		0.6 per 100ml	
diet	Asda	0.20		
	Safeway	1		
	Whites	2	5 per 250ml bottle	
low calorie	Diet Corona	1	0.5 per 100ml	
	Schweppes Slimline		0.38 per 100ml	
	Tesco	4	1	
	Waitrose	5	1	
old fashioned	Waitrose	43	13	
traditional	Corona	39	12	
Lemonade and beer shandy				
low calorie	Schweppes Slimline	6	2	
Lemonade and cider	Top Deck	38	11	
Lemonade dipper	Barratt	341	97	
Lemonade shandy	Safeway	13	43 per 330ml can	
	Schweppes	25	7	

Product	Brand	Calories per 100g/ 100ml	Calories per oz/ pack/ portion
	Top Deck	25	7
Lemonade with beer, low calorie	Diet Top Deck	11	3
Lemonade-flavoured concentrate	Safeway	193	57
low calorie	Safeway	41	12
Lemons			
juice, fresh		7	2
whole		15	4
Lentil and bacon	Safeway	55	235 per 425g can
soup	Sainsbury's	47	200 per 425g can
Lentil and vegetable casserole	Granose	100	425 per can
Lentil dish	Granose	114	32
Lentil soup		99	28
	Asda	41	
	Baxters	52	225 per 425g can
	Campbell's Bumper Harvest	45	200 per 425g can
	Heinz Whole Soup	38	115 per 300g can
	Tesco	37	160 per 425g can
condensed	Campbell's	88	260 per 300g can
Lentils			
brown, raw		371	104
brown, cooked		114	32
green, raw		332	93

Product	Brand	Calories per 100g/ 100ml	Calories per oz/ pack/ portion
green, cooked		125	35
red, raw		307	86
red, cooked		100	28
Lettuce			
raw		12	3
iceberg	Tesco	13	4
round Cos crisp	Tesco	12	3
Lhabia and mushroom bhajee	Sharwood	94	400 per can
Licorice chewing gum PK			6 per pellet
Lilva, canned, drained		65	18
Lime, fresh, raw		36	10
Lime cordial	Safeway	100	28
Lime flavour jelly	Waitrose	272	77
Lime jelly	Safeway	268	76
	Tesco	57	16
table	Littlewoods	260	74
Lime juice cordial undiluted		112	32
Lime marmalade	Rose's	260	74
Limeade	Asda	23	
	Corona·	23	7
	Safeway	24	7
	Tesco	20	6
Limeade and lager	Top Deck	32	9

Product	Brand	Calories per 100g/ 100ml	Calories per oz/ pack/ portion
Limmits apricot lunchpack	Limmits		210 per pack
Limon, sparkling low calorie	Schweppes	44	13
	Schweppes Slimline	1	
Lincoln biscuits	Peek Frean	486	35 per biscuit
	Tesco	485	137
diabetic	Boots	402	114
Lincoln pea soup, dried			262 per pint pack as sold
	Batchelors	312	
Lincolnshire sausage	St Michael	350	99
Linguine	Napolina	320	80
Lion bar	Rowntree Mackintosh	495	210 per bar
Cub	Rowntree Mackintosh	495	80 per bar
Liqueur truffles	St Michael	519	147
fresh cream	St Michael	522	148
Liquid cherry	Rowntree Mackintosh		30 per sweet
Liquorice allsorts		313	89
	Trebor Bassett	342	97
	St Michael	361	102
	Waitrose	368	104
Liquorice comfits	Trebor Bassett	354	100

Product	Brand	Calories per 100g/ 100ml	Calories per oz/ pack/ portion
Liquorice drops	Boots	402	133 per 33g stick pack
Liquorice Granymels	Itona	395	112
Liquorice novelties	Tesco	321	91
Liquorice pipes	Barratt	295	84
Liquorice powder		212	60
Liquorice toffees	Littlewoods	414	117
	Trebor Bassett	456	31 per sweet
Liquorice torpedoes	Trebor Bassett	354	100
Liquorice twists	Tesco	349	99
Lite fat-reduced spread	St Michael	540	153
Little Big Feet jellies	Trebor Bassett	289	13 per sweet
Liver			
calf, raw		153	43
calf, fried		254	72
chicken, raw		135	38
chicken, fried		194	55
lamb, raw		179	51
lamb, fried		232	66
ox, raw		163	46
pig, raw		154	44
Liver and bacon	Sainsbury's		470 per pack
frozen	Sainsbury's		350 per pack
Liver and bacon bake	Asda	138	
Liver and bacon paste	Shippams	194	68 per 35g pack

Product	Brand	Calories per 100g/ 100ml	Calories per oz/ pack/ portion
Liver casserole cooking mix	Colman's	350	99
Liver sausage		310	88
Liver with onion and gravy	Birds Eye MenuMaster		190 per pack
Lobster			
boiled		119	34
boiled (with shell)		42	12
Lobster bisque	Baxters	59	251 per 425g can
	Sainsbury's	61	260 per 425g can
	Tesco	62	264 per 425g can
Lockets	Mars	351	100
Loganberries			
raw		17	5
stewed without sugar		16	5
stewed with sugar		54	15
canned		101	29
Lollies assorted	Safeway		40 each
Lollyades	Trebor Bassett	363	109 per sweet
London grill(canned)	Crosse & Blackwell	157	45
Long grain and wild rice, made with butter	Uncle Ben's	112	32
Long grain rice (cooked)	Tesco	356	101
	Tesco	99	28
	Whitworths	361	102

Product	Brand	Calories per 100g/ 100ml	Calories per oz/ pack/ portion
American	St Michael	349	99
cooked	Uncle Ben's	115	32
frozen, cooked	Uncle Ben's	131	37
three minute, cooked			
(canned)	Uncle Ben's	113	32
Longan			
canned		63	18
dried		256	73
Loquats (Japanese medlar), canned		84	24
Lorne sausage			
sliced	McKellar Watt		165 per portion
sliced Scottish	St Michael	355	101
Lotus tubers, canned		15	4
Low fat spread		366	104
	Safeway	365	103
	Tesco	340	96
Low sugar drink, concentrated	Kia-Ora	26	8
Lucozade		68	19
	Beecham	72	21
Luncheon meat			
canned		313	89
sliced	Tesco	310	88
Luxury all butter rich fruit cake	Tesco	345	98
Luxury cheesecake mix(Tesco): *see flavours*			

Product	Brand	Calories per 100g/ 100ml	Calories per oz/ pack/ portion
Luxury mincemeat with brandy, glace cherries and almonds	Safeway	267	76
	Waitrose	275	78
Luxury cheese and onion pizza	Safeway	200	56
Luxury cheese and tomato pizza	Safeway	200	56
Luxury meat pizza	Tesco	204	57
Luxury pepperoni pizza	Safeway	202	56
Luxury sponge mix	Granny Smiths	342	1216 per 355g pack made up
	Whitworths	425	120
dry	Tesco	431	122
made up	Tesco	370	105
Lychee yoghurt	Safeway	94	141 per 150g pack
Lychees			
fresh, raw		64	18
canned in syrup		68	19
Lymeswold cheese: *see Cheese*			

Product	Brand	Calories per 100g/ 100ml	Calories per oz/ pack/ portion
M & Ms			
peanut	Mars	500	142
plain	Mars	483	137
Maasdam cheese: *see Cheese*			
Macadamia nuts	Holland and Barrett	760	215
	St Michael	691	196
Macaroni			
raw		348	99
boiled		117	33
wholewheat	Waitrose	325	92
Macaroni cheese		174	49
	Asda	105	
	Birds Eye MenuMaster		470 per pack
canned	Heinz	106	220 per 210g can
Macaroni, creamed	Ambrosia	92	405 per 439g can
Macaroni Verdi, Quick-Cook	Tesco	343	97
Mackerel			
raw		223	63
fried		188	53
fried (with bones)		138	39
canned in brine	Shippams	201	854 per 425g can
canned in tomato sauce	Shippams	198	842 per 425g can
frozen, cooked	Tesco	310	88
frozen, raw	Tesco	302	86

Product	Brand	Calories per 100g/ 100ml	Calories per oz/ pack/ portion
hot peppered			
(frozen), cooked	Tesco	363	103
kippered	Young's	323	92
kippered fillets	Ross	210	60
	St Michael	310	88
peppered	Young's	333	94
smoked fillets	Asda	341	
	Ross	300	85
	St Michael	300	85
	Waitrose	256	73
smoked, with crushed			
peppercorns	Waitrose	256	73
steaks canned in			
brine	Armour	229	458 per 200g can
whole	Young's	275	78
Madeira cake		393	111
	Tesco	365	103
	Waitrose	437	124
all butter	Safeway	376	107
	Waitrose	370	105
butter	Lyons	378	107
cherry	Tesco	350	99
lemon iced	St Michael	415	118
with buttercream			
filling	Waitrose	309	88
Madeira cake mix			
classic	Green's	431	135 per portion made up

Product	Brand	Calories per 100g/ 100ml	Calories per oz/ pack/ portion
lemon	Granny Smiths	326	1190 per 365g pack made up
Madeira sandwich cake, iced	Waitrose	423	120
Madeira wine Cooking-in Sauce	Baxters	63	268 per 425g can
Madeleines apricot	Lyons	335	95
raspberry	Lyons	333	94
Madras Classic curry sauce	Homepride	82	314 per 383g pack
Madras curry, dry	Beanfeast	269	76
Madras curry mix	Tesco	337	96
Madras medium curry cooking mix	Colman's	335	140 per pack
Main Course soups (Campbell's): *see flavours*			
Maize flour	Holland and Barrett	370	105
Major Grey chutney	Sharwood	217	62
Makes Five Pints	Tesco	485	137
Malaysian chicken and sweetcorn soup	Knorr		220 per pint packet
Mallows coconut	Peek Frean	384	46 per biscuit

Product	Brand	Calories per 100g/ 100ml	Calories per oz/ pack/ portion
jamboree	Peek Frean	382	77 per biscuit
milk coated	Peek Frean	433	52 per biscuit
orange coated	Peek Frean	433	52 per biscuit
Malt crunch biscuits	Peek Frean	420	35 per biscuit
Malt loaf	St Michael	267	76
	Sunblest Sun Malt	262	74
fruited	Waitrose	243	69
wholemeal	Allinson	247	70
Malt loaf bread	Tesco	262	74
Malt vinegar	Tesco	4	1
	Waitrose	4	1
traditional	Tesco	4	1
Malted chocolate drink	Tesco	390	111
Malted drink	Boots	358	101
	Tesco	398	113
	Waitrose	385	109
instant	Boots	394	112
instant, with honey flavour	Boots	392	111
Malted food drink	Horlicks	386	114
low fat, instant	Horlicks	382	113
Malted milk (as sold)	Safeway	385	109
Malted milk biscuits	Asda	472	
	St Michael	466	132
	Tesco	501	142

Product	Brand	Calories per 100g/ 100ml	Calories per oz/ pack/ portion
	Waitrose	466	132
Malted milk chocolate sandwich bar	St Michael	496	141
Malted milk creams	Tesco	474	134
Malted white drink	Wander	385	109
Maltesers	Mars	500	142
Maltlets	Horlicks	386	109
Mandalay korma	Sainsbury's	131	395 per pack
Mandarin crush	St Michael	44	13
Mandarin juice			
freshly squeezed	St Michael	50	14
long life	Safeway	38	11
Mandarin oranges			
canned in syrup		56	16
in light syrup	Waitrose	67	19
in natural juice	Waitrose	45	13
Mandarin trifle	St Ivel		165 per carton
Mandarin yoghurt	Safeway	93	140 per 150g pack
	St Ivel Shape	42	12
	Waitrose	93	140 per 150g pack
low fat	Diet Ski	56	84 per 150g pack
	Littlewoods	82	123 per 150g pack
Mange tout fresh, cooked	Tesco	34	10
Mango and ginger chutney	Sharwood	223	63

Product	Brand	Calories per 100g/ 100ml	Calories per oz/ pack/ portion
Mango chutney			
oily, whole contents		285	81
	Pan Yan	196	56
	Waitrose	221	63
Green Label	Sharwood	217	62
Mango juice		44	12
Mangoes			
fresh, raw		59	17
canned in syrup		77	22
Mangosteen		30	8
Maple and walnut ice cream	Safeway	234	66
	Tesco	186	53
American style	Waitrose	171	51
Maple syrup		250	70
Marathon	Mars	508	144
Marble cake	Tesco	429	122
Marcona almonds	St Michael	565	160
Margarine, all kinds		730	207
	Granose	750	213
	Holland and Barrett	730	207
	Littlewoods	2960	839
	Rakusen	740	210
	Tesco	734	208
blended	Waitrose	730	207
blended soft	Waitrose	735	208

Product	Brand	Calories per 100g/ 100ml	Calories per oz/ pack/ portion
Blue Band	Van den Berghs	740	210
cooking	Safeway	726	206
de Luxe	Safeway	733	208
Echo	Van den Berghs	740	210
Flora Sunflower	Van den Berghs	740	210
Gold	St Ivel	390	111
Krona	Van den Berghs	740	210
Krona Silver	Van den Berghs	740	210
low fat spread	Littlewoods	1480	420
low salt	Granose	750	213
Luxury	Kraft	730	207
premier	Tesco	734	208
salt free	Tesco	734	208
soft	Tesco	734	208
soft, Dutch	Littlewoods	733	208
soya	Safeway	730	207
soya soft	Waitrose	735	208
special soft tub	Kraft	730	207
Stork	Van den Berghs	740	210
Stork Special Blend	Van den Berghs	740	210
sunflower	Asda	729	
	Granose	720	204
	Littlewoods	740	210
	Safeway	735	208
	Tesco	734	208
	Waitrose	735	208
sunflower salt-free	Safeway	735	208
sunflower soft	St Michael	730	207
Superfine	Kraft	730	207
supersoft	Tesco	734	208

Product	Brand	Calories per 100g/ 100ml	Calories per oz/ pack/ portion
superspread soft	St Michael	730	207
table	Safeway	733	208
Tomor	Van den Berghs	740	210
Vitalite sunflower	Kraft	730	207
Margherita pizza	St Michael	218	62
Marie biscuits	Tesco	441	125
Marie Rose dressing	St Michael	740	210
Mariner's bake	St Michael	107	470 per pack
Mariners pasta gratin	Birds Eye MenuMaster		370 per pack
Marmalade		261	74
	Moorhouse	250	40 per portion
all flavours	Chivers	255	40 per portion
	Roses	255	40 per portion
all other varieties	Robertson's	251	71
chunky	Safeway	251	71
coarse cut	Safeway	251	71
diabetic	Dietade	230	65
diabetic, fine cut	Boots	239	68
diabetic, thick cut	Boots	239	68
fine cut	Tesco	290	82
fresh fruit	St Michael	240	68
ginger preserve	Tesco	275	78
Golden Shred	Robertson's	251	71
lemon shred	Safeway	251	71
	Tesco	286	81
lime	Safeway	251	71
lime shred	Tesco	278	79

Product	Brand	Calories per 100g/ 100ml	Calories per oz/ pack/ portion
mature thick cut	Tesco	250	71
	Safeway	251	71
medium cut	Safeway	251	71
no added sugar	Safeway	139	39
no sugar	Whole Earth	120	34
orange	Tesco	243	69
orange shred	Safeway	251	71
orange, thin cut, reduced sugar	Heinz Weight Watchers	124	7 per 6ml
original thick cut	Robertson's	251	71
Pure Fruits, all flavours	Hartley's	255	40 per portion
reduced sugar	Asda	125	
	Boots	154	44
Silver Shred	Robertson's	251	71
thick cut	Tesco	279	79
	Waitrose	248	70

Marmite		179	51
	Beecham	179	51

Marrow			
canned, drained		11	3
raw		16	5
boiled		7	2
large, raw		16	5
small parwal, fresh, raw			144

Marrowfat peas: *see Peas, marrowfat*

Mars Bar		441	125
	Mars	454	129

Product	Brand	Calories per 100g/ 100ml	Calories per oz/ pack/ portion
Marshmallow	Tesco	383	109
Marvel	Cadbury's	355	10 per portion
Marzipan (almond paste)		443	126
	Asda	412	
	Safeway	408	116
	Tesco	437	124
(almond)	Whitworths	412	117
golden	Waitrose	408	116
white	Waitrose	408	116
Marzipan bars, diabetic	Boots	465	132
Mascarpone: *see Cheese*			
Mashed potatoes: *see also Instant*			
Masur savoury snack		644	183
Matchmakers, long all flavours	Rowntree Mackintosh	485	20 per sweet
Matoki: *see Plantain*			
Matzo		384	109
Matzo crackers	Rakusen	347	17 per biscuit
wheaten	Rakusen	340	17 per biscuit
Mayonnaise		718	204
	Heinz	530	150
	Littlewoods	734	208
	Safeway	745	211
	St Michael	734	208

Product	Brand	Calories per 100g/ 100ml	Calories per oz/ pack/ portion
	Tesco	711	202
	Waistline	378	107
	Waitrose	734	208
French	St Michael	753	213
French reduced calorie	Asda	386	
garlic	Hellmanns	720	204
	Safeway	745	211
	Waitrose	734	208
lemon	Hellmanns	720	204
	Safeway	745	211
	Waitrose	734	208
low calorie	Boots Shapers	382	108
	St Michael	298	84
Real	Hellmanns	720	204
reduced calorie	Hellmanns	293	83
reduced calorie	Waitrose	734	208
Meat and potato pie	Safeway		410 per pie
Meat paste		173	49
Meatballs			
beef gravy	Campbell's	82	23
curry sauce	Campbell's	114	32
onion gravy	Campbell's	84	24
spicey, in tomato sauce	Waitrose	150	525 per 350g pack
tomato sauce	Campbell's	96	27
Meatballs and pasta in barbecue sauce	Tyne Brand	133	38

Product	Brand	Calories per 100g/ 100ml	Calories per oz/ pack/ portion
in tomato sauce	Tyne Brand	130	37
Meatless savoury cuts	Granose	88	25
Meatloaf style soya mix	Hera	480	136
Mediterranean juice	St Ivel Real	35	10
Mediterranean vegetable soup	St Michael	37	10
Medium curry cooking sauce	St Michael	41	12
Medium curry Cooking-in Sauce	Baxters	91	387 per 425g can
Medlars		42	12
Megabars	Peek Frean	376	97 per biscuit
Mela Menthe	Bertorelli	306	213 per 70g pack
Mela Parisienne	Bertorelli	302	211 per 70g pack
Mela Stregata	Bertorelli	298	208 per 70g pack
Melba toast	Buitoni	382	108
Melbury cheese: *see Cheese*			
Mellora	Carnation	425	40 per 9g sachet
Melon			
cantaloupe, flesh only		25	7
cantaloupe, with skin		14	4
charentais, flesh only		18	5
galia, flesh only		28	8
galia, with skin		21	6

Product	Brand	Calories per 100g/ 100ml	Calories per oz/ pack/ portion
honey dew/yellow, flesh only		21	6
honey dew/yellow, with skin		14	4
Ogden, with skin		18	5
watermelon, flesh only		21	6
watermelon, with skin		10	3
Melon seeds		581	165
Melon yogurt low calorie	Diet Ski	55	83 per 150g pack
Melton Mowbray pie	Tesco	358	101
Melton Mowbray pork pie	St Michael	402	114
	Waitrose	403	114
individual	Waitrose	377	479 per 127g pie
large	St Michael	353	100
Menthol Eucalyptus	Boots	363	120 per 33g stick pack
Menthol mints	Boots	363	120 per 33g stick pack
MenuMaster meals (Birds Eye): *see flavours*			
Meringue nests	Littlewoods	311	88
	Safeway	312	17 per meringue
	St Michael	380	108
	Tesco	371	105
Meringues		380	108
fresh cream	St Michael	338	96
Mexican bean stew	Granose	130	555 per can

Product	Brand	Calories per 100g/ 100ml	Calories per oz/ pack/ portion
Mexican chilli (dry)	Beanfeast	292	83
Mexican honey, set	Safeway	300	85
Mexican chilli beef stir fry	Ross	108	370 per pack
Mexican style chicken	St Michael	270	615 per pack
Micro chips	McCain		230 per pack
Mignons morceaux	Phileas Fogg		205 per 40g pack
Milanese sauce	Buitoni	47	133 per 283g can
	Tesco	76	22
	Waitrose	62	264 per 425g can
Milanese souffle	Young's	245	69
Mild curry (dry)	Beanfeast	282	80
Mild curry dressing	Heinz All Seasons	276	78
Mild curry rice, frozen, cooked	Uncle Ben's	136	39
Mild curry Saucy Noodles			375 per 115g pack as sold
	Batchelors	326	
Mild curry savoury rice			463 per 137g sachet as sold
	Batchelors	338	
Mild Curry Super Noodles			460 per pack as sold
	Batchelors	465	

Product	Brand	Calories per 100g/ 100ml	Calories per oz/ pack/ portion
Mild mustard pickle	Heinz Ploughman's	114	32
Mild mustard relish	Tesco	128	36
Mild vegetable curry	Sharwood	65	265 per can
Milk			
buttermilk			210 per pint
Channel Island/Gold Top			445 per pint
evaporated, full cream			360 per pint
goats'			340 per pint
instant dried, skimmed			280 per pint
instant dried, low fat			100 per oz
long life/UHT			380 per pint
pasteurized silver top			380 per pint
semi-skimmed			260 per pint
skimmed			190 per pint
sterlized			380 per pint
Milk assorted biscuits	Cadbury's	495	60 per biscuit
Milk caramel wafers	Safeway	567	161
Milk choc ices	Waitrose	290	86
Milk chocolate		529	150
Milk chocolate Bounty	Mars	483	137
Milk chocolate brazil nuts	Littlewoods	553	157
Milk chocolate Brazils	Tesco	565	160
Milk chocolate buttons	St Michael	510	145

Product	Brand	Calories per 100g/ 100ml	Calories per oz/ pack/ portion
Milk chocolate caramel biscuits	Safeway		125 per biscuit
Milk chocolate caramel shortcake	Safeway Tesco		95 per biscuit 120 per biscuit
Milk chocolate coated rings	Tesco	503	143
Milk chocolate caramel wafer	St Michael		95 per biscuit
Milk chocolate caramel finger wafer	Safeway		45 per biscuit
Milk chocolate covered roll	Waitrose	428	121
Milk chocolate currant topped caramel wafer	St Michael		120 per wafer
Milk chocolate digestive biscuits	Cadbury's St Michael	490	50 per biscuit 65 per biscuit
Milk chocolate drops diabetic	Tesco Boots	507 512	144 145
Milk chocolate eclairs	Cadbury's	450	20 each pocket pack, standard pack 40
	St Michael	445	126
Milk chocolate finger wafers	St Michael		45 per wafer
Milk chocolate fingers	Safeway	528	150

Product	Brand	Calories per 100g/ 100ml	Calories per oz/ pack/ portion
Milk chocolate ginger cookie	St Michael		85 per biscuit
Milk chocolate hazelnut wafer	St Michael		180 per wafer
Milk chocolate honeycomb orange bar	Safeway		140 per bar
Milk chocolate honeycomb sandwich bar	Safeway		145 per bar
Milk chocolate oat crunchie	St Michael		75 per biscuit
Milk chocolate orange sandwich bar	St Michael		130 per bar
Milk chocolate rolls with raspberry filling	Waitrose	365	103
with vanilla filling	Waitrose	453	128
Milk chocolate sandwich bar	Waitrose	516	146
Milk chocolate sandwich biscuits	Gateway Tesco		125 per biscuit 125 per biscuit
Milk chocolate snack fingers	Tesco	556	158
Milk chocolate sunota biscuits(half-coated)	Safeway	500	142
Milk chocolate tea cakes	Safeway		50 each

Product	Brand	Calories per 100g/ 100ml	Calories per oz/ pack/ portion
	St Michael		80 each
	Tesco		60 each
Milk chocolate toffee shortbread	St Michael		80 per biscuit
Milk chocolate truffle	Rowntree Mackintosh		40 per sweet
Milk chocolate wafer bar	Boots Shapers Meal	520	147
Milk chocolate, diabetic			
filled with coffee cream	Boots	574	163
filled with strawberry cream	Boots	552	156
filled with yogurt cream	Boots	556	158
hazelnut	Boots	518	147
Milk chocolates	Nestle	534	151
Milk Club biscuits	Jacobs	510	117 per biscuit
Milk coated mallows	Peek Frean	433	52 per biscuit
Milk drink	St Ivel Shape	45	13
Milk half coated digestive biscuits	Huntley & Palmer	502	65 per biscuit
Milk pudding		131	37
rice		91	26
Milk, goats': *see Milk*			
Milk, soya	Granose	50	15

Product	Brand	Calories per 100g/ 100ml	Calories per oz/ pack/ portion
carob	Granose	59	17
coconut	Granose	70	21
strawberry	Granose	64	19
sugar free	Granose	42	12
Milk, human			
mature		69	20
transitional		67	19
Milky bar chocolates	Nestlé	540	153
Milky Way	Mars	433	123
Millet	Holland and Barrett	380	108
Millet flakes	Holland and Barrett	381	108
Milquik	St Ivel	34	200 per pint made up
powder	St Ivel	355	101
Mince Bolognese	Tyne Brand	122	480 per can
Mince pies		435	123
	Littlewoods	369	105
	Tesco	394	112
	Waitrose	369	105
deep	Safeway	380	108
puff pastry	Waitrose	391	111
wholemeal	Waitrose	401	114
Minced beef and dumplings	Tesco	168	765 per pack

Product	Brand	Calories per 100g/ 100ml	Calories per oz/ pack/ portion
Minced beef and onion	Tesco	146	290 per 198g can
	Tyne Brand	116	230 per 198g can
Minced beef and onion pie			
canned	Tyne Brand	193	55
family (frozen)	Ross	290	82
	Tesco	277	79
frozen	Safeway	294	83
individual	Waitrose	287	81
individual (frozen)	Tesco	315	89
large oval	Waitrose	282	80
Minced beef and onion roll (chilled)	Tesco	295	84
Minced beef and pasta bake	St Michael	130	370 per pack
Minced beef and vegetable pie value	Birds Eye		325 per pie
Minced beef and vegetable plate pie	St Michael	265	75
Minced beef and vegetables (canned)	Campbell's	99	420 per 425g can
Minced beef in rich gravy (canned)	St Michael	150	640 per 425g can
Minced beef lattice roll with cheese, tomato and herb filling	Waitrose	293	83

Product	Brand	Calories per 100g/ 100ml	Calories per oz/ pack/ portion
Minced beef pancakes	Birds Eye Snacks		130 each shallow-fried
	Findus	159	105 each
Minced beef pie	Waitrose	267	380 per 142g pie
	Waitrose	298	1344 per 454g pie
topcrust	St Michael	210	60
traditional, small	St Michael	336	95
Minced beef roll	St Michael	297	84
Minced beef rolls with mustard	Waitrose	333	94
Minced beef savoury toasts	Findus	199	56
Minced beef with vegetables in gravy	Birds Eye MenuMaster		150 per pack
Minced lamb rolls	Waitrose	341	97
Minced soya and onion	Protoveg Menu	359	102
Minced steak and onion pie filling	Fray Bentos	196	56
Mincemeat		235	67
	Moorhouse	285	45 per portion
	Safeway	271	77
	Waitrose	275	78
luxury	Safeway	267	76
	Tesco	272	77

Product	Brand	Calories per 100g/ 100ml	Calories per oz/ pack/ portion
luxury, with brandy cherries and			
almonds	Waitrose	275	78
ordinary	Tesco	338	96
Pure Fruit	Hartley's	285	45 per portion
standard	Robertson's	266	75
traditional	Robertson's	266	75
Minestrone soup			
canned	Baxters	36	155 per 425g can
	Campbell's Bumper Harvest	43	185 per 425g can
	Heinz	31	95 per 300g can
	Tesco	50	140 per 425g can
dried	Batchelors	275	132 per 48g pint pack as sold
	Hera		480 per pack
	Knorr		225 per 1 1/2 pint pack
dried, instant	Tesco	338	75 per sachet
dried, with croutons	Batchelors Cup-a-Soup Special	339	78 per 23g pack as sold
Mini Milk ice cream			
strawberry	Wall's		40 per portion
vanilla	Wall's		35 per portion
Mini pizza	St Michael	282	80
Mini waffles	Birds Eye		22 per pack baked or grilled, fried 27

Product	Brand	Calories per 100g/ 100ml	Calories per oz/ pack/ portion
Ministick chocolate bars			
fruits of the forest	St Michael	473	134
hazelnut	St Michael	550	156
Ministicks			
mint	St Michael	476	135
Mocca	St Michael	554	157
Minstrels	Mars	500	142
Mint assortment	St Michael	375	106
	Waitrose	377	107
Mint carob bar	Kalibu	413	310 per 75g bar
Mint chews	St Michael	370	105
Mint choc cheesecake	Tesco	39	109
Mint choc chip Cornetto	Wall's		235 per cone
Mint choc chip dessert	Birds Eye Supermousse		140 per tub
Mint choc chip ice cream	Lyons Maid Gold Seal	196	56
	Lyons Maid Napoli	224	64
Mint choc ices	Waitrose	290	86
Mint choc King Cone	Lyons Maid		195 per cone
Mint choc ice cream	Wall's Gino Ginelli Tubs	221	62

Product	Brand	Calories per 100g/ 100ml	Calories per oz/ pack/ portion
Mint chocolate chip ice cream, American style	Waitrose	199	59
Mint chocolate dessert	Waitrose	432	122
Mint Club biscuits	Jacobs	495	113 per biscuit
Mint creams	Trebor Bassett	342	32 per sweet
Mint Crisp	Lyons Maid		180 each
Mint Crisp block	Needlers	508	229 per 45g pack
Mint crisp chocolates	Waitrose	489	139
Mint Granymels	Itona	370	105
Mint humbugs	Boots	371	122 per 33g stick pack
	Waitrose	362	103
soft centre	Needlers	356	101
Mint imperials	Needlers	389	110
	Tesco	379	107
diabetic	Boots	380	108
	Boots	371	105
Mint jelly	Baxters	257	449 per 175g jar
	Colman's	265	75
	Safeway	265	75
	Tesco	266	75
Mint ministicks	St Michael	476	135
Mint relish, spicy	Branston	113	32
Mint sauce	Baxters	121	175 per 145g jar
	Safeway	17	5

Product	Brand	Calories per 100g/ 100ml	Calories per oz/ pack/ portion
	Tesco	100	28
	Waitrose	80	23
fresh garden	Colman's	10	3
garden	Safeway	10	3
sweet, concentrated	O.K.	40	11
Mint sensations	Needlers	435	123
Mint sticks	Tesco	519	147
Mint toffees	Trebor Bassett	456	31 per sweet
Mint truffles	St Michael	605	172
Minted peas (frozen)	Safeway	80	23
Mintola	Rowntree Mackintosh	450	25 per sweet
Mints			
Extra strong	Needlers	364	103
extra strong roll	Trebor Bassett	378	10 per sweet
Miracle whip dressing	Kraft	440	125
Miso sauce	Sunwheel	161	46
Mississippi mud pie	California cake & Cookie Company		280 per square
Mr Men			
all flavours	Lyons Maid	45	20 each
Mr Men Cartoons cake mix (as sold)	Green's	409	64 made up per portion
Mr Men fruit gums	Trebor Bassett	308	87
Mr Men yogurt(Raines): *see flavours*			

Product	Brand	Calories per 100g/ 100ml	Calories per oz/ pack/ portion
Mivvi			
pineapple super	Lyons Maid		82 each
raspberry Fun Size	Lyons Maid	120	50 each
strawberry	Lyons Maid		77 each
Mixed bean salad	Safeway	82	350 per can
Mixed fruit	Waitrose	243	69
dried	Safeway	247	70
	Tesco	306	87
Mixed fruit bar	Granose	384	192 per 50g bar
Mixed fruit drink	Tesco	48	14
Mixed fruit drops	Boots	363	120 per 33g stick pack
Mixed fruits in natural syrup, chunky	Libby	52	15
Mixed fruit jam	Safeway	248	70
Mixed fruit pickle, spiced	Baxters	159	484 per 305g jar
Mixed fruit sponge pudding	Heinz	298	84
Mixed fruit trifle, individual	Young's	150	43
Mixed grain kasha	Bewell Amazing Grains	364	103
Mixed nuts			
chopped	Whitworths	564	160
raw	Tesco	611	173

Product	Brand	Calories per 100g/ 100ml	Calories per oz/ pack/ portion	263
salted	Tesco	641	182	
	Waitrose	655	186	
salted/roasted	Safeway	532	151	
Mixed nuts and fruit	Safeway	536	152	
Mixed nuts and raisins	Sooner	488	122 per 25g pack	
	Waitrose	535	152	
bag	Tesco	464	132	
no salt	Tesco	566	160	
tub	Tesco	516	146	
Mixed nuts, raisins and chocolate chips	Tesco	489	139	
Mixed peel	Asda	252		
	Whitworths	244	69	
cut	Safeway	252	71	
	Tesco	249	71	
	Waitrose	212	60	
Mixed peppers				
chopped	Waitrose	20	6	
dried	Tesco	205	58	
	Whitworths	212	60	
frozen	Ross	20	6	
	Safeway	14	4	
Mixed pickle	Haywards	9	3	
	Waitrose	21	6	
clear	Safeway	8	2	
Continental	Safeway	19	5	

Product	Brand	Calories per 100g/ 100ml	Calories per oz/ pack/ portion
in mild vinegar	Haywards New Seasons	33	9
Mixed salad			
Continental	Sainsbury's	13	20 per pack
fresh	Safeway	34	85 per pack
with apple, raisin and walnut	Sainsbury's	50	100 per pack
with beans and radichio	Sainsbury's	50	100 per pack
with chinese leaf	Sainsbury's	32	65
and sweetcorn	Sainsbury's	32	65
	Seasons	38	11
Mixed spice	Safeway	367	104
	Tesco	281	80
Mixed toffees		430	122
Mixed vegetable curry		181	51
Mixed vegetable savoury rice			416 per 125g sachet as sold
	Batchelors	333	
	Safeway	333	416 per 125g pack
	Whitworths	310	88
special	Batchelors	326	388 per 119g sachet as sold
Mixed vegetables	Safeway	37	105 per 284g pack
	Waitrose	68	304 per 454g pack
	Waitrose	35	320 per 907g pack
canned	Hartley's	55	60 per 109g can
	Tesco	44	12

Product	Brand	Calories per 100g/ 100ml	Calories per oz/ pack/ portion
	Waitrose	43	129 per 300g can
casserole mix	Tesco	34	10
casserole vegetables	Birds Eye	35	10
cauliflower, peas and carrots	Birds Eye	35	10
Continental	Safeway	57	16
Continental vegetable mix	Tesco	313	89
country mix	Findus	55	16
dried	Batchelors		203 per 88g sachet as sold
	Surprise	231	sold
	Tesco	360	102
	Whitworths	258	73
farmhouse	Ross	30	9
original	Birds Eye	53	15
peas and baby carrots	Birds Eye	35	10
petits pois, button sprouts baby carrots	Birds Eye	42	12
rice, peas and mushrooms, boiled	Birds Eye	123	35
rice, sweetcorn peas and carrots, boiled	Birds Eye	123	35
special	Tesco	68	19
special mix	Ross	40	11
stewpack	Ross	20	6
summer(canned)	Tesco	50	14
summer harvest mix	Findus	72	20

Product	Brand	Calories per 100g/ 100ml	Calories per oz/ pack/ portion
sweet corn, peas and carrots	Birds Eye	53	15
Mocca ministicks	St Michael	554	157
Mocha almond ice cream	Safeway	248	73
Mocha cake mix (as sold)	Green's	396	258 made up per portion
Moghulai Korma curry sauce	Sharwood	190	85 per sachet
Molasses	Holland and Barrett	200	57
Molasses snack bar carob coated	Sunwheel Kalibu	437	131 per 30g bar
Monkfish raw, fish only smoked steamed, fish only		71 110 100	20 31 28
Monkey nuts	Tesco	615	174
Montelimar	Rowntree Mackintosh		45 per sweet
Mooli: *see Radish, white*			
Moon Waffles	McCain		100 each
Moong dahi chilki		83	24
Moong gram, whole		66	19

Product	Brand	Calories per 100g/ 100ml	Calories per oz/ pack/ portion
Morello cherry and apple juice	Copella	35	10
Morello cherry and cream cheesecake	Young's	240	68
Morello cherry conserve	Safeway	248	70
	Waitrose	250	71
Morello cherry Fruit For-All	Chivers	110	85 per portion
Morello cherry jam, reduced sugar	Waitrose	124	35
Morello cherry juice	Copella	34	10
Morello cherry yoghurt, low fat	Waitrose	90	135 per 150g pack
Morning coffee biscuits	Tesco	471	134
Mortadella: see Sausages, delicatessen			
Moules bonne femme	St Michael	97	27
Moussaka		195	55
	Findus	145	435 per pack
	Safeway	128	385 per pack
	Tesco	116	530 per pack
Mousse: see flavours			
Mozzarella: see Cheese			
Muesli		368	104
	Holland and Barrett	370	105

Product	Brand	Calories per 100g/ 100ml	Calories per oz/ pack/ portion
"Eight" fruit	Granose	408	116
Bircher	Granose	379	107
bran	Prewetts	320	91
country	Jordans	345	98
Crispy	Jordans	307	86
deluxe	Sunwheel	390	111
	Prewetts	360	102
fruit and fibre	Waitrose	293	83
fruit and nut, 35%	Safeway	326	92
harvest mix	Sunwheel	389	109
high fibre	Holland and Barrett	340	96
honey	Boots Second Nature	417	118
no added sugar	Boots Second Nature	362	103
no sugar/salt	Asda	333	
Swiss style	Asda	380	
special recipe	Jordans	330	94
sugar free	Holland and Barrett	380	108
	Prewetts	340	96
traditional	St Michael	362	103
tropical	Prewetts	340	96
unsweetened	St Michael	340	96
wholegrain fruit	Granose	408	116
wholewheat	Tesco	346	98
Muesli and fruit biscuits	Boots Second Nature	461	131

Product	Brand	Calories per 100g/ 100ml	Calories per oz/ pack/ portion
Muesli bar			
apple	Granose	416	104 per 25g bar
chocolate chip	Granose	484	121 per 25g bar
chocolate coated	Tesco	510	145
fruit	Prewetts	310	130 per 42g bar
hazelnut	Granose	476	119 per 25g bar
hazelnut and almond	Granose	460	115 per 25g bar
Swiss style	Boots	350	99
Muesli bar square snack	Holly Mill		216 per bar
Muesli base	Prewetts	340	96
	Sunwheel	370	105
Muesli biscuits	Holland and Barrett		60 per biscuit
diabetic	Boots	437	124
Muesli cereal	Boots Second Nature	361	102
Muesli cookies	St Michael	476	135
	Tesco	464	132
	Waitrose	448	127
Muesli snack bar carob coated	Sunwheel Kalibu	397	119 per 30g bar
Muesli stuffing mix	Knorr	385	109
Muesli tub	Allinson	380	108
banana and brazil	Jordans	430	122

Product	Brand	Calories per 100g/ 100ml	Calories per oz/ pack/ portion
coconut and sultana	Jordans	366	104
Muesli yoghurt	Safeway	101	152 per 150g pack
	St Ivel Shape	45	13
Muffins	Sunblest Muffin Man	233	158 per muffin
plain	Tesco	225	64
wholemeal	Asda	202	
	Sunblest Muffin Man	214	154 per muffin
Mulberries		36	10
Mullet			
grey, fillet, raw		142	40
grey, fillet, steamed		125	35
red, fillet, raw		160	45
Mulligatawny soup	Heinz Spicy Soups	48	145 per 300g can
Munch biscuits	Moorlands		50 per biscuit
wholewheat fruit	Moorlands		60 per biscuit
Munch Bunch yogurts(Eden Vale): *see flavours*			
Munchies	Rowntree Mackintosh	505	25 per sweet
Mung (moong) beans: *see Beans*			
Mung (moong) beansprouts			
fresh, raw		35	10
canned		9	3
Murray Fruits	Cadbury's	390	25 per Fruit

Product	Brand	Calories per 100g/ 100ml	Calories per oz/ pack/ portion
Murray Mints	Cadbury's	400	25 per mint pocket pack, others 20
Muscovado sugar	Safeway	394	112
dark	Waitrose	360	102
light	Waitrose	378	107
Mushroom *straw, canned, drained*			309
Mushroom and bacon Toast Topper	Heinz	131	37
Mushroom and pasta italienne	Birds Eye MenuMaster		303 per pack
Mushroom and peppers savoury rice	Safeway	341	426 per 125g pack
Mushroom and ricotta cheese cannelloni	Sainsbury's	157	410 per pack
Mushroom cream soup	Knorr "No Simmer"	484	137
Mushroom en croute	St Michael	207	830 per pack
Mushroom pancakes	St Michael	140	320 per pack
Mushroom pate	Vessen	256	115 per 45g pack
Mushroom Pour Over sauce mix	Colman's	335	100 per pack
Mushroom quiche	St Michael	277	79
Mushroom sandwich cream	Granose	360	102

Product	Brand	Calories per 100g/ 100ml	Calories per oz/ pack/ portion
Mushroom savoury rice	Batchelors	346	450 per 130g sachet as sold
Mushroom snack pizza	Tesco	222	63
Mushroom soup	Asda	57	
	Batchelors Cup-a-Soup	415	108 per 26g sachet as sold
	Campbell's Granny Soups	37	160 per 425g can
dried	Safeway	355	101
	Tesco	382	108
	Waitrose	340	139 per 41g pack
instant special (made up)	Safeway	45	13
low calorie	Heinz Weight Watchers	24	70 per 292g can
	Waitrose	16	47 per 295g pack
Mushroom Super Noodles	Batchelors	465	460 per pack as sold
Mushrooms			
Chinese, dried		284	81
raw		13	4
fried		210	60
button, whole	Safeway	13	200g/7oz pack
	Waitrose	20	6
canned	Tesco	32	9
chopped	Waitrose	20	6
creamed(canned)	Asda	78	

Product	Brand	Calories per 100g/ 100ml	Calories per oz/ pack/ portion
	Tesco	87	25
dried	Tesco	325	92
dried, sliced	Whitworths	133	38
fresh, fried	Tesco	210	60
fresh, raw	Tesco	13	4
sliced	Safeway	13	4
	Waitrose	20	6
stir fry	Safeway	80	23

Mushrooms sandwich spread | Granose | 337 | 96 |

Mushy peas: *see Peas, mushy*

Mussels			
raw		66	19
boiled		87	25
boiled (with shells)		26	7
cooked	Dan Maid	75	21
frozen, raw	Tesco	82	23

Mustard			
American	Colman's	110	31
Burger mild	Colman's	110	31
chive	Colman's	170	48
Dijon	Colman's	170	48
English	Colman's	180	51
	Safeway	95	27
French	Colman's	115	33
	Safeway	75	21
German	Colman's	135	38
horseradish	Colman's	140	40

Product	Brand	Calories per 100g/ 100ml	Calories per oz/ pack/ portion
sage and onion	Colman's	175	50
whole grain	Colman's	145	41
Mustard and cress, raw		10	3
Mustard and vinaigrette dressing	Tesco	503	143
Mustard leaves, raw		34	10
Mustard oil dressing	Safeway	440	130
Mustard powder		452	128
English DSF	Colman's	480	136
whole grain	Colman's	505	143
Mustard relish	Safeway	118	33
mild	Tesco	128	36
Mustard seeds		469	133
My Little Pony Cartoons cake mix (as sold)	Green's	412	64 made up per portion

Product	Brand	Calories per 100g/ 100ml	Calories per oz/ pack/ portion
Naan bread	Tesco	273	380 per serving
Naan bread mix	Sharwood	360	102
Nachips	Old El Paso	550	156
Napoletana sauce	Asda	45	
	St Michael	34	10
	Tesco	40	11
	Waitrose	35	10
Napoli	Whole Earth Pasta Pots		260 per pot
Napoli dairy ice cream (Lyons Maid): *see flavours*			
Napolitan sauce	Buitoni	24	68 per 283g can
	Waitrose	27	114 per 424g can
Natch cider	Taunton	34	200 per pint
Natural cottage cheese	Asda	97	
	Eden Vale	97	27
	St Ivel	94	27
Natural country bran	Jordans	167	47
Natural flavour vegetarian chunks	Direct Foods	251	71
Natural flavour vegetarian mince	Direct Foods	250	71
Natural original crunchy	Jordans	405	115
Natural seed bar poppy	Boots	439	124
sesame	Boots	464	132

Product	Brand	Calories per 100g/ 100ml	Calories per oz/ pack/ portion
sunflower	Boots	464	132
Natural set yogurt	Safeway	47	71 per 150g pack
low fat	Waitrose	59	89 per 150g pack
low fat, unsweetened	Waitrose	59	295 per 500g pack
whole milk	Waitrose	75	113 per 150g pack
Natural wheatgerm	Jordans	325	92
Natural yogurt	Eden Vale	70	105 per 150g pack
	Safeway	47	71 per 150g pack
	St Ivel	60	17
	St Michael	69	20
	St Ivel Shape	50	14
low fat	Littlewoods	45	68 per 150g pack
	Tesco	64	18
	Waitrose	47	71 per 150g pack
unsweetened	Raines	55	16
whole milk, French	St Michael	68	19
Neapolitan ice cream	Lyons Maid	179	51
	Tesco	179	51
	Waitrose	157	46
sliceable	Wall's Gino Ginelli		50
soft scoop	Lyons Maid	178	50
Neapolitan vegetable sauce	Prewetts	304	86
Neapolitan wafers	Peek Frean	504	36 per biscuit
Nectarines raw		50	14

Product	Brand	Calories per 100g/ 100ml	Calories per oz/ pack/ portion
raw (with stones)		46	13
Nectarines and orange yogurt	St Michael	98	28
Neeps and tatties	Sainsbury's	100	300 per pack
Nice biscuits	Boots Peek Frean	449	30 per biscuit 44 per biscuit
Nice creams	Peek Frean Tesco	484	57 per biscuit 60 per biscuit
Night cap	Boots	359	102
Nik Naks, spicy	St Michael	540	153
Nik-Naks	Sooner	497	149 per 30g pack
90% beefburgers	Findus	283	80
No bake egg custard dessert mix (as sold)	Green's	380	148 per portion made up
No Simmer soups (Knorr): see flavours			
Noiseberry fruits: see Sapota			
Noisette pate	Rowntree Mackintosh		40 per sweet
Noisettes	Ross St Michael	180 323	51 92
Non-dairy cream	Tesco	253	72
Non-dairy ice cream		165	47
Non-dairy vanilla ice cream	Tesco	179	51

Product	Brand	Calories per 100g/ 100ml	Calories per oz/ pack/ portion
Noodle Doodles spaghetti shapes in tomato sauce	Heinz	59	17
Noodles *egg, dried, raw* *wheat, dried, raw*		391 388	111 110
Noots	Itona	420	119
Nottingham pie	Tesco	326	92
Nougat	Barratt	355	101
Number 7 cider	Bulmer	35	100 per half pint
Nut and raisin carob bar	Kalibu	453	340 per 75g bar
Nut and raisin confectionery bar, no added sugar	Sunwheel Kalibu	500	210 per 42g bar
Nut burger mix	Tomorrow Foods	353	100
Nut loaf	Granose	176	50
Nut luncheon	Mapletons	380	540 per 142g pack
Nut roast	Granose	488	138
Nut toffee creme	Rowntree Mackintosh		45 per sweet
Nutbrawn	Granose	212	60
Nutmeg *powder*	Tesco	525 456	149 129

Product	Brand	Calories per 100g/ 100ml	Calories per oz/ pack/ portion
ground	Safeway	556	158
whole	Safeway	556	158
Nutrigrain			
brown rice and rye with raisins	Kellogg's Nutrigrain	342	97
rye and oats with hazelnuts	Kellogg's Nutrigrain	368	104
wholewheat with raisins	Kellogg's Nutrigrain	326	92
Nuts and fruit, yogurt coated	Waitrose	570	162
Nuts and raisins	Whitworths	462	131
Nuttolene	Granose	298	84
Nutty bar	Rowntree Mackintosh	495	255 per bar
Nutty choc choc bar	Wall's		190 per bar
Nutty toffee dairy ice cream	Lyons Maid Napoli	205	30

Product	Brand	Calories per 100g/ 100ml	Calories per oz/ pack/ portion
Oat and honey crunch bar	Boots Second Nature	432	122
Oat cereal, instant	Tesco	382	108
Oatcakes		441	125
bran	Allinson		50 per biscuit
Scottish rough	Asda	450	
Oatcakes and bran biscuits	Mitchelhill		50 per biscuit
Oaten crunch biscuits	Safeway	459	130
Oatmeal			
raw		401	114
medium	Whitworths	401	114
Oatmeal/oats	Holland and Barrett	400	113
Oatmeal and raisin cookies	Barbaras		220 per biscuit
Oatmeal biscuits	Holland and Barrett		60 per biscuit
carob coated	Holland and Barrett		70 per biscuit
Ocean pie	St Michael	107	245 per pie
Octopus, raw		68	19
Oil-free French dressing	Waistline	13	4
Okra (lady's fingers)			
raw		17	5

Product	Brand	Calories per 100g/ 100ml	Calories per oz/ pack/ portion
canned, drained		15	4
Okra curry		259	73
Old English ginger beer	Idris	35	10
with lemonade	Idris	37	11
Olde English chutney	Pan Yan	176	50
Old fashioned mixture drops	Boots	363	120 per 33g stick pack
Olive oil		900	255
	Asda	899	
	Boots	899	255
	Crosse & Blackwell	900	255
	Holland and Barrett	720	213
	Safeway	887	263
	Tesco	875	248
	Waitrose	900	266
extra virgin	Safeway	887	263
first cold pressed, unrefined	Sunwheel	900	255
Olive sandwich cream	Granose	340	96
Olives			
in brine		103	29
in brine (with stones)		82	23
stuffed	Tesco	160	45

Product	Brand	Calories per 100g/ 100ml	Calories per oz/ pack/ portion
Olives sandwich spread	Granose	308	87
100% beefburgers	Birds Eye Steakhouse		120 each, grilled or fried
Onion and cheddar cottage cheese	St Ivel	113	32
	St Ivel Shape	85	24
Onion and chives cottage cheese	Eden Vale	95	27
	St Ivel	85	24
	St Ivel Shape	72	20
	Waitrose	85	24
Onion and pepper cottage cheese	Safeway	92	26
Onion and watercress spreading cheese	Medley	284	81
Onion bhajia mix	Sharwood	310	88
Onion bhajjis	Asda	228	
	St Michael	211	60
	Waitrose	226	64
Onion chutney	Waitrose	154	44
Onion crocs	Asda	466	133
Onion flavour Chinese noodles, instant	Sharwood	487	138
Onion kites	St Michael	463	131
Onion relish	Branston	126	36
	Crosse & Blackwell	135	38

Product	Brand	Calories per 100g/ 100ml	Calories per oz/ pack/ portion
	Tesco	135	38
Onion ring crisps	Littlewoods	500	250 per 50g pack
Onion rings	Safeway	516	258 per 50g pack
	Tesco	494	140
	Waitrose	483	137
battered	Asda	176	
Onion sauce		99	28
Onion sauce mix	Knorr	343	100 per pocket
fresh	Safeway	364	109 per 30g pack
	Tesco	78	22
Pour Over	Colman's	330	110 per pack
Onion sour cream dressing	St Michael	385	109
Onions			
raw		25	7
boiled		14	4
sliced, fried		160	45
onion rings			
in batter		517	145
dried		280	79
whole, medium, raw			28 (113g/4oz)
pickled			5 each
cocktail			1 each
spring onion			3 each
Opals	Mars	391	111

Product	Brand	Calories per 100g/ 100ml	Calories per oz/ pack/ portion
Orange and apricot drink			
chilled	Safeway	43	13
	Waitrose	41	12
long life	Safeway	45	13
Orange and cointreau yogurt	St Ivel Cabaret	101	29
Orange and sherry Chinese barbecue sauce	Sharwood	140	40
Orange and pineapple drink	Britvic	40	133 per 330ml can
	Quosh		50 per carton
concentrated	Kia-Ora	105	31
sparkling	Tango	44	13
sparkling, low calorie	Diet Tango	2	1
undiluted	Corona	93	28
Orange and pineapple fruit juice	Del Monte	46	14
Orange and pineapple juice, longlife	Tesco	45	13
Orange bar	Granose	376	188 per 50g bar
Orange barley crush, sparkling	Lucozade	72	21
Orange barley drink	Boots	130	38
	Robinsons	30	9
Orange barley water	Robinsons	110	33

Product	Brand	Calories per 100g/ 100ml	Calories per oz/ pack/ portion
	Safeway	90	27
Orange 'C' reduced calories	Libby	28	8
sweetened	Libby	51	14
Orange C drink, long life	Safeway	35	10
Orange cakes, chocolate topped	Waitrose	381	108
Orange carob bar no added sugar	Sunwheel Kalibu	493	296 per 60g bar
with raw sugar	Sunwheel Kalibu	518	311 per 60g bar
Orange chicken	Sainsbury's	116	350 per pack
Orange chocolate coated wafers, diabetic	Boots	555	157
Orange chocolate wafer bar	Boots Shapers Meal	519	147
Orange Club biscuits	Jacobs	497	113 per biscuit
Orange coated mallows	Peek Frean	433	52 per biscuit
Orange cream (Black Magic)	Rowntree Mackintosh		45 per sweet
(Quality Street)	Rowntree		

Product	Brand	Calories per 100g/ 100ml	Calories per oz/ pack/ portion
	Mackintosh		40 per sweet
Orange creams	Tesco		65 per biscuit
Orange creme biscuits	Cadbury's	500	80 per biscuit
Orange crisp block	Needlers	508	144
Orange crunch breakfast cereal	Whole Earth	400	113
Orange crush	St Michael	43	12
50% juice	St Michael	53	15
low calorie	St Michael	3	1
	Slimsta	5	9 per 180ml pack
Orange drink			
undiluted		107	30
	Britvic	44	145 per 330ml
	Quosh	34	10
	Robinsons	35	10
	Safeway	50	165 per 330ml
	St Michael	49	14
	Waitrose	104	31
concentrated	Kia-Ora	97	29
diet	Asda	6	
dilutable	Safeway	99	29
Jaffa	St Michael	110	33
long life	Waitrose	40	100 per 250ml carton
low calorie	Littlewoods	4	1
	Quosh	5	1
	Safeway	17	5
	Tesco	24	7

Product	Brand	Calories per 100g/ 100ml	Calories per oz/ pack/ portion
	Waitrose	15	4
low calorie, sparkling	Diet Tango	3	1
original, ready to drink	Robinsons	40	12
sparkling	St Michael	45	13
	Schweppes	40	12
	Tango	46	14
	Waitrose	48	14
sparkling, low calorie	Schweppes Slimline	2	1
undiluted	Tesco	107	32
whole	Boots	102	30
	Corona	90	27
	Quosh	90	27
	Sqeez	34	10
	Tesco	38	11
whole, diabetic	Boots	7	2
Orange-filled bars, chocolate coated	Tesco	503	143
Orange flavour dessert mix	Dietade	264	75
Orange flavour jelly crystals	Waitrose	272	77
	Dietade	290	82
Orange-flavoured concentrate	Safeway	196	58
Orange fruit drink undiluted	Baby Ribena	316	94

Product	Brand	Calories per 100g/ 100ml	Calories per oz/ pack/ portion
Orange fruit juice	Del Monte	42	12
Orange Fruite	Wall's		60 per portion
Orange jelly	Littlewoods	260	74
	Safeway	268	76
	Tesco	57	16
Orange jelly crystals, diabetic	Boots	365	103
Orange jelly marmalade, fine cut	Waitrose	248	70
Orange juice			
sweetened, canned		51	14
unsweetened, canned		33	9
Orange juice	Boots	33	10
	Britvic	44	49 per 133ml pack
	Hycal	243	72
	Prewetts	33	10
	Safeway	40	12
	St Ivel Real	38	11
	Tesco	42	12
	Volonte	40	12
concentrated	Tesco	136	40
concentrated (frozen)	Waitrose	40	12
freshly squeezed	Tesco	42	12
	Waitrose	31	9
Jaffa	St Michael	35	10
Jaffa, concentrated	St Michael	38	11
long life	Waitrose	37	11

Product	Brand	Calories per 100g/ 100ml	Calories per oz/ pack/ portion
	Tesco	42	12
natural	Schweppes	47	14
pure	St Michael	38	11
	Waitrose	35	10
pure, chilled	Waitrose	35	10
pure, long life	Safeway	42	12
sparkling	Orangina	38	109 per half pint
sweetened	Hunts	52	15
	Libby	51	14
	Schweppes	56	17
unsweetened	Hunts	38	11
	Libby	33	9
Orange juice bar	Lyons Maid	70	39 each
Orange, lemon and pineapple whole fruit drink	Robinsons	95	28
Orange Maid	Lyons Maid		43 each
Orange marmalade	Tesco	243	69
fine shred	Baxters	253	72
fresh, thick cut	Waitrose	248	70
matured, thick cut	Waitrose	248	70
reduced sugar, thin cut	Heinz Weight Watchers	124	35
reduced sugar, thin cut	Waitrose	124	35
vintage	Baxters	248	70
Orange marmalade preserve reduced sugar	Robertson's	150	43

Product	Brand	Calories per 100g/ 100ml	Calories per oz/ pack/ portion
Orange, pineapple and lemon drink	Robinsons	35	10
Orange pure fruit spread, fine cut	Robertson's	120	34
Orange Quick-Set Jel	Tesco	365	103
Orange ripple yogurt	St Michael	126	36
Orange segments in orange juice (canned)	St Michael	45	13
Orange shred marmalade	Safeway	251	71
Orange sorbet ice cream	Tesco	62	18
Orange souffle	St Ivel	163	46
Orange squash concentrated	St Michael	169	48
	Rose's High Juice	160	47
	Schweppes	111	33
diluted	Britvic	22	6
diluted	Britvic High Juice	26	7
	Quosh	48	14
low calorie	Dietade	10	3
real, undiluted	Quosh	143	42
undiluted	Britvic	108	31
	Britvic High Juice	129	37
Orange squosh	Waitrose	134	40

Product	Brand	Calories per 100g/ 100ml	Calories per oz/ pack/ portion
Orange Surprise	Bertorelli	220	176 per 80g pack
Orange water ice	Bertorelli	110	31
Orange whole fruit drink	Robinsons	95	28
original	Robinsons	155	46
Orange yogurt	St Ivel Real	81	23
	Ski	82	123 per 150g pack
whole milk	Safeway	63	95 per 150g pack
Orangeade	Corona	27	8
	Safeway	33	9
	Tesco	18	5
	Whites	23	7
diabetic	Boots	1	0.6 per 100ml
low calorie	Canada Dry Slim	3	5 per 175ml pack
Orangeade sparkles	Wall's		30 per portion
Oranges			
raw		35	10
raw (with peel and pips)			267
juice, fresh		38	11
Orangina sparkling orange juice	Bulmer	38	109 per half pint
Orbit Nutra sweet chewing gum	Wrigley		7 per stick
Oregano powder		306	87

Product	Brand	Calories per 100g/ 100ml	Calories per oz/ pack/ portion
Oriental prawns (chilled)	Young's	110	31
Oriental stir fry mix, cooked	Tesco	92	26
Original beefburgers	Birds Eye Steakhouse		130 each grilled or fried
Original cheesecake mix (as sold)	Green's	425	236 made up per portion
Original cider	Bulmer	37	104 per half pint
Original Cookies	Cadbury's	480	50 per biscuit
Original crunchy	Jordans	416	118
bran and apple	Jordans	369	105
honey, almond and raisins	Jordans	396	112
natural	Jordans	405	115
original	Jordans	416	118
Original crunchy bar			
apple and bran	Jordans	394	132 per bar
coconut and honey	Jordans	416	138 per bar
honey and almond	Jordans	412	135 per bar
Original Dolmio (as sold)	Dolmio	41	11
Original mixed vegetables	Birds Eye	53	15
Original pickle	Pan Yan	133	38
Original Ready Brek	Lyons	391	111

Product	Brand	Calories per 100g/ 100ml	Calories per oz/ pack/ portion
Ortanique juice, freshly squeezed	Safeway	40	11
Ortaniques, raw		49	14
Outline dairy spread, low fat	Van den Berghs	370	105
Ovaltine		378	107
	Wander	378	107
instant	Wander	392	111
Ovaltine drinking chocolate	Wander	387	110
instant	Wander	400	113
Oven chips	Safeway	150	43
	Tesco	150	43
	Waitrose	158	45
baked or grilled	Birds Eye	194	55
cooked	Tesco	235	67
crisp 'n' golden	McCain	150	42
Oven cod, battered	Ross	200	57
Oven crispy cod steaks	Birds Eye		215 each baked or grilled
Oven crispy fish 'n' chips	Birds Eye		470 per pack baked
Oven crispy haddock steaks	Birds Eye		215 each baked or grilled
Oven croquettes	McCain		40 each

Product	Brand	Calories per 100g/ 100ml	Calories per oz/ pack/ portion
Oven Stars			
baked or grilled	Birds Eye	229	65
fried	Birds Eye	300	85
Ox tongue	Waitrose	143	41
canned	Asda	195	
sliced	St Michael	170	48
	Tesco	280	79
Oxo beef drink	Brooke Bond		
	Oxo	100	28
Oxo cubes		229	65
chicken	Brooke Bond		
	Oxo	210	60
red	Brooke Bond		
	Oxo	245	69
Oxtail			
raw		171	48
stewed		243	69
stewed (with bones)		92	26
Oxtail soup			
canned		44	12
dried		356	101
dried, as served		27	8
	Campbell's Bumper Harvest	44	185 per 425g can
	Crosse & Blackwell	35	100 per 283g can
	Heinz	43	125 per 300g can
	Safeway	36	155 per 425g can

Product	Brand	Calories per 100g/ 100ml	Calories per oz/ pack/ portion
condensed	Campbell's	86	215 per 295g can
dried	Knorr	329	250 per 1 1/2 pint pack
	Knorr Quick Soup		60 per sachet
	Batchelors Cup-a-Soup	388	93 per 24g sachet
Oyster Chinese pouring sauce	Sharwood	66	19
Oyster crackers	Safeway	431	3 per biscuit
Oyster sauce		80	23
Oysters			
raw		51	14
raw (with shell)		6	2

P

Product	Brand	Calories per 100g/ 100ml	Calories per oz/ pack/ portion
Pacific drink (chilled)	Tesco	49	15
Pacific pilchards in tomato sauce	Armour	126	285 per 227g can
Paella	Vesta	399	638 per 160g pack for two as served
low calorie	Batchelors Slim-a-Meal	346	230 per 66.5g pack
Paglia-e-fieno (as sold)	Signor Rossi	271	77
Pakoras (bhajia)		183	52
	Waitrose	226	64
Pale ale, bottled		32	9
Pan: see Betel leaves			
Pancake mix	Whitworths	348	99
Pancake roll, Chinese crispy	St Michael	178	50
Pancakes		307	87
plain	Tesco	247	70
Pancakes: see also flavours			
Pancho peanuts	Trebor Bassett	545	6 per sweet
Pancho raisins	Trebor Bassett	545	6 per sweet
Papaya: see Paw-paw			
Papaya chunks in syrup	Del Monte	57	16

Product	Brand	Calories per 100g/ 100ml	Calories per oz/ pack/ portion
Papri beans			
fresh, raw		40	11
canned, drained		26	7
Parathas	Tesco	324	454 per serving
Parkin cut cake	St Michael	329	93
Parmesan cheese: *see Cheese*			
Parsley			
dried		276	78
raw		21	6
Parsley and thyme	Safeway	350	297 per 85g pack
stuffing mix	Whitworths	355	300 per 85g pack
Parsley sauce mix	Knorr		65 per pack
	Safeway		75 per sachet
Pour Over	Colman's		65 per pack
Parsnips			
raw		49	14
boiled		56	16
Partridge			
roast		212	60
roast (with bone)	127	36	
fresh	Waitrose	400	1000 per 250g bird
Party rings	Safeway	443	126
Party Twigs	Waitrose	399	113
Parwal: *see Marrow*			
Passata	Sainsbury's		165 per jar

Product	Brand	Calories per 100g/ 100ml	Calories per oz/ pack/ portion
	Tesco		145 per carton
	Waitrose	21	84 per 400g pack
Passion cake	Tesco	366	102
Passion Splitz	Canada Dry	45	113 per 250ml pack
Passionfruit			
raw		34	10
raw (with skin)		14	4
Passionfruit and melon yogurt	Safeway	89	135 per 150g pack
low fat	Waitrose	89	134 per 150g pack
Passionfruit and raspberry yogurt	Ski	83	125 per 150g pack
Passionfruit sorbet	Waitrose	125	625 per 500ml pack
Pasta	Waitrose	378	107
bows	Buitoni	340	96
	Safeway	344	98
	Waitrose	378	107
cooked (typical figures)	Tesco	138	39
quills	Buitoni	340	96
	Safeway	344	98
shells	Buitoni	340	96
	Buitoni Country Harvest	318	90
	Safeway	344	98
	St Michael	359	102

Product	Brand	Calories per 100g/ 100ml	Calories per oz/ pack/ portion
	Waitrose	378	107
shells, cooked	Tesco	150	cooked
shells, green and white	Signor Rossi	309	88
shells, uncooked	Tesco	348	99
spirals, wholewheat	Signor Rossi	275	as sold
tubes	Waitrose	378	107
twists	Buitoni	340	96
	Buitoni Country Harvest	318	90
	Safeway	344	98
	Waitrose	378	107
uncooked (typical figures)	Tesco	348	99
wheels	Waitrose	378	107
whirls	Buitoni Country Harvest	318	90
Pasta and tuna bake	Asda	93	
Pasta and vegetable bake	St Michael	104	295 per pack
Pasta Bolognese	Safeway Microwave Ready Meals		275 per pack
Pasta Choice (Crosse & Blackwell): *see flavours*			
Pasta florentine	St Michael	176	50
Pasta Italienno	Birds Eye Snack Shots		255 per meal
Pasta salad	Sainsbury's	195	54

Product	Brand	Calories per 100g/ 100ml	Calories per oz/ pack/ portion
Pasta shells, wholewheat, in spicy tomato sauce	Heinz	65	18
Pasta shells with vegetables and prawns	Heinz		225 per pack
Pasta with tuna salad	Tesco	231	64
Pasties			
cheese and onion	Freshbake	250	230 each
chicken	Ross		240 each
Cornish	Ross		240 each
individual	St Michael		83 each
fresh vegetable	St Michael		77 each
jumbo traditional	Ross		405 each
Pastilles		253	72
	Bassett's	322	91
Pastrami		232	65
Pastry			
choux, raw		214	61
choux, baked		335	94
flaky, raw		432	121
flaky, baked		571	160
phyllo, raw		335	94
puff, frozen, raw		410	115
shortcrust, raw		460	129
shortcrust, baked		532	149
wholemeal, raw		446	125
wholemeal, baked		517	145
Pastry mix	Whitworths	484	137

Product	Brand	Calories per 100g/ 100ml	Calories per oz/ pack/ portion
flaky	Tesco	558	158
short	Safeway	495	140
shortcrust (dry)	Tesco	484	137
shortcrust (made up)	Tesco	450	128
Pate			
with herbs	Vessen	244	110 per 45g pack
with peppers	Vessen	211	95 per 45g pack
Pate en croute	Waitrose	221	63
Patent cornflour	Brown and Polson	330	94
Patra leaves		26	7
Pavlova: *see flavours*			
Paw-paw (Papaya)			
fresh, raw		45	13
canned, whole contents		65	18
Pea and ham soup	Baxters	58	250 per 425g can
	Heinz Whole Soups	51	155 per 300g can
	St Michael	60	255 per 425g can
condensed	Campbell's	123	365 per 245g can
Pea with ham soup (dried)	Knorr		200 per 1 1/2 pint pack
	Knorr Quick Soup		70 per sachet

Product	Brand	Calories per 100g/ 100ml	Calories per oz/ pack/ portion
Peach and papaya yogurt	Safeway	93	140 per 150g pack
Peach and passionfruit cheesecake	St Michael	273	76
Peach and passionfruit trifle	St Michael	160	45
Peach and redcurrant yogurt	Safeway	91	137 per 150g pack
Peach blancmange mix	Brown and Polson	330	94
Peach chutney	Sharwood	173	49
	Tesco	146	41
	Waitrose	221	63
Peach halves	Safeway	87	358 per 411g can
in fruit juice	Del Monte	46	13
in natural syrup	Libby	47	13
in syrup	Del Monte	69	20
	Waitrose	62	255 per 411g can
Peach jelly	Tesco	57	16
Peach melba dairy ice cream	Lyons Maid Napoli	172	49
Peach melba ice cream	Lyons Maid	177	50
soft scoop	Lyons Maid	180	51
Peach Melba super mousse	Tesco		125 each

Product	Brand	Calories per 100g/ 100ml	Calories per oz/ pack/ portion
Peach melba yogurt	Mr Men	93	26
	Raines	96	27
	Safeway	103	155 per 150g pack
	St Ivel Rainbow		7120
	St Michael	90	26
	Ski	82	123 per 150g pack
	Diet Ski	54	81 per 150g pack
	St Ivel Shape	41	12
low fat	Asda	88	
	Littlewoods	87	131 per 150g pack
	Tesco	102	29
	Waitrose	103	155 per 150g pack
whole milk	Safeway	62	93 per 150g pack
Peach slices	Safeway	87	358 per 411g can
diabetic	Boots	20	6
in fruit juice	Del Monte	46	13
in juice	Asda	47	
	Waitrose	35	77 per 220g can
in natural syrup	Libby	49	14
in syrup	Del Monte	69	20
	Waitrose	62	255 per 411g can
Peach trifle	St Ivel	145	41
Peach yogurt	Ski	83	125 per 150g pack
Peaches			
canned in syrup			25
canned in natural juice			13
dried			60
fresh			10

Product	Brand	Calories per 100g/ 100ml	Calories per oz/ pack/ portion
fresh with stone			9
Peaches and pears in syrup	Safeway	82	337 per 411g can
	Waitrose	95	390 per 411g can
Peanut butter			
smooth		623	177
	Whole Earth	580	164
crunchy	Boots Second Nature	605	172
	Gales	600	170
	Safeway	600	170
	Sun-Pat	607	172
	Tesco	610	173
	Waitrose	600	170
natural	Prewetts	620	176
smooth	Boots Second Nature	605	172
	Gales	600	170
	Safeway	600	170
	Sun-Pat	607	172
	Tesco	610	173
	Waitrose	600	170
Peanut butter cookies	Waitrose	300	85
Peanut butter/ crumble	Granose	586	166
Peanut butter spread	Sunwheel	559	158
Peanut carob bar no added sugar	Sunwheel Kalibu	507	304 per 60g bar

Product	Brand	Calories per 100g/ 100ml	Calories per oz/ pack/ portion
with raw sugar	Sunwheel Kalibu	528	317 per 60g bar
Peanut crackle	Tesco	487	138
Peanut crisp block	Needlers	513	145
Peanut crunch biscuits	Tesco	485	137
Peanut crunch cake	Lyons		130 per cake
Peanut M & Ms	Mars	500	142
Peanut nougat	Rowntree Mackintosh		45 per sweet
Peanut, raisin and chocolate chips	Waitrose	480	136
Peanut Sunsnack	Sunwheel	622	176
Peanuts			
(weighed with shells)		394	112
fresh		570	162
roasted and salted		570	162
	Holland and Barrett	560	159
	St Michael	600	170
blanched	Tesco	605	172
chocolate covered	Littlewoods	497	141
crunchy coated	Sooner	490	196 per 40g pack
dry roast	St Michael	544	154
	Sooner	602	301 per 50g pack
dry roasted	Safeway	570	162
	Tesco	616	175

Product	Brand	Calories per 100g/ 100ml	Calories per oz/ pack/ portion
	Waitrose	625	177
kernels	Littlewoods	570	162
	Whitworths	570	162
roast salted	St Michael	600	170
roasted salted	Waitrose	610	173
roasted salted large	Waitrose	650	184
salted	Sooner	572	143 per 25g pack
	Sun-Pat	615	174
	Tesco	627	178
salted snacks	Littlewoods	570	162
salted, large	Waitrose	598	170
salted/roasted	Safeway	570	162
shelled	Safeway	570	162
	Waitrose	610	173
yogurt coated, no added sugar	Sunwheel	559	158
Peanuts and raisins	Safeway	495	140
	St Michael	410	116
	Waitrose	495	140
blanched	Tesco	500	142
carob coated	Sunwheel		
	Kalibu	503	143
chocolate	Tesco	489	139
plain	Sooner	476	119 per 25g pack
yogurt coated, no added sugar	Sunwheel	477	135
Pear 'n' apple fruit spread	Sunwheel	239	68

Product	Brand	Calories per 100g/ 100ml	Calories per oz/ pack/ portion
Pear 'n' apple jam	Whole Earth	280	79
Pear and apple juice	Copella	40	12
Pear 'n' apricot fruit spread	Sunwheel	264	75
Pear 'n' black cherry fruit spread	Sunwheel	258	73
Pear and raspberry yogurt	Safeway	89	per 150g pack 134
Pear 'n' strawberry fruit spread	Sunwheel	242	69
Pear chews	Trebor	375	per sweet 15
Pear dessert	Boots Baby Foods	62	18
	Heinz Baby Foods	56	per 128g can 72
Pear drops	Trebor	366	per sweet 15
roll	Trebor	351	per sweet
Pear flan, continental style	St Michael	233	66
Pear flavour drops	Littlewoods	366	104
Pear fruit cream trifle	Safeway	135	38
Pear halves	Libby	69	20
	Safeway	77	per 411g can 316
dried	Tesco	308	87
in fruit juice	Del Monte	48	14
in juice	Waitrose	50	per 425g can 213

Product	Brand	Calories per 100g/ 100ml	Calories per oz/ pack/ portion
in natural syrup	Libby	49	14
in syrup	Del Monte	63	18
	Waitrose	71	per 411g can 292
Pear Helene slice	Waitrose	215	61
Pear Helene sundae	Eden Vale	132	per 125g pack 165
Pear quarters			
diabetic	Boots	21	6
in juice	Waitrose	50	per 220g can 110
in syrup	Safeway	77	per 227g can 175
	Waitrose	71	per 220g can 156
Pear tart	St Michael	240	67
Pear yogurt	Ski	80	120 per 150g pack
Pearl barley: *see Barley, pearl*			
Pears			
canned in syrup		77	22
canned in natural juice		107	30
cooking		36	10
dried		160	45
eating		41	12
eating (weighed with skin and core)		29	8
Peas: *see also mange tout, petits pois*			
Peas			
fresh, boiled		52	15
fresh, raw		67	19
frozen, boiled		41	12

Product	Brand	Calories per 100g/ 100ml	Calories per oz/ pack/ portion
frozen, raw		53	15
canned, garden		47	13
canned, processed		80	23
dried, boiled		103	29
dried, raw		286	81
Split, boiled		118	33
Split, raw		310	88
Peas, blackeye			
dried	Holland and Barrett	340	96
Peas, chick			
Bengal gram, raw		320	91
chana dahl		97	27
dahl, cooked		144	41
	Waitrose	75	21
dried	Holland and Barrett	300	85
Peas, marrowfat	Morton	90	26
	Safeway	78	222 per 284g can
	Tesco	314	89
	Waitrose	95	285 per 300g can
canned	Asda	80	
	Tesco	78	22
dried	Waitrose	286	81
dried, boiled	Whitworths	103	29
dried, raw	Whitworths	286	81
Peas, mushy	Morton	80	23
canned	Batchelors	84	24

Product	Brand	Calories per 100g/ 100ml	Calories per oz/ pack/ portion
Chip Shop (canned)	Asda	74	
	Batchelors	76	22
mint flavour (canned)	Batchelors	83	24
Peas, red pigeon, raw		301	85
Peas and baby carrots	Birds Eye	35	10
Peas, corn and peppers	Waitrose	68	304 per 454g pack
Pease pudding (canned)	Batchelors	103	29
Pecan nuts	Holland and Barrett	680	193
Pecan Danish pastry	St Michael	418	117
Pecan pie	Tesco	425	119
Peking Classic Chinese sauce			
aromatic	Homepride	91	348 per 383g pack
barbecue	Homepride	94	360 per 383g pack
Penne	Napolina	320	80
Penne all'arrabbiata	Tesco		220 per pack
Pepper		308	87
black ground	Tesco	275	78
black whole	Tesco	275	78
white	Tesco	275	78
Pepper and onion relish	Branston	137	39

Product	Brand	Calories per 100g/ 100ml	Calories per oz/ pack/ portion
Pepper salami	Waitrose	427	423 per 99g pack
Peppered mackerel (chilled)	Young's	333	94
hot (frozen), cooked	Tesco	363	103
Peppermint carob bar no added sugar	Sunwheel Kalibu	493	296 per 60g bar
with raw sugar	Sunwheel Kalibu	518	311 per 60g bar
Peppermint chewing gum	PK		6 per pellet
	Wrigley Freedent		9 per stick
Peppermint cordial diluted	Britvic	18	5
non-alchoholic, concentrated	Schweppes	104	31
undiluted	Britvic	92	26
Peppermint cream bar	Cadbury's	420	210 per 50g bar
Peppermint creams	Littlewoods	350	99
Peppermint lumps	Littlewoods	380	108
Peppermint pastilles, diabetic	Boots	99	28
Peppermint sweet chewing gum	Wrigley Orbit Nutra		7 per stick
Peppermints		392	111

Product	Brand	Calories per 100g/ 100ml	Calories per oz/ pack/ portion
Pepperoni luxury pizza (frozen)	Safeway	205	58
Peppers (Pimentos)			
red, raw		15	4
green, raw		15	4
yellow, raw		35	10
Peppers, red/chilli, raw		116	33
Perry	Bulmer	43	122 per half pint
Pesto	Whole Earth Pasta Pots	230 per pot	
Petit beurre biscuits	Waitrose	468	133
Petits pois			
canned	Morton	58	16
	Safeway	99	196 per 198g can
	Tesco	89	25
frozen	Findus	63	18
	Safeway	53	480 per 907g pack
	Tesco	73	21
	Waitrose	53	240 per 454g pack
Petits pois and baby carrots	Waitrose	65	258 per 397g pack
Petits pois and carrots (bottled)	Tesco	55	16
Petits pois, button sprouts and baby carrots	Birds Eye	42	12

Product	Brand	Calories per 100g/ 100ml	Calories per oz/ pack/ portion
Petticoat shortbread biscuits	Tesco	502	142
Petticoat tails	Safeway	465	50 each
	Waitrose	515	65 each
Pheasant			
roast		213	60
roast (with bone)		134	38
Philadelphia soft cheese: *see Cheese*			
Piccalilli		33	9
	Haywards	29	8
	Heinz		
	Ploughman's	85	24
	Littlewoods	47	13
	Pan Yan	68	19
	Safeway	35	10
	Tesco	56	16
	Waitrose	48	14
chunky sweet	Safeway	98	28
sweet	Haywards	75	21
	Tesco	103	29
	Waitrose	48	14
Pickle			
chilli		271	77
chow chow, sour		29	8
chow chow, sweet		116	33
lime		178	50
mango		177	50
sweet		134	38

Product	Brand	Calories per 100g/ 100ml	Calories per oz/ pack/ portion
	Heinz Ploughman's	120	34
original	Pan Yan	133	38
sweet	Branston	131	37
	Littlewoods	160	45
	Safeway	91	26
	Tesco	172	49
	Waitrose	215	61
sweet, low calorie	Boots Shapers	66	19
Pickle crisps, natural	Hedgehog	407	110 per 27g pack
Pickled beetroot			
baby	Waitrose	35	10
sliced	Littlewoods	37	10
	Waitrose	37	10
sliced, in sweet vinegar	Waitrose	55	16
Pickled dill cucumber	Tesco	14	4
Pickled gherkins	Safeway	6	2
Pickled Jalapenos	Old El Paso	32	91 per 283g can
Pickled onion crisps	Hunters	520	130 per 26g bag
Pickled onions	Haywards	16	5
	Littlewoods	19	5
	Safeway	37	10
	St Michael	23	7
	Tesco	18	5
	Waitrose	19	5
silverskin	Littlewoods	27	8
sweet	Haywards	25	7

Product	Brand	Calories per 100g/ 100ml	Calories per oz/ pack/ portion
	Tesco	28	8
	Waitrose	38	11
Pickled red cabbage	Waitrose	21	6
Pickles			
gherkin		13	4
mixed, clear	Safeway	8	2
mixed, Continental	Safeway	19	5
Picnic	Cadbury's	495	230 per 46g bar
Picnic eggs	St Michael	293	83
Pie filling mixes: *see flavours*			
Piermont soft drink	Taunton	18	100 per pint
Pigeon			
roast		230	65
roast (with bone)		101	29
Pigeon peas/Red gram, raw		301	85
Pilchard and tomato paste	Shippams	169	127 per 75g pack
Pilchards			
canned in tomato sauce		126	36
in tomato sauce	Shippams	162	689 per 425g can
Pacific, in tomato sauce	Armour	126	197 per 156g can
Pina colada cocktail	St Michael Shakers		285 per 25cl can 235 per 160ml bottle

Product	Brand	Calories per 100g/ 100ml	Calories per oz/ pack/ portion
Pina colada dairy ice cream	Safeway	225	67
Pina colada yogurt	St Ivel Cabaret	105	30
Pine kernels	Holland and Barrett	580	164
Pineapple canned in syrup		77	22
canned in natural juice		53	15
fresh, raw		46	13
Pineapple and coconut choc ices	Waitrose	288	85
Pineapple and coconut drink	Safeway	90	27
Pineapple and coconut yoghurt, low fat	Waitrose	87	131 per 150g pack
Pineapple and grapefruit drink, low calorie	St Michael	4	1
Pineapple and grapefruit juice	Appella	42	12
	Del Monte	46	14
Pineapple and grapefruit yogurt	St Michael	106	30
Pineapple and ham cottage cheese	Waitrose	96	27
Pineapple 'C'	Libby	44	12
Pineapple Chunks	Trebor Bassett	354	17 per sweet

Product	Brand	Calories per 100g/ 100ml	Calories per oz/ pack/ portion
Pineapple chunks in juice	Del Monte	61	17
Pineapple cottage cheese	Eden Vale	98	28
	Safeway	98	28
	St Ivel	91	26
	St Ivel Shape	74	21
Pineapple crush, low calorie	Slimsta	5	1
Pineapple fruit filling	Morton	64	18
Pineapple fruit harvest ice cream	Lyons Maid	150	43
Pineapple fruit juice	Del Monte	50	15
	Heinz	57	17
Pineapple, grapefruit and lemon fruit drink	Del Monte Island Blend	46	14
Pineapple jam	Waitrose	248	70
Pineapple juice *canned*		53	15
Pineapple juice	Britvic	50	57 per 113ml pack
	Libby	53	15
	St Ivel Real	40	12
	Schweppes	48	14
	Volonte	49	15
chilled	Safeway	43	13
	Tesco	42	12
longlife	Tesco	42	12
	Waitrose	44	13

Product	Brand	Calories per 100g/ 100ml	Calories per oz/ pack/ portion
pure	St Michael	49	14
pure, chilled	Waitrose	43	13
pure, longlife	Safeway	49	15
sweetened	Hunts	54	16
Pineapple juice bar	Lyons Maid		42 each
Pineapple, lemon and lime fruit drink	Del Monte Island Blend	41	12
Pineapple, orange and mandarin fruit drink	Del Monte Island Blend	46	14
Pineapple pancakes	St Michael	161	46
Pineapple Pavlova	Ross	290	82
Pineapple preserve	Tesco	255	72
Pineapple split	Wall's		81 per split
Pineapple Super Mivvi	Lyons Maid		82 each
Pineapple sweet and sour chutney	Sharwood	61	17
Pineapple tidbits	Libby	58	16
Pineapple yogurt	Safeway	90	135 per 150g pack
	St Ivel Real	82	23
	Ski	83	125 per 150g pack
low fat	Littlewoods	86	129 per 150g pack
	Tesco	83	24
Pink salmon (canned)	Asda	140	
Pinto beans: *see Beans*			

Product	Brand	Calories per 100g/ 100ml	Calories per oz/ pack/ portion
Pistachio nuts		626	177
Pitta bread			
white		257	72
wholemeal		235	66
Pizza: *see flavours*			
Pizza base mix			
(as sold)	Granny Smiths	248	595 per 240g pack made up
(as sold)	Tesco	363	103
(made up)	Tesco	250	71
Pizza bites snacks	Littlewoods	547	274 per 50g pack
Pizza bits Italian style	St Michael	473	134
Pizza pleesors	Burton's		125 per pack
Pizza style cheese	St Ivel	405	115
Pizza topping Prego sauce	Campbell's	76	22
Pizzaiola Prego sauce	Campbell's	37	10
PK chewing gum			
arrowmint	Wrigley		6 per pellet
licorice	Wrigley		6 per pellet
peppermint	Wrigley		6 per pellet
Plaice			
fried in batter		279	79
fried in crumbs		228	65
raw		91	26
steamed		93	26

Product	Brand	Calories per 100g/ 100ml	Calories per oz/ pack/ portion
steamed (with bones and skin)		50	14
fillet	Co-op	89	25
fillet in oven crisp breadcrumbs	Tesco	300	84
in lemon and parsley crumbs	Tesco	210	59
in ovencrisp crumbs	St Michael	264	74
kiev	Tesco	198	695 per portion
portion	Sainsbury's		90 each
stuffed with prawn/mushroom	Sainsbury's		300 per portion
whole	St Michael		600 per pack
Plain cake mix, diabetic (as sold)	Boots	459	130
Plain carob bar			
no added sugar	Sunwheel Kalibu	493	296 per 60g bar
with raw sugar	Sunwheel Kalibu	518	311 per 60g bar
Plain chocolate		525	149
diabetic	Boots	500	142
Plain chocolate bar	Boots Shapers Meal	506	143
	St Michael	531	151
	Tesco	540	153
Plain chocolate biscuit thins	St Michael	470	133

Product	Brand	Calories per 100g/ 100ml	Calories per oz/ pack/ portion
Plain chocolate Bounty	Mars	485	137
Plain chocolate Brazils	Tesco	581	165
Plain chocolate breaktime biscuit	Waitrose	588	167
Plain chocolate crunch biscuits (half-coated)	Safeway	478	136
Plain chocolate digestive biscuits	Safeway	500	142
	St Michael	505	143
	Tesco	508	144
	Waitrose	505	143
half-coated	Huntley & Palmer	496	65 per biscuit
Plain chocolate drops	Tesco	516	146
Plain chocolate fingers	Safeway	562	159
Plain chocolate ginger biscuits	St Michael	490	139
Plain chocolate Melt in the Bag cake covering	Lyons	572	162
Plain chocolate mint sandwich bar	St Michael	491	139
	Waitrose	519	147

Product	Brand	Calories per 100g/ 100ml	Calories per oz/ pack/ portion
Plain chocolate petit beurre biscuits	Waitrose	470	133
Plain chocolate Polka Dots	Lyons	507	144
Plain chocolate wafer fingers	Waitrose	504	143
Plain chocolate with hazelnuts	Waitrose	554	157
Plain Club biscuits	Jacobs	494	112 per biscuit
Plain confectionery bar, no added sugar	Sunwheel Kalibu	517	217 per 42g bar
Plain digestive biscuits		471	134
Plain fruit cake		354	100
Plain luxury cheesecake mix (as sold)	430		236 made up per portion
Plain M & Ms	Mars	483	137
Plain mint wafer fingers	Waitrose	510	145
Plain peanuts and raisins	Sooner	476	119 per 25g pack
Plain superfine chocolates	Nestle	546	155
Plantain			
boiled		122	35
green, raw		112	32

Product	Brand	Calories per 100g/ 100ml	Calories per oz/ pack/ portion
ripe, fried		267	76
Plantain (Green banana, matoki)		89	25
PLJ lemon juice less sharp, undiluted	Beecham	25	7
original sharp, undiluted	. Beecham	25	7
Ploughman's Ideal sauce	Heinz	106	30
Ploughman's mild mustard pickle	Heinz	114	32
Ploughman's piccalilli	Heinz	85	24
Ploughman's pickle	Heinz	120	34
Ploughman's sandwiches	Safeway Tesco		400 per pack 385 per pack
Ploughman's tangy pickle spread	Heinz Ploughman's	118	33
Ploughman's tomato pickle	Heinz	95	27
Plum and walnut yoghurt	Safeway	106	159 per 150g pack
Plum jam	Safeway	251	71
Plum preserve	Tesco	255	72
Plum yoghurt	Safeway	96	144 per 150g pack
Plums cooking, raw		26	7

Product	Brand	Calories per 100g/ 100ml	Calories per oz/ pack/ portion
cooking, raw (with stones)		23	7
cooking, stewed with sugar		59	17
cooking, stewed with sugar (with stones)		55	16
cooking, stewed without sugar		22	6
cooking, stewed without (with stones)		20	6
Victoria dessert, raw		38	11
Victoria dessert, raw (with stones)		36	10
dessert, without stones, fresh	Littlewoods	38	11
golden	Waitrose	58	16
Victoria	Waitrose	80	23
Poached salmon sandwiches	Waitrose		375 per pack
Poacher's broth	Baxters	35	149 per 425g can
Polar mints	Trebor Bassett	365	19 per sweet
Polka Dots			
milk chocolate	Lyons	493	140
plain chocolate	Lyons	507	144
Polo fruits	Rowntree Mackintosh	380	8 per sweet
Polo peppermints	Rowntree Mackintosh	395	6 per sweet
Polony: see Sausages, delicatessen			
Pomagne			
medium dry	Bulmer	52	148 per half pint

Product	Brand	Calories per 100g/ 100ml	Calories per oz/ pack/ portion
medium sweet	Bulmer	65	185 per half pint
Pomegranate, raw, fresh			7220
Pomegranate juice, fresh			4412
Pomelo, fresh	Tesco	36	10
Pommia cider, dry	Taunton	54	310 per pint
sweet	Taunton	65	370 per pint
Pontefract cakes	Trebor Bassett	296	84
Popcorn			
Butterkist	Tesco	390	111
chocolate	Tesco	414	117
Poppadoms, raw		272	77
Popping corn	Holland and Barrett	375	106
Poppy and sesame	Asda	519	
crackers	Tesco	511	145
Poppy seed bar			
natural	Boots	439	124
Popular pies			
apple	Lyons	349	99
apple and blackcurrant	Lyons	353	100
apricot	Lyons	361	102
Pork			
crackling		722	202
fillet, raw, lean		125	35
leg, raw, lean and fat		269	76

Product	Brand	Calories per 100g/ 100ml	Calories per oz/ pack/ portion
leg, roast, lean and fat		286	81
loin, raw		329	93
loin chips, grilled, lean and fat		332	94
loin chips, grilled, lean and fat (with bone)		258	73
loin chips, grilled, lean only		226	64
mince, raw		232	65
mince, raw, lean		196	55
rump belly, raw, lean		142	40
rump loin, raw, lean		125	35
shoulder, raw, lean only		107	30
shoulder, roast, lean only		142	40
tenderloin, raw, lean only		125	35
Pork and apple pastry roll	Jus-Rol	300	84
Pork and bean pastry roll	Jus-Rol	285	80
Pork and beef chipolatas	Tesco	314	89
Pork and beef luncheon sausage	Waitrose	256	73
Pork and beef sausages	Asda	246	
	St Michael	370	105
	Tesco		125 per sausage grilled
large	Sainsbury's		125 per sausage grilled

Product	Brand	Calories per 100g/ 100ml	Calories per oz/ pack/ portion
skinless, mini	Safeway		30 per sausage grilled
skinless, thin	Safeway		55 per sausage grilled
thick	Safeway		120 per sausage grilled
	Sainsbury's		135 per sausage grilled
thin	Safeway		70 per sausage grilled
low fat, large	Sainsbury's		90 per sausage grilled
low fat, small	Sainsbury's		50 per sausage grilled
Pork and chicken pie	Waitrose	226	64
Pork and egg pie	Tesco	370	105
large	St Michael	324	92
sliced	St Michael	385	109
Pork and ham roulade with cheese	Waitrose	262	74
Pork and herb sausages, thick	Safeway		145 per sausage grilled
thin	Safeway		65 per sausage grilled
Pork and pepper kebab	Waitrose	150	43

Product	Brand	Calories per 100g/ 100ml	Calories per oz/ pack/ portion
Pork and pepper roll	Asda	295	
Pork brochettes	Waitrose	207	59
Pork buffet pie	Bowyers		260 per pie
	Co-op		220 per pie
Pork casserole cooking mix	Colman's	295	125 per pack
Pork, cheese and pickle pie	Sainsbury's		230 each
Pork chipolatas	Tesco	338	96
	Waitrose	358	101
Cumberland	Waitrose	320	91
premium	Tesco	343	97
	Waitrose	310	88
skinless	Waitrose	326	92
Pork crackling crisps	Hunters	520	130 per 26g bag
Pork crunchies	Tesco	462	131
Pork, ham and egg pie gala	Waitrose	221	63
Pork lattice pie			
individual	Littlewoods	351	404 per 115g pie
large	Littlewoods	321	1079 per 336g pie
Pork luncheon meat	Asda	340	
	Waitrose	356	113g/4oz pack
Pork luncheon meat, Chinese		288	82
Pork mixed grill	Waitrose	207	59

Product	Brand	Calories per 100g/ 100ml	Calories per oz/ pack/ portion
Pork pie			
individual		376	107
country style	Asda	350	98
crisp bake	St Michael		520 per pie
	Tesco	352	98
individual	St Michael	450	126
lattice top			
crisp bake	St Michael	371	104
Melton Mowbray	Asda	346	97
	Safeway	389	109
	Sainsbury's	342	95
Melton Mowbray,			
mini	St Michael	425	119
premium	Sainsbury's	302	87
with herbs	Asda	400	112
with onion	Asda	382	107
Pork provencale **(canned)**	St Michael	110	31
Pork roll			
stuffed (canned)	Tyne Brand	153	43
stuffed, sliced	Tesco	316	90
with egg, sliced	Tesco	294	83
Pork, sage and onion **stuffing**	St Michael	200	57
Pork sate stick	Waitrose	160	45
Pork sausage meat	Bowyers	375	105
premium	Sainsbury's	314	88
Pork sausages	Bowyers		215 each, as sold

Product	Brand	Calories per 100g/ 100ml	Calories per oz/ pack/ portion
	Gateway	275	77
	Tesco		160 per sausage grilled
Cumberland	Asda	285	
	Sainsbury's		180 per sausage grilled
	Tesco		145 per sausage grilled
large	Sainsbury's		175 per sausage grilled
low fat	St Michael		115 per sausage grilled
	Tesco		80 per sausage grilled
premium, large	Sainsbury's		130 sausage grilled
small	Sainsbury's		70 per sausage grilled
thick	Co-op		170 per sausage
thin	Co-op		85 per sausage
skinless	Bowyers		95 each, as sold
	Sainsbury's		75 per sausage grilled
	Tesco		60 per sausage grilled
traditional	Tesco		130 per sausage grilled
Pork, chopped slices, cured	St Michael	194	55

Product	Brand	Calories per 100g/ 100ml	Calories per oz/ pack/ portion
Pork, cured (canned)	St Michael	270	77
Porridge		44	12
Porridge oats	Tesco	366	104
	Waitrose	355	101
cooked	Whitworths	44	12
uncooked	Whitworths	401	114
with bran	Tesco	370	105
Port		157	45
Port Salut cheese: see Cheese			
Pot au chocolat	St Michael		265 per carton
	Tesco		240 per carton
Potato and chive salad	Eden Vale	163	46
Potato and sweetcorn salad	Sainsbury's	170	33
Potato and leek soup, homestyle	Heinz Ready to Serve	36	10
Potato and onion salad	Waitrose	141	320 per 227g pack
Potato Bake country	Birds Eye		435 per pack
Potato and pea curry	Sharwood	106	440 per can
Potato cake Swiss style	Findus	80	23
Potato, celery and dill salad	Littlewoods	153	347 per 227g pack

Product	Brand	Calories per 100g/ 100ml	Calories per oz/ pack/ portion
Potato, cheese and asparagus pancakes	Waitrose	156	44
Potato cheesies	Birds Eye		75 each grilled
Potato crisps: *see also Crisps and flavours*		533	151
all flavours	Littlewoods	520	130 per 25g pack
Potato Crispy Crosses	Ross	180	51
Potato croquettes	Asda	152	
	Birds Eye		50 each baked
	Sainsbury's		50 each baked
	Tesco		50 each
Potato curry		167	47
Potato dauphinoise	Sainsbury's	128	400 per pack
Potato fritters crispy, grilled, fried or baked	Birds Eye	212	60
Potato lamb cutlet	Waitrose	226	64
Potato, leek and celery bake	Sainsbury's	108	490 per pack
Potato leek soup	Granny's	44	29 as served
Potato mix, instant	Tesco	327	93
Potato pancakes: see also flavours	Ross	210	60
Potato rings	St Michael	510	145
	Tesco	532	151
	Waitrose	516	146

Product	Brand	Calories per 100g/ 100ml	Calories per oz/ pack/ portion
Potato salad	Asda	133	
	Heinz	168	48
	Safeway	209	59
	St Michael	322	91
	Tesco	114	32
in reduced calorie dressing	Tesco	85	24
in reduced calorie dressing, others	Tesco	90	26
mild	Eden Vale	224	64
other recipes	Tesco	150	43
spicy	Safeway	184	52
Potato scones	St Michael	210	60
	Tesco	235	67
Potato shells	Tesco	563	160
Potato sticks	Waitrose	508	144
ready salted	Safeway	505	143
	St Michael	505	143
Potato thins, ready salted	St Michael	472	134
Potato topped Cumberland pie	St Michael	142	505 per pie
Potato topped Savoury pie	Sainsbury's	86	130 per pie
Potato triangle biscuits	Tesco	467	132

Product	Brand	Calories per 100g/ 100ml	Calories per oz/ pack/ portion
Potato twirls, salt and vinegar	Waitrose	423	120
Potato waffles	Birds Eye		115 each baked/ grilled
	Safeway		80 each
	St Michael		110 each
Potato, instant mashed			
made up		70	20
powder		318	90
Potatoes			
new, boiled		76	22
new, canned		53	15
old, baked		105	30
old, baked (with skins)		85	24
old, boiled		80	23
old, chips		253	72
old, chips, frozen		109	31
old, chips, frozen, fried		291	82
old, mashed		119	34
old, raw		87	25
old, roast		157	45
Potted beef (canned)	St Michael	170	48
Potted salmon with butter (canned)	St Michael	166	47
Pouch batter mix (as sold)	Green's	348	99
Pour Over sauce (Crosse & Blackwell): *see flavours*			

Product	Brand	Calories per 100g/ 100ml	Calories per oz/ pack/ portion
Pour Over sauce mix (Colman's): *see flavours*			
Pouring syrup	Tate and Lyle	284	81
Poussin	Waitrose	232	66
Praline and apricot gateau	Safeway	365	103
Praline and toffee dairy ice cream	Safeway	230	68
Praline dairy ice cream	Bertorelli	210	60
Praline truffles, diabetic	Boots	582	165
Prawn and marie rose sandwiches	Waitrose		275 per pack
Prawn and cocktail sauce sandwiches	St Michael		285 per pack
Prawn and cucumber dressing sandwiches	St Michael		235 per pack
Prawn, apple and celery sandwiches	Boots Shapers		245 per pack
Prawn cocktail crisps	Christies	520	130 per 26g bag
	Hunters	520	130 per 26g bag
	Tesco	550	156
Prawn cocktail sauce	O.K.	380	108
Prawn cocktail snacks	St Michael	486	138
	Tesco	492	139
	Waitrose	520	147

Product	Brand	Calories per 100g/ 100ml	Calories per oz/ pack/ portion
Prawn crackers	St Michael	435	123
	Sharwood	350	99
Prawn curry	Vesta	349	340 per 211g pack for two as served
with parsley rice	Findus		340 per pack
with rice	Birds Eye		
	Menu Master		350 per pack
Prawn mayonnaise sandwiches	Safeway		415 per pack
Prawn provencal with piquant rice	Heinz	82	280 per pack
Prawn salad	Asda	159	
	Eden Vale	155	44
	St Ivel	155	44
	Tesco	119	34
	Waitrose	144	41
other recipes	Tesco	155	44
Prawn sambal	Sainsbury's	82	205 per pack
Prawns			
boiled		107	30
boiled (with shell)		41	12
dried		362	103
raw, fresh		87	25
Prawns cottage cheese Waitrose		112	32
Prego sauce (Campbell's): *see flavours*			

Product	Brand	Calories per 100g/ 100ml	Calories per oz/ pack/ portion
Premier pizza (chilled)	Tesco	195	55
Preserves	Thursday Cottage	280	79
diabetic	Thursday Cottage	140	40
Preserving sugar	Tate and Lyle	394	112
Prizesteak	Birds Eye Steakhouse		235 each grilled or shallow-fried
Processed cheese	Waitrose	260	74
Cheddar slices	Kraft	326	92
Cheshire slices	Kraft	335	95
Family Favourites (average)	St Ivel	280	79
Gold Spinner	St Ivel	280	79
singles slices	Kraft	302	86
slices	Safeway	300	85
slices, reduced fat	Heinz Weight Watchers	195	40 per slice
with walnut	Tesco	344	98
Processed cheese spread			
dairy	St Michael	300	85
soft, with butter	St Michael	360	102
walnut	St Michael	310	88
Processed peas: *see Peas*			
Profiteroles	Waitrose	425	120
and chocolate sauce	Young's	330	94

Product	Brand	Calories per 100g/ 100ml	Calories per oz/ pack/ portion
Protein bar square snack	Holly Mill		184 per bar
Protose	Granose	159	45
Provamel soya dessert	Provamel	94	28
Provencale Cooking-in Sauce	Baxters	116	493 per 425g can
Prune juice	Leisure Drinks	82	24
Prunes			
dried, raw		161	46
dried, raw (with stones)		134	38
dried, stewed with sugar		104	29
dried, stewed with sugar (with stones)		95	27
dried, stewed without sugar		82	23
dried, stewed without sugar (and stones)		74	21
canned	Del Monte	117	33
	Hartley's	95	105 per 111g can
canned in syrup	Tesco	109	235 per 213g can
	Waitrose	117	497 per 425g can
dried, no need to soak	Tesco	127	36
Pudding mix, steamed/baked	Creamola	352	100
Pudding rice, cooked	Tesco	153	43
Puff pastry (frozen): *see Pastry*			

Product	Brand	Calories per 100g/ 100ml	Calories per oz/ pack/ portion
Puff pastry sausage rolls	St Michael	409	116
Puff pastry (frozen) sheets	Birds Eye		360 per sheet
Puffed Wheat		325	92
Pumpkin, raw		15	4
Pumpkin seeds	Holland and Barrett	400	113
Pure fruit jam, all flavours	Hartley's	255	40 per portion
Pure Fruit jelly jam, all flavours	Hartley's	260	40 per portion
Pure Fruit lemon cheese	Hartley's	295	45 per portion
Pure Fruit mincemeat	Hartley's	285	45 per portion
Pure fruit spread (Robertson's): *see flavours*			
Pure Fruits marmalade, all flavours	Hartley's	255	40 per portion

Q

Product	Brand	Calories per 100g/ 100ml	Calories per oz/ pack/ portion
Quality Street assortment			
caramel	Rowntree Mackintosh		30 per sweet
coconut eclair	Rowntree Mackintosh		45 per sweet
coffee cup	Rowntree Mackintosh		40 per sweet
cracknel	Rowntree Mackintosh		40 per sweet
dairy toffee	Rowntree Mackintosh		30 per sweet
fudge	Rowntree Mackintosh		45 per sweet
gooseberry cream	Rowntree Mackintosh		40 per sweet
milk chocolate truffle	Rowntree Mackintosh		40 per sweet
noisette pate	Rowntree Mackintosh		40 per sweet
nut toffee creme	Rowntree Mackintosh		45 per sweet
orange cream	Rowntree Mackintosh		40 per sweet
peanut nougat	Rowntree Mackintosh		45 per sweet
strawberry cream	Rowntree Mackintosh		45 per sweet
toffee cup	Rowntree Mackintosh		40 per sweet

Product	Brand	Calories per 100g/ 100ml	Calories per oz/ pack/ portion
toffee de luxe	Rowntree Mackintosh		45 per sweet
toffee finger	Rowntree Mackintosh		30 per sweet
toffee pat	Rowntree Mackintosh		30 per sweet
Quark: *see Cheese*			
Quarter pounders	Asda		250 each
	Birds Eye Steakhouse		235 each grilled
lean beef	Findus		175 each grilled
Queen of puddings		216	61
Quenchers	Trebor Bassett	326	92
Quiche: *see also flavours*			
Quiche lorraine		391	111
	Asda	235	66
	St Michael	300	85
Quiche with cheese and onion	St Michael	300	85
Quiche with tomato and cheese	St Michael	270	77
Quick batter mix	Whitworths	338	96
Quick chilli sauce mix			
Cook In	Colman's	335	115 per pack
Pour Over	Colman's	335	115 per pack
Quick Cook (Tesco): *see flavours*			

Product	Brand	Calories per 100g/ 100ml	Calories per oz/ pack/ portion
Quick cooking oats	Safeway	377	107
Quick custard	Batchelors	424	382 per 90g jar/sachet
Quick Jel dessert mix, all flavours (as sold)	Green's	360	22 made up per portion
Quick macaroni (as sold)	Buitoni	340	96
Quick Soups (Knorr): *see flavours*			
Quick-Cook egg lasagne			
cooked	Tesco	135	38
uncooked	Tesco	343	97
Quick-Cook macaroni			
cooked	Tesco	152	43
uncooked	Tesco	348	99
Quick-Cook spaghetti	Tesco	355	101
Quick-Set Jel (Tesco): *see flavours*			
Quinces, raw		25	7

R

Product	Brand	Calories per 100g/ 100ml	Calories per oz/ pack/ portion
Rabbit			
raw		124	35
stewed		179	51
stewed (with bone)		91	26
Radicchio		10	3
Radish			
red, raw		15	4
white/mooli, raw		24	7
Rainbow trout			
	St Michael	135	38
smoked	St Michael	135	38
whole	Waitrose	130	37
with mushrooms and onion stuffing	Waitrose	244	69
Raisin and bran crunchy bars	Asda	452	
Raisin and lemon pancakes	Tesco	306	87
Raisin biscuits	Huntley & Palmer	454	59 per biscuit
Raisin bran buns	Vitbe	313	166 per bun
Raisin fudge	Trebor Bassett	425	40 per sweet
Raisin snack bar, yogurt coated	Sunwheel Kalibu	340	102 per 30g bar
Raisins			
dried		246	70
(canned or dried)	Tesco	451	128

Product	Brand	Calories per 100g/ 100ml	Calories per oz/ pack/ portion
yogurt coated	Tesco	451	128
yogurt coated, no added sugar	Sunwheel	396	112
Rapeseed oil	Boots	899	255
	Tesco	884	247
	Sainsbury's	900	252
Raspberries			
canned in syrup		87	25
canned in natural juice		35	10
fresh/frozen		25	7
stewed with sugar		68	19
stewed without sugar		26	7
Raspberry and melon yoghurt, creamy	Waitrose	146	183 per 125g pack
Raspberry and passionfruit yogurt	Safeway	91	137 per 150g pack
	St Michael	105	30
Raspberry and redcurrant brulee	Young's	310	88
Raspberry and redcurrant cheesecake	St Michael	285	81
Raspberry and redcurrant fruit crunch	Young's	255	72
Raspberry and redcurrant oat crunch	Young's	250	71

Product	Brand	Calories per 100g/ 100ml	Calories per oz/ pack/ portion
Raspberry and vanilla Swiss roll	Lyons	338	96
Raspberry baked roll	Waitrose	356	101
Raspberry blancmange	Brown and Polson	330	94
Raspberry cheesecake individual slice	Eden Vale Young's St Michael	194 250	55 71 450 each
Raspberry conserve	Safeway Tesco Waitrose	248 268 250	70 76 71
Raspberry cream dessert	Young's	200	57
Raspberry cream gateau	Waitrose	263	75
Raspberry cream supreme	St Michael	146	41
Raspberry dessert sauce	Lyons Maid	266	75
Raspberry drink	Safeway	140	41
Raspberry flan filling	Armour	119	946 per 795g pack
Raspberry flavour dessert mix	Dietade	264	75
Raspberry flavour jelly crystals	Waitrose Dietade	272 290	77 82

Product	Brand	Calories per 100g/ 100ml	Calories per oz/ pack/ portion
Raspberry fruit harvest ice cream	Lyons Maid	174	49
Raspberry fruit spread	Waitrose	124	35
Raspberry ice cream tub	Tesco	430	122
Raspberry jam	Robertson's	251	71
	Safeway	251	71
	Waitrose	248	70
diabetic	Boots	240	68
	Dietade	234	66
no added sugar	Safeway	139	39
reduced sugar	Asda	126	
	Heinz Weight Watchers	124	35
	Waitrose	124	35
seedless	Safeway	251	71
	Waitrose	248	70
Raspberry jam sponge pudding	Heinz	285	81
Raspberry jelly	Safeway	268	76
	Tesco	57	16
crystals, diabetic	Boots	365	103
table	Littlewoods	260	74
Raspberry juice	Hycal	243	72
Raspberry madeleines	Lyons	333	94

Product	Brand	Calories per 100g/ 100ml	Calories per oz/ pack/ portion
Raspberry Mivvi, Fun Size	Lyons Maid	120	34
Raspberry mousse tub dessert	Safeway	159	47
	Birds Eye		110 per tub
Raspberry peach sundae ice cream	Lyons Maid Gold Seal	139	39
Raspberry preserve	Baxters	242	69
	Tesco	255	72
reduced sugar	Robertson's	150	43
Raspberry pavlova mini	St Michael	297	83
	St Michael		110 each
Raspberry puff	St Michael	380	106
Raspberry pure fruit spread	Robertson's	120	34
Raspberry ring dessert	St Michael	136	39
Raspberry ripple ice cream	Asda	156	
	Ross	170	48
	Safeway	164	49
	Tesco	176	50
	Waitrose	193	57
	Wall's Gino Ginelli sliceable	178	50
Raspberry ripple mousse	Findus	171	48
	Ross		90 each
	Tesco	173	49

Product	Brand	Calories per 100g/ 100ml	Calories per oz/ pack/ portion
	Waitrose	157	45
Raspberry ripple yogurt	St Michael	126	36
Raspberry ruffles	Tesco	385	109
Raspberry sauce	Tesco	323	92
Raspberry sponge roll	St Michael	342	97
Raspberry sponge sandwich cake	Asda Lyons	373 314	89
Raspberry sponge with buttercream	Safeway	380	108
Raspberry sundae cups	Lyons Maid		89 each
Raspberry Swiss roll	Lyons	295	84
Raspberry Topsy Turvy	Ambrosia	103	29
Raspberry trifle	Eden Vale Sainsbury's St Ivel St Michael		155 per carton 155 per carton 165 per carton 190 per carton
Raspberry water ice	Bertorelli	101	29
Raspberry yogurt	Mr Men Munch Bunch Raines Safeway Ski St Ivel Rainbow	94 99 89 94 83 69	27 124 per 125g pack 25 141 per 150g pack 125 per 150g pack 20

Product	Brand	Calories per 100g/ 100ml	Calories per oz/ pack/ portion
	St Ivel Real	82	23
French style	Littlewoods	102	153 per 150g pack
low fat	Diet Ski	55	83 per 150g pack
	Littlewoods	83	125 per 150g pack
	St Ivel Shape	41	12
	St Michael Lite	39	11
	Tesco	96	27
	Waitrose	90	135 per 150g pack
whole milk	Safeway	62	93 per 150g pack
Raspberry yogurt snack bar, carob coated	Sunwheel Kalibu	410	123 per 30g bar
Ratatouille	Boots Ready Meal	30	9
	Safeway	55	15
	St Michael	61	17
	Tesco	36	10
canned	Buitoni	37	139 per 375g can
	Safeway	46	179 per 390g can
	Sainsbury's	38	130 per 340g can
Ravioli			
as sold	Signor Rossi	277	78
canned	Buitoni	82	164 per 200g can
	Granose	64	270 per 425g can
in beef and tomato sauce	Heinz	76	165 per 215g can
in meat and tomato sauce	Waitrose	83	332 per 400g can
in tomato sauce	Heinz	75	160 per 215g can

Product	Brand	Calories per 100g/ 100ml	Calories per oz/ pack/ portion
pomodoro (as sold)	Signor Rossi	230	65
wholewheat (canned)	Buitoni	84	336 per 400g can
Raw sugar marzipan snack bar, carob coated	Sunwheel Kalibu	433	130 per 30g bar
Ready Brek		390	111
Coco	Lyons	388	110
Golden	Lyons	391	111
Original	Lyons	391	111
Ready Eddie	Lyons Maid		85 each
Ready salted chips	Tesco	524	149
Ready salted crisps	Christies	520	130 per 26g bag
	Hunters	520	130 per 26g bag
	Littlewoods	561	140 per 25g pack
	Nature's Snack	530	265 per 50g pack
	Safeway	500	125 per 25g pack
	St Michael	545	155
	Tesco	547	155
	Waitrose	520	390 per 75g pack
crinkle cut	Littlewoods	534	401 per 75g pack
	Safeway	543	407 per 75g pack
lower-fat	St Michael	485	137
Ready salted crispy squares	Safeway	472	236 per 50g pack
Ready salted crunchy sticks	Safeway	481	361 per 75g pack
	Tesco	442	125

Product	Brand	Calories per 100g/ 100ml	Calories per oz/ pack/ portion
Ready salted potato sticks	Safeway	505	379 per 75g pack
	St Michael	505	143
Ready salted potato thins	St Michael	472	134
Real fruit gums	Trebor Bassett	293	83
	St Michael	340	96
Real fruit jellies	Trebor Bassett	320	31 per sweet
Real fruit pastilles	Trebor Bassett	303	86
Real fruit teddy bear gums	St Michael	340	96
Real juice, squash, yogurt, etc: *see also flavours*			
Real mayonnaise	Hellmanns	720	204
Real milk ice strawberry	Lyons Maid		49 each
vanilla	Lyons Maid		50 each
Red cabbage: *see also Cabbage, red*			
Red Cabbage salad	St Michael	114	32
Red cheese and pineapple salad	Asda	165	
	Littlewoods	172	49
Red cherries in syrup	Waitrose	78	332 per 425g pack
Red cherry cheesecake	Young's	235	67

Product	Brand	Calories per 100g/ 100ml	Calories per oz/ pack/ portion
Red cherry fruit filling	Morton	82	23
	Waitrose	82	328 per 400g pack
Red cherry luxury cheesecake mix (as sold)	Green's	266	243 made up per portion
Red cubes	Oxo	245	69
Red gram: *see Peas, red*			
Red grape juice	Schloer	49	15
	Waitrose	55	16
Red grape fruit juice, longlife	Safeway		45 per 1/4 pint
Red kidney beans: *see Beans*			
Red Leicester cheese: *see Cheese*			
Red palm oil		875	248
Red peppers	Tesco	24	7
Red peppers sweet	Waitrose	18	5
Red plums in syrup	Asda	77	
Red Quick-Set Jel	Tesco	365	103
Red salmon (canned)	Asda	210	
Red snapper/malabar, raw		99	28
Red sockeye salmon, canned	Waitrose	163	347 per 213g can

Product	Brand	Calories per 100g/ 100ml	Calories per oz/ pack/ portion
Red wine		68	19
Red wine Cook in Sauce	Homepride	76	286 per 376g pack
Red wine cooking sauce	St Michael	55	16
Red wine sauce	Knorr		330 per carton
Redcurrant and raspberry fruit filling	Morton	56	16
Redcurrant jelly	Crosse & Blackwell	259	73
	Tesco	290	82
Redcurrant sauce	O.K.	290	82
Redcurrants			
raw		21	6
stewed without sugar		18	5
stewed with sugar		53	15
Reduced calorie dressing	Asda	125	
	Heinz Weight Watchers	148	42
Reduced fat spread	Heinz Weight Watchers	360	102
Refreshers	Trebor Bassett	375	6 per sweet
Refried beans	Old El Paso	92	417 per 453g can
Revels	Mars	478	136

Product	Brand	Calories per 100g/ 100ml	Calories per oz/ pack/ portion
Rhubarb			
raw		6	2
stewed with sugar		45	13
stewed without sugar		6	2
in syrup	Tesco	60	17
	Waitrose	51	275 per 539g can
Rhubarb and ginger preserve	Baxters	246	70
Rhubarb fruit fool	St Michael	133	38
Rhubarb yogurt	Raines	81	23
	Safeway	95	143 per 150g pack
	St Michael	95	27
low fat	Diet Ski	52	78 per 150g pack
	Littlewoods	81	122 per 150g pack
	St Ivel Shape	39	11
	Tesco	89	25
Ribena			
undiluted		229	65
Baby, undiluted	Beecham	316	94
concentrated	Beecham	293	87
Ribena juice drinks (Beecham): see flavours			
Rice			
brown, raw		353	99
brown, boiled		117	33
Chinese		364	102
ground, raw		357	100
white, raw		364	102
white, boiled		125	35

Product	Brand	Calories per 100g/ 100ml	Calories per oz/ pack/ portion
wild, raw		375	105
wild, boiled		175	49
Rice and vegetable salad	Tesco	135	38
Rice and whole food salad	St Michael	202	56
Rice cakes	La Source de Vie	384	109
carob original	Newform		133 per cake
carob, sugar free	Newform		130 per cake
Rice, creamed	Ambrosia	91	395 per 439g can
	Libby	89	390 per 439g can
Rice creamola	Creamola	357	101
Rice crisp with raisins cake	St Michael	321	91
Rice crunchies	Safeway	342	96
	Waitrose	350	101
Rice dessert and apricot puree	St Michael	178	150 per carton
Rice Krispies		372	105
	Kellogg's	351	100
Rice, peas and mushrooms, boiled	Birds Eye	123	35
Rice pudding	Itona	70	297 per 425g can
	Tesco	87	25
creamed	Asda	88	

Product	Brand	Calories per 100g/ 100ml	Calories per oz/ pack/ portion
low fat, no added sugar	Heinz Weight Watchers	70	154 per 220g can
traditional	Ambrosia	102	450 per 439g can
Rice salad and mushrooms	St Michael	211	59
Rice snaps	Asda	359	
Rice, sweetcorn, peas and carrots, boiled	Birds Eye	123	35
Rice, basmati raw		359	102
Rich beef casserole	St Michael	69	20
Rich chocolate ripple Napoli ice cream	Lyons Maid	178	50
Rich fruit cake		332	94
iced		352	100
	Waitrose	354	100
with marzipan	Tesco	389	110
Rich fruit Christmas cake	Safeway	375	106
and marzipan	Safeway	389	110
Rich fruit loaf	St Michael	245	69
Rich Osborne biscuits	Peek Frean	437	35 per biscuit
Rich shortie biscuits	Asda	486	
Rich table water biscuits	Jacobs	411	30 per biscuit

Product	Brand	Calories per 100g/ 100ml	Calories per oz/ pack/ portion
Rich tea biscuits	Littlewoods	450	43 per biscuit
	Peek Frean	438	25 per biscuit
	Safeway	451	35 per biscuit
Rich tea finger biscuits	St Michael		25 per biscuit
Rich tea finger creams	St Michael		50 per biscuit
Ricicles	Kellogg's	354	100
Ricotta cheese: *see Cheese*			
Rigatoni	Napolina	320	80
Ripple	Mars	547	155
Risotto Ready Meal, vegetarian	Boots	133	38
Rissoles, savoury	Birds Eye Snacks		190 each grilled or fried
Rissolnut	Granose	376	107
Risotto style pot meal	Boots Shapers		220 per pot
Ritz crackers	Nabisco	495	16 per biscuit
cheese	Nabisco	480	16 per biscuit
Roast almond bar	Cadbury's	540	153
Roast beef and salad sandwich	St Michael		315 per pack
Roast beef crisps	Christies	520	130 per 26g bag
	Hunters	520	130 per 26g bag

Product	Brand	Calories per 100g/ 100ml	Calories per oz/ pack/ portion
Roast beef dinner	Birds Eye MenuMaster		360 per tray
Roast beef in gravy	Sainsbury's	103	115 per pack
Roast beef platter	Birds Eye MenuMaster		375 per meal
Roast chicken and broccoli meal	St Michael	104	445 per pack
Roast chicken and gravy	Birds Eye MenuMaster	84	190 per 227g pack
Roast chicken and salad sandwiches	St Michael		390 per pack
Roast chicken plate pie	St Michael	254	72
Roast chicken platter	Birds Eye MenuMaster		360 per meal
Roast pork loin, sliced	St Michael	159	45
Roast turkey and ham plate pie	St Michael	220	62
Rock Edinburgh seaside		364 339	102 95
Rock cake mix made up	Tesco Tesco	354 411	100 117
Rock cakes		394	112
Roe cod (hard), raw		113	32

Product	Brand	Calories per 100g/ 100ml	Calories per oz/ pack/ portion
cod, fried	.	202	57
herring (soft), raw		80	23
herring, fried		244	69
Rogan josh beef	Asda	126	
lamb	Asda	183	
Rogan Josh curry sauce	Sharwood	117	330 per can
Classic	Homepride	85	326 per 383g pack
Rolls: see Bread rolls			
Rolo	Rowntree Mackintosh	450	25 per sweet
Romagna Prego sauce	Campbell's	64	18
Roquefort: see Cheese			
Rose coco beans, dried	Holland and Barrett	271	77
Rose wine, medium		71	20
Rosehip bar	Granose	382	191 per 50g bar
Rosehip syrup, undiluted		232	66
Rose's lime juice cordial, concentrated	Rose's	101	30
Roses marmalade, all flavours	Roses	255	40 per portion
Roule cheese	Tesco	383	109
	Waitrose	335	95

Product	Brand	Calories per 100g/ 100ml	Calories per oz/ pack/ portion
Round shorties	St Michael	494	140
Rounders	Sooner		102 per packet
Royal Game soup	Baxters	37	157 per 425g can
Royale King Cone	Lyons Maid		203 per cone
Royale truffles	St Michael	553	157
Rum			50 per 1/6 gill
Rum and raisin crunch mix (as sold)	Royal	264	1266 per 480g pack made up
Rum and raisin ice cream	Lyons Maid Gold Seal	184	52
Rum baba cake, fresh cream	Tesco	256	73
Rum babas, mini	St Michael	240	68
Runner beans: see Beans			
Rusks			
original	Farley	397	67 per rusk
Oster Rusks	Farley	404	34 per rusk
round	Boots Baby Foods	401	114
with wholemeal	Farley	396	67 per rusk
Rusks, low sugar	Boots Baby Foods	401	114
	Farley	408	69 per rusk
apricot	Boots Baby Foods	400	113
Russchian	Schweppes	23	7

Product	Brand	Calories per 100g/ 100ml	Calories per oz/ pack/ portion
Rydal biscuits	Safeway	475	135
Rye and oats with hazelnuts	Kellogg's Nutrigrain	368	104
Rye crispbread light whole	St Michael Boots Shapers Tesco	375 391 375	106 111 106
Rye flakes	Holland and Barrett	316	90
Rye flour	Holland and Barrett	335	95
Rye flour (100%)		335	95

S

Product	Brand	Calories per 100g/ 100ml	Calories per oz/ pack/ portion
Saccharin tablets	Boots		per tablet negligible
Safflower oil	Holland and Barrett	720	213
	Sunwheel	900	255
	Waitrose	900	266
Saffron (Kaisar)		310	88
Sag, cooked dish		100	28
Sage and onion mustard	Colman's	175	50
Sage and onion stuffing mix	Asda	350	
	Safeway	350	99
	Tesco	359	102
	Waitrose	325	92
	Whitworths	342	97
Sage, onion and bacon stuffing mix	Knorr	404	115
Sago			
raw		355	101
cooked	Tesco	137	39
raw	Tesco	328	93
Sago, creamed	Ambrosia	81	355 per can
Sago pudding	Whitworths	131	37
St Jaques dressing	Hellmanns	316	90
Saithe			
raw		73	21

Product	Brand	Calories per 100g/ 100ml	Calories per oz/ pack/ portion
steamed		99	28
steamed (with bones and skin)		84	24
Salad cream		311	88
	Asda	318	
	Crosse & Blackwell	346	98
	Heinz	342	97
	Littlewoods	330	94
	Safeway	310	88
	Tesco	387	110
	Waitrose	324	92
Salad dressing, herb	St Michael	105	30
Salami		491	139
Danish	Asda	558	
	Waitrose	520	147
Danish, sliced	Tesco	529	150
German	Asda	391	
	Waitrose	427	121
German spiced	Waitrose	422	120
German, sliced	Tesco	405	115
Hungarian	Waitrose	520	147
Italian	Waitrose	411	117
Italian thin sliced	St Michael	491	139
Land	Waitrose	436	124
pepper	Waitrose	427	121
Salmon			
canned		155	44
raw		182	52

Product	Brand	Calories per 100g/ 100ml	Calories per oz/ pack/ portion
smoked		142	40
steamed		197	56
steamed (with bones and skin)		160	45
Salmon and broccoli pie	St Michael	132	37
Salmon and broccoli mornay	Birds Eye MenuMaster		320 per pack
Salmon and cucumber cottage cheese	Eden Vale Safeway	110 129	31 37
Salmon and cottage cheese sandwiches	Tesco		295 per pack
Salmon and cucumber sandwiches	St Michael Tesco		265 per pack 310 per pack
Salmon and shrimp paste	Littlewoods Safeway Shippams Tesco	128 206 173 150	45 per 35g pack 155 per 75g pack 61 per 35g pack 43
Salmon en croute	Sainsbury's St Michael Young's	250 292 270	70 82 77
Salmon joints, Scottish	Young's	148	42
Salmon soup	Tesco	57	245 per can
Salmon spread	Littlewoods Shippams	126 159	44 per 35g pack 56 per 35g pack

Product	Brand	Calories per 100g/ 100ml	Calories per oz/ pack/ portion
Salmon steak au gratin	Birds Eye MenuMaster		460 per pack
Salmon steaks with herb butter	St Michael	259	72
Salmon tagliatelle	Sainsbury's	115	630 per pack
Salsify boiled		18	5
Salt		0	
Salt substitute	Boots	0	
Salt and pepper fries	Littlewoods	440	221 per 50g pack
Salt and pepper Super Fries	Hunters	441	106 per 24g pack
Salt and vinegar chiplets	St Michael	487	138
Salt and vinegar chips	Tesco	466	132
Salt and vinegar crisps	Christies	520	130 per 26g bag
	Hunters	520	130 per 26g bag
	Safeway	500	125 per 25g pack
	St Michael	525	149
	Tesco	520	147
	Waitrose	520	147
Salt and vinegar crispy squares	Safeway	472	236 per 50g pack
Salt and vinegar crunchy sticks	Safeway	487	365 per 75g pack
	Tesco	466	132

Product	Brand	Calories per 100g/ 100ml	Calories per oz/ pack/ portion
Salt and vinegar new ringos	Golden Wonder	339	95
Salt and vinegar potato twirls	Waitrose	423	120
Salt and vinegar savoury sticks	Waitrose	483	137
Salt and vinegar twirls	Safeway	444	222 per 50g pack
Salted cashew nuts: *see Cashew nuts*			
Salted fish, Chinese, steamed, bone removed		155	44
Salted mixed nuts	Waitrose	655	186
Salted peanuts: *see Peanuts*			
Samosas			
minced lamb (Asian)		578	164
chicken	Waitrose	226	64
lamb	Waitrose	226	64
six vegetable	Waitrose	191	54
vegetable	Asda	204	
	Waitrose	226	64
Samsoe cheese, Danish	Waitrose	344	98
Sandwiches: *see flavours*			
Sandwich bar biscuits, chocolate coated	Tesco	512	145
Sandwich bar biscuits		513	145

Product	Brand	Calories per 100g/ 100ml	Calories per oz/ pack/ portion
cheese	Nabisco	528	48 per biscuit
cheese and onion	Nabisco	522	47 per biscuit
Sandwich biscuits: *see also flavours*			
Sandwich cakes: *see flavours*			
Sandwich cake mixes: *see flavours*			
Sandwich cream			
mushroom	Granose	360	102
olive	Granose	340	96
Sandwich spread	Heinz	206	58
cereals	Granose	225	64
cucumber	Heinz	183	52
herbs	Granose	263	75
mushrooms	Granose	337	96
olives	Granose	308	87
Sandwich wafer biscuits, chocolate flavour filling	Waitrose	571	162
Sandwichmaker (Shippams): *see flavours*			
Sapota (sapodilla, noiseberry fruits), raw		76	22
Sardine and tomato paste	Littlewoods	125	44 per 35g pack
	Tesco	160	45
Sardine and tomato spread	Shippams	183	64 per 35g pack
Sardines			
canned in oil, fish only		217	62

Product	Brand	Calories per 100g/ 100ml	Calories per oz/ pack/ portion
canned in oil, fish plus oil		334	95
canned in tomato sauce		177	50
raw		196	55
Sata pastries, assorted		538	153
Sate sauce	Waitrose	165	47
Satsumas		42	12
Satsumas in syrup	Tesco	63	18
Sauce tartare: *see Tartare sauce*			
Sauces: *see also flavours*			
Sauerkraut		18	5
Sausage **Scottish lorne,** sliced	St Michael	355	101
sliced round	Littlewoods	396	140 per slice
smoked, sliced	Tesco	339	96
top quality	St Michael	400	113
Sausage and bacon plait	Waitrose	314	89
Sausage and bacon rissole	Waitrose	232	66
Sausage casserole Cook in the Pot	Crosse & Blackwell	353	140 per packet
Sausage casserole cooking mix	Colman's	345	125 per pack
Sausage roll pie	Littlewoods	546	155

Product	Brand	Calories per 100g/ 100ml	Calories per oz/ pack/ portion
Sausage rolls			
flaky pastry		479	136
short pastry		463	131
	Ross		150 each
cocktail	Kraft		80 each
	Ross		75 each
	Sainsbury's		65 each
	St Michael		55 each
jumbo size	Ross		255 each
king size	Co-op	319	89
	Kraft		185 each
lattice	Asda	371	104
	St Michael	400	112
party size	Asda	367	103
	Kraft		60 each
puff pastry	St Michael	414	116
small	Sainsbury's		125 each
Sausagemeat	St Michael	350	99
low fat	Asda	172	

Sausages: *see also Beef, Pork, etc*

Sausages, beef			
fried		269	76
grilled		265	75
raw		299	85
Sausages, delicatessen			
Bierwurst		267	75
Bockwurst		642	180
Cervelat		500	140

Product	Brand	Calories per 100g/ 100ml	Calories per oz/ pack/ portion
chorizo		500	140
French Garlic Sausage		321	90
garlic sausage		250	70
ham sausage		160	45
Kabanos		410	115
Krakowska		285	80
Mortadella		375	105
Polony		285	80
Sausages, pork			
fried		317	90
grilled		318	90
raw		367	104
Sausalatas	Granose	137	390 per 284g pack
Sausfry	Granose	492	139
Saute potatoes	Findus	97	27
with eggs, onion and bacon	Waitrose	170	850 per 500g pack
with onion and smoked bacon	Waitrose	135	540 per 400g pack
with onion, sausages and cheese	Waitrose	120	600 per 500g pack
Saveloy		262	74
Saviand	Granose	199	56
Savoury beef rice	Tesco	345	98
Savoury chicken rice	Tesco	350	99

Product	Brand	Calories per 100g/ 100ml	Calories per oz/ pack/ portion
Savoury cocktail biscuit assortment	St Michael	575	163
Savoury crackers	Waitrose	495	140
Savoury curried rice	Crosse & Blackwell	105	30
Savoury curry rice hot	Tesco	334	95
mild	Tesco	327	93
Savoury cuts, meatless	Granose	88	25
Savoury mince	Tyne Brand	86	335 per can
Savoury minced beef pasties	Waitrose	264	75
Savoury minced beef with onions in gravy	Fray Bentos	168	660 per can
Savoury mixed vegetables rice	Tesco	249	71
Savoury pudding	Granose	207	59
country style	Granose	167	47
Savoury puffs	Safeway	600	300 per 50g pack
cheese flavoured	Waitrose	526	149
Savoury rice and mushrooms	Crosse & Blackwell	106	30
and peppers	Crosse & Blackwell	106	30

Product	Brand	Calories per 100g/ 100ml	Calories per oz/ pack/ portion
and vegetables	Crosse & Blackwell	105	30
Savoury rice: *see also flavours*			
Savoury rissoles	Birds Eye Snacks		190 each grilled or fried
Savoury Scotch eggs	Tesco	298	84
Savoury snaps	St Michael	490	139
Savoury spread	Boots	205	58
	Safeway	194	220 per 113g pack
Savoury sticks	Tesco	422	120
	Waitrose	483	137
Savoury toasts (Findus): *see flavours*			
Savoury tomato rice	Tesco	329	93
Savoury twigs	Safeway	391	196 per 50g pack
Savoury vinegar crunchy sticks	Tesco	466	132
Savoury white sauce mix	Knorr	360	102
Savoy cabbage			
raw		26	7
boiled		9	3
Scalloped potatoes	Whitworths	355	101
au gratin	Whitworths		531 per pack, 813 made up
with savoury white			544 per pack

Product	Brand	Calories per 100g/ 100ml	Calories per oz/ pack/ portion
sauce	Whitworths		826 made up
with sour cream and			565 per pack,
chives	Whitworths		847 made up
Scallops			
raw, without shells		71	20
steamed, without shells		107	30
Scampi			
fried		316	90
raw		107	30
breaded, baked	Sainsbury's	210	58
	Tesco	200	56
Scampi provencale			
(chilled)	Young's	65	18
Scampi tails, chilled	Young's	87	25
whole, in			
breadcrumbs	Young's	203	58
Scampi with Patna rice			
americaine	Baxters	125	390 per 312g pack
francaise	Baxters	114	356 per 312g pack
indienne	Baxters	113	355 per 312g pack
provencale	Baxters	90	280 per 312g pack
thermidor	Baxters	114	356 per 312g pack
Scamps	St Michael	493	140
Scone mix (as sold)	Granny Smiths	330	666 per 202g pack made up
	Tesco	396	112
	Whitworths	433	123

Product	Brand	Calories per 100g/ 100ml	Calories per oz/ pack/ portion
made up	Tesco	395	112
Scones		371	105
cream	St Michael		300 each
Scotch broth	Asda	41	
	Baxters	47	200 per 425g can
	Campbell's		
	Bumper Harvest	40	170 per 425g can
	Granny's	67	285 per 425g can
	Heinz Farmhouse		
	Soups	36	110 per 300g can
	Safeway	42	179 per 425g can
	Waitrose	37	157 per 425g can
condensed	Campbell's	71	230 per 300g can
Scotch eggs		279	79
	Asda	256	
	St Michael	315	89
	Tesco	286	81
savoury	Tesco	298	84
Scotch mince	Baxters	93	395 per 432g can
Scotch orange marmalade	Baxters	248	843 per 340g jar
Scotch pancakes		283	80
	St Michael	305	86
Scotch pie			
fresh	McKellar Watt		320 per pie
frozen	Mckellar Watt		365 per pie
Scotch salmon bisque	Baxters	69	293 per 425g can

Product	Brand	Calories per 100g/ 100ml	Calories per oz/ pack/ portion
Scotch vegetable soup	Baxters	28	117 per 425g can
Scottish buns	Tesco	316	90
Scottish crumpets	Tesco	260	74
Scottish haggis	Baxters	172	731 per 411g can
Scottish raspberries: *see Raspberries*			
Scottish salmon: *see Salmon*			
Scottish vegetable soup with lentils	Heinz Ready to Serve	43	185 per 435g can
Sea kale		8	2
Sea-salt and cider vinegar crisps	Hedgehog	407	110 per 27g pack
Sea-salt crisps natural	Hedgehog	407	110 per 27g pack
Seafood and prawn cocktail dressing	Safeway	325	92
Seafood cottage cheese	Eden Vale	92	26
Seafood dressing	Safeway	385	109
	Tesco	301	85
Seafood flaky bake pie	Birds Eye MenuMaster		445 per pie
Seafood in cream and wine sauce	Findus Lean Cuisine		255 per pack
Seafood lasagne	Young's	110	31
Seafood paella	St Michael	151	42
Seafood pasta	Tesco	111	31

Product	Brand	Calories per 100g/ 100ml	Calories per oz/ pack/ portion
	Young's	120	34
Seafood sticks	Young's	85	24
Seafood tagliatelle	St Michael	111	31
Second Nature biscuits (Boots): *see flavours*			
Semi-skimmed chocolate drink	St Michael	66	19
Semi-skimmed strawberry drink	St Michael	57	16
Semolina raw		350	99
cooked	Tesco	98	28
Semolina, creamed	Ambrosia	83	365 per 439g can
Semolina pudding	Whitworths	131	37
Sesame and sunflower biscuits	Prewetts		83 per biscuit
Sesame chicken with special fried rice and sweetcorn	Findus Lean Cuisine		300 per meal
Sesame crackers	Sainsbury's		20 each
	Tesco		20 each
Sesame nut crunch	Tesco	583	165
Sesame oil		881	250
	Holland and Barrett	900	266
	Sunwheel	900	255

Product	Brand	Calories per 100g/ 100ml	Calories per oz/ pack/ portion
Sesame seed bar, natural	Boots	464	132
Sesame seeds		588	167
	Holland and Barrett	560	159
Sesame spread	Sunwheel	563	160
Sev (ganthia), savoury, Asian		485	137
Sevyiaan (sweet), Asian		443	126
Shakers crisps	St Michael	56	16
Shallot, raw		48	14
Shandy	Barr	26	85 per 330ml can
	Britvic	25	81 per 330ml can
	Corona	25	7
	St Michael	22	7
	Tesco	23	7
	Tesco	33	10
Shandy bass	Canada Dry	26	65 per 250ml can
Shandy cider	Canada Dry	26	65 per 250ml can
Shandy drink	Littlewoods	25	83 per 330ml pack
Shandy pilsner	Canada Dry	26	65 per 250ml can
Shanghai beef noodles	Vesta	388	672 per 173g pack for two as served
Shanghai nuts	Phileas Fogg	515	144

Product	Brand	Calories per 100g/ 100ml	Calories per oz/ pack/ portion
Shape cheese (wedge)	St Ivel	260	74
Shape coleslaw	St Ivel	38	11
Shape cottage cheese (St Ivel): *see flavours*			
Shape milk drink	St Ivel	45	13
Shape yogurts (St Ivel): *see flavours*			
Shapers (Boots): *see flavours*			
Shapers Sugarlite	Boots	391	111
Sharon fruit		78	22
Shawburger mix	Hera	340	96
Shepherd's pie	Birds Eye MenuMaster	119	270 per 227g pack
	Safeway	110	250 per 227g pack
	Sainsbury's		310 per pack
	Tesco	125	570 per 454g pack
Shepherd's pie Cook in the Pot	Crosse & Blackwell	339	160 per packet
Shepherd's pie filling	Tyne Brand	113	435 per 392g can
Sherbet lemon yogurt	Munch Bunch	92	115 per 125g pack
Sherbet dip dabs	Barratt	346	98
Sherbet fountain	Barratt	328	93
Sherbet lemons	Trebor Bassett	359	23 per sweet

Product	Brand	Calories per 100g/ 100ml	Calories per oz/ pack/ portion
Sherry			
dry		116	33
medium		118	33
sweet		136	39
Sherry trifle	St Michael	157	45
Shish kebab	Asda	285	
Short pastry mix (as sold)	Granny Smiths	497	1327 per 225g pack made up
	Safeway	495	140
Shortbread biscuits		504	143
Shortbread fingers	Safeway		90 per finger
	Sainsbury's		100 per finger
	Waitrose		110 per finger
wholemeal	Waitrose		105 per finger
Shortbread mix (as sold)	Granny Smiths	487	1240 per 255g pack made up
	Tesco	381	108
made up	Tesco	508	144
Shortcake bar biscuits, chocolate coated	Tesco	498	141
Shortcake biscuits	Peek Frean	454	49 per biscuit
	Sainsbury's		65 per biscuit
	Tesco		45 per biscuit
Dutch	Huntley & Palmer	539	40 per biscuit

Product	Brand	Calories per 100g/ 100ml	Calories per oz/ pack/ portion
fruit	Peek Frean	443	36 per biscuit
Shortcake snack	Cadbury's	490	35 per biscuit
Shortcrust pastry: *see Pastry*			
Shredded Wheat		324	92
Shrimps			
boiled		117	33
boiled (with shell)		39	11
canned		94	27
dried		245	69
frozen, shell removed		73	21
Shrimps/prawns	Armour	94	188 per 200g can
Siciliana sauce	Buitoni	74	209 per 283g can
	Waitrose	54	230 per 425g can
Siciliana spaghetti sauce	Campbell's	53	160 per 300g can
Silky smooth choc ice	Lyons Maid		132 each
Silver mints	Littlewoods	374	106
Silver Shred marmalade	Robertson's	251	71
Silverskin onions	Haywards	20	6
	Heinz	13	4
	Safeway	21	6
Simply topping mix	Royal	179	330 per 1.85g pack made up

Product	Brand	Calories per 100g/ 100ml	Calories per oz/ pack/ portion
Singapore curry Classic Chinese sauce	Homepride	95	364 per 383g pack
Singapore curry Chinese sauce mix	Sharwood	290	190 per sachet
Six grain biscuits	Boots Second Nature	441	125
Sizzles, vegetarian	Protoveg Menu	587	166
Skate			
fried (with waste)		163	46
fried in batter		199	56
Ski yogurts (Eden Vale): *see flavours*			
Skippy	Cadbury's	455	190 per 42g bar
Slender (as sold)			
chocolate	Carnation	360	229 per sachet + 190ml milk
coffee, strawberry, vanilla	Carnation	350	99
lemon, raspberry, yogurt	Carnation		227 per sachet + 190ml milk
Slender bars			
chocolate and coffee	Carnation	430	250 per 2-bar meal
fruit country	Carnation	393	111
natural country	Carnation	500	250 per 2-bar meal

Product	Brand	Calories per 100g/ 100ml	Calories per oz/ pack/ portion
Slender Slim chocolate drink	Carnation	365	40 per serving
Slender soup, all flavours	Carnation	335	40 per serving
Sliced sausage, round	Littlewoods	396	140 per slice
Slim-a-Soups (Batchelors): *see flavours*			
Slim drinks (Canada Dry): *see flavours*			
Slimline drinks (Schweppes): *see flavours*			
Slippery Elm food	Lanes	337	96
Smash	Cadbury's	265	55 per portion
Smatana, creamed	Raines	129	37
Smoked almonds	Tesco	630	179
Smoked cheese	Waitrose	305	86
Austrian	St Ivel	315	89
with ham	Waitrose	305	86
Smoked fish: *see also Cod, Haddock, etc*			
Smoked fish kebabs	Young's	134	38
Smoked haddock and egg flan	Sainsbury's	300	84
Smoked haddock croquettes	Young's	188	53
Smoked haddock crumble	Tesco	186	53
Smoked haddock mousse	Tesco	242	68

Product	Brand	Calories per 100g/ 100ml	Calories per oz/ pack/ portion
Smoked ham	Waitrose	121	(appr) 136 per 113g pack
Smoked mackerel mousse	Tesco	321	90
Smoked mackerel pate	St Michael	321	90
Smoked pork sausage	Tesco	344	98
	Waitrose	328	93
cooked	Littlewoods	320	91
Smoked salmon and cream cheese sandwiches	Safeway		375 per pack
Smoked salmon pate	St Michael	236	67
	Tesco	296	83
Smoked sausage, sliced	Tesco	339	96
Smoky bacon pancakes	Findus	140	40
Smoky cheese spread	Sun-Pat	268	76
Snack-a-Soups (Batchelors): *see flavours*			
Snack crackers	Tesco	445	126
Snack meals (Tesco): *see flavours*			
Snackbar, carob coated	Allinson	469	150 per 32g bar

Product	Brand	Calories per 100g/ 100ml	Calories per oz/ pack/ portion
Snow White Cartoons cake mix (as sold)	Green's	414	64 made up per portion
Snow Ball biscuits	Peek Frean	418	131 per biscuit
	Safeway	251	71
Snowballs	Safeway		85 each
	Sainsbury's		105 each
	Tesco		100 each
Snowcaps	St Michael	344	98
Soda scones, plain	Tesco	286	81
Soft and smooth caramels	St Michael	485	137
Soft cheese			
dairy	Tesco	271	77
dairy, with chives	Tesco	290	82
dairy, with			
pineapple	Tesco	358	101
full fat	Raines	288	82
	Waitrose	296	84
medium fat	Raines	173	49
skimmed milk	Asda	78	
	Raines	76	22
Soft fruit gums	Wilkinson	319	90
Softmints	Trebor Bassett	374	16 per sweet
Sojal	Hera	45	13
Sole, breaded	Waitrose	116	33

Product	Brand	Calories per 100g/ 100ml	Calories per oz/ pack/ portion
Somerset pie	Waitrose	91	468 per 510g pie
Sonata dessert log	Wall's		130 per 1/6 log
Sorbitol (fructose)	Holland and Barrett	400	113
Sosmix, vegetarian	Ranch House Meals	598	170
Soup in Seconds (Prewetts): *see flavours*			
Soup mix, dried	Boots	328	93
Soup mixture	Whitworths	332	94
Sour cream and chives flavour crisps	Waitrose	520	390 per 75g pack
Sour cream dressing, onion	St Michael	385	109
Southern Comfort			70 per 1/6 gill
Southern fried Coat and cook sauce	Homepride		180 per 43g sachet
Soutsoukakia	Waitrose	226	64
Soy Chinese pouring sauce			
light	Sharwood	24	7
rich	Sharwood	60	17
Soy sauce			
dark, thick		86	24
light, thin		64	18
Soya flour			
full fat		447	127

Product	Brand	Calories per 100g/ 100ml	Calories per oz/ pack/ portion
low fat		352	100
Soya bean curd: *see Tofu*			
Soya bean flakes	Holland and Barrett	384	109
Soya bean oil	Holland and Barrett	920	272
	Waitrose	900	266
Soya bean paste	Granose	140	40
Soya beans: *see Beans*			
Soya bolognese mix	Protoveg Menu	275	78
Soya bran	Granose	100	28
	Itona	220	62
Soya chocolate dessert	Granose	72	20
Soya curd/Tofu			
canned, fried		302	86
steamed		70	20
Soya flour	Holland and		
low fat	Barrett	350	99
Soya franks	Granose	272	77
Soya margarine	Asda	724	
	Safeway	730	207
Soya milk		39	11
	Granose	51	15
carob	Granose	59	17
coconut	Granose	70	21
concentrate	Plamil	103	30

Product	Brand	Calories per 100g/ 100ml	Calories per oz/ pack/ portion
honey and malt	Provamel	50	15
powdered	Soyagen	496	141
strawberry	Granose	64	19
sugar free	Granose	42	12
unsweetened	Granose	42	HB
Soya mince with onion, dried	Beanfeast	334	95
Soya mix, meatloaf style	Hera	480	136
Soya oil	Boots	899	255
	Safeway	900	266
Soya strawberry dessert	Granose	72	20
Soya thread (Foo-juk), dried		387	110
Soya vanilla dessert	Granose	72	20
Soya wurst, chicken flavour	Granose	300	85
Soyagen	Granose	496	141
Soyal dessert	Provamel	94	28
Soyapro slices			
beef	Granose	210	60
chicken	Granose	210	60
Soyapro wieners	Granose	210	60
Soybrits	Hofels	367	55 per 15g pack
Soysage mix	Hera	410	116

Product	Brand	Calories per 100g/ 100ml	Calories per oz/ pack/ portion
Soyvita	Healtheries	517	147
Spaghetti			
boiled		117	33
raw		342	97
Spaghetti, canned in tomato sauce		59	17
	Asda	64	
	Crosse &		
	Blackwell	57	140 per 213g can
	Heinz	68	145 per 215g can
	Heinz Invaders	65	140 per 215g can
	Safeway	59	251 per 425g can
	Tesco	61	265 per 425g can
	Waitrose	55	241 per 439g can
hoops	Heinz	64	140 per 215g can
no added sugar	Heinz Weight		
	Watchers	53	117 per 220g can
reduced sugar			
and salt	Asda	53	
rings	Crosse &		
	Blackwell	61	140 per 213g can
	Safeway	59	126 per 213g can
	Waitrose	67	143 per 213g can
shapes	Heinz Haunted		
	House	72	150 per 215g can
shapes	Heinz Noodle		
	Doodles	59	125 per 215g can
shapes and	Heinz Invaders		
meatballs	and Meteors	89	25

Product	Brand	Calories per 100g/ 100ml	Calories per oz/ pack/ portion
wholewheat	Crosse & Blackwell	65	130 per 213g can
Spaghetti bolognaise	Safeway		230 per pack
Spaghetti bolognese	Asda	139	
	Birds Eye MenuMaster		420 per pack
	Findus Lean Cuisine		240 per pack
	Heinz		280 per pack
	Tesco		265 per pack
canned	Heinz		170 per 210g can
Spaghetti bolognese sauce mix			
Cook In	Colman's	370	130 per pack
Pour Over	Colman's	370	130 per pack
Spaghetti sauce			
bolognese	Campbell's	90	26
siciliana	Campbell's	70	20
tomato and mushroom	Campbell's	68	19
Spaghetti sauce mix	Knorr	334	145 per pack
Spaghetti verdi	Tesco	338	96
	Waitrose	350	99
cooked	Tesco	110	31
Spanish fig cake	Wilcox and Lomer	556	250 per 45g pack
Spanish mandarins (canned)	Safeway	56	176 per 312g can

Product	Brand	Calories per 100g/ 100ml	Calories per oz/ pack/ portion
Spanish orange trifle	Eden Vale	155	44
Spanish salad	Eden Vale	112	32
	Safeway	170	384 per 227g pack
Spanish savoury rice	Safeway	334	95
Sparkles, all flavours	Wall's		30 per portion
Sparkling drinks: *see flavours*			
Sparkling fruits	Tesco	380	108
Sparkling mints	Tesco	380	108
Sparks bar	St Michael	480	136
Spearmint chewing gum	Wrigley		9 per stick
Freedent	Wrigley		9 per stick
sweet	Wrigley Orbit		
	Nutra		7 per stick
Spearmint chews	Littlewoods	366	104
Special fried rice	Safeway	146	497 per pack
	Sainsbury's	140	560 per pack
Special K		388	110
	Kellogg's	355	101
Special mixed vegetables	Safeway	46	13
Special recipe muesli	Jordans	330	94
Special reserve cider	Bulmer	52	148 per half pint
Special savoury rice (Batchelors): *see flavours*			

Product	Brand	Calories per 100g/ 100ml	Calories per oz/ pack/ portion
Special tea, infused	Safeway	1	
Special Vat cider	Taunton	44	250 per pint
Speciality assortment biscuits	St Michael	504	143
Specialty soup			
Consomme	Crosse & Blackwell	22	90 per 425g can
Vichyssoise	Crosse & Blackwell	47	220 per 425g can
Spiced mixed fruit pickle	Baxters	159	484 per 305g jar
Spicy barbecue fried special savoury rice	Batchelors	456	129
Spicy beef and pork lasagne	Findus	175	525 per 300g pack
Spicy brown sauce	Waitrose	60	374 per 624g jar
Spicy cake mix (as sold)	Granny Smiths	324	1199 per 370g pack made up
Spicy chicken crisps	Hunters	520	130 per 26g bag
Spicy lamb/beef marinade	Knorr	279	79
Spicy meatballs in tomato sauce	Waitrose	150	525 per 350g can
Spicy mint relish	Branston	113	32
Spicy Nik Naks	St Michael	540	153

Product	Brand	Calories per 100g/ 100ml	Calories per oz/ pack/ portion
Spicy potato salad	Safeway	184	416 per 227g pack
Spicy rice salad	Asda	121	
Spicy risotto	Vesta	312	640 per 205g pack for two as served
Spicy sauce	Branston	112	32
	O.K.	95	27
	Safeway	94	27
traditional	Tesco	147	42
Spicy vegebanger	Real Eats	828	235
Spinach			
boiled		30	9
canned, drained		24	7
fresh, raw		26	7
Spinach tortelloni with ricotta filling (as sold)	Signor Rossi	286	81
Spirits 70% proof		222	63
Split lentils, peas: *see Lentils, Peas*			
Sponges: *see also flavours*			
Sponge bar cake, fresh cream	Tesco	332	94
Sponge cake			
jam filled		302	86
with fat		464	132

Product	Brand	Calories per 100g/ 100ml	Calories per oz/ pack/ portion
without fat		301	85
Sponge cake mix (as sold)			
Devon	Green's	396	223 made up per portion
traditional recipe	Green's	354	93 made up per portion
Sponge cake mixes: *see also flavours*			
Sponge finger biscuits	Huntley & Palmer	388	21 per biscuit
Sponge fingers	Tesco		20 each
Sponge gateau with buttercream and jam	St Michael	391	111
with chocolate and buttercream	St Michael	413	117
Sponge mix, luxury (as sold)	Granny Smiths	342	1216 per 355g pack made up
	Whitworths	425	120
Sponge pudding, steamed		344	98
Sponge puddings: *see also flavours*			
Sponge sandwich cake with buttercream and jam	St Michael	424	120
Sponge slice cake	Littlewoods	334	95
Sponge trifle	Lyons	308	87

Product	Brand	Calories per 100g/ 100ml	Calories per oz/ pack/ portion
Sports biscuits	Safeway	473	134
Spotted Dick	Ross	350	99
	St Michael	339	96
Sprats			
dried		168	48
fresh, raw		100	28
fried		441	125
fried (with bones)		388	110
Spread, low fat	Tesco	340	96
with cheese	Sun-Pat	176	50
with cheese and garden herbs	Sun-Pat	176	50
Spread, reduced fat	Heinz Weight Watchers	360	102
Spread with cheese and onion low fat	Sun-Pat	176	50
Spreading cheese (Medley): *see flavours*			
Spring cabbage, boiled		7	2
Spring greens *boiled*		10	3
Spring onion crisps	Christies	520	130 per 26g bag
	Hunters	520	130 per 26g bag
	Littlewoods	548	411 per 75g pack
	St Michael	546	155
Spring onion dressing	Heinz All Seasons	264	75

Product	Brand	Calories per 100g/ 100ml	Calories per oz/ pack/ portion
Spring onions			
bulbs and tops, raw		28	8
flesh of bulb only, raw		35	10
Spring roll	St Michael		150 each
with chicken	Safeway		125 each
with vegetables	Safeway		125 each
Spring vegetable soup	Heinz Ready to Serve	33	140 per 435g can
	Heinz Weight Watchers	22	65 per can
dried	Batchelors	268	102 per 38g pint pack as sold
	Littlewoods	320	118 per 37g pint packet
	Safeway	317	90
	Tesco	334	95
	Waitrose	286	114 per 40g pack
dried, low calorie	Knorr Quick Soup	285	30 per sachet made up
Sprouts (frozen)	Tesco	35	10
medium	Waitrose	18	80 per 454g pack
Sprouts: see also Brussels sprouts			
Square snack			
muesli bar	Holly Mill		216 per bar
protein bar	Holly Mill		184 per bar
Squash: see Courgettes			

Product	Brand	Calories per 100g/ 100ml	Calories per oz/ pack/ portion
Squid			
dried		328	93
fresh, raw		75	21
frozen, raw		66	19
St Paulin cheese	Safeway	300	85
	Tesco	289	82
	Waitrose	300	85
Stackers	Cadbury's	450	5 per crisp
Star Bar	Cadbury's	495	260 per 53g bar
Start	Kellogg's	340	96
Steak, flash fry	St Michael	128	36
Steak and kidney pancakes	Findus	141	40
Steak and kidney pie	Asda	309	
	Fray Bentos	220	935 per 425g pie
	Ross		450 per pie
	Safeway	303	610 per 198g pie
	Sainsbury's	320	455 per 142g pie
individual	Birds Eye		370 per pie
	Bowyers	300	480 per 160g pie
large	Tesco	272	1550 per 570g pie
	Tesco	161	710 per 440g pie
plate pie	Tesco	275	77
puff pastry	St Michael	279	475 per 170g pie
rich pastry	St Michael	266	1280 per 480g pie
small	St Michael	290	610 per 210g pie

Product	Brand	Calories per 100g/ 100ml	Calories per oz/ pack/ portion
Steak and kidney pie filling	Fray Bentos	147	575 per 397g can
Steak and kidney pie meal with carrots		199	665 per meal
Steak and kidney pudding	Fray Bentos	212	900 per 425g pudding
	Ross		280 each
	Safeway	226	430 per 190g pudding
individual	Tesco		370 each
small	Tesco		390 each
Steak and kidney stew	Campbell's	64	18
Steak and mushroom flaky bake pie	Birds Eye MenuMaster		505 per pie
Steak and mushroom pie filling	Fray Bentos	144	565 per 392g can
Steak and vegetable top crust pie	St Michael	218	61
Steak burger, prime	Safeway	250	71
Steak, kidney and vegetables soup	Campbell's Main Course	55	195 per 425g can
Steak, mushroom and red wine pie	Waitrose	239	68
Steak pie	Sainsbury's		415 each
	Tesco	309	440 per 142g pie

Product	Brand	Calories per 100g/ 100ml	Calories per oz/ pack/ portion
	Tesco	254	1155 per 454g pie
Steakhouse chips	Tesco	207	59
Steaklet, ground beef	St Michael	128	36
Stem ginger in syrup	Waitrose	260	1105 per 425g can
Stem ginger biscuits	Prewetts		77 per biscuit
Stem ginger cookies	Tesco	478	136
	Waitrose	487	138
Sterilized cream	Tesco	227	64
Stewed steak with gravy (canned)		176	50
	Asda	98	
Stewpack vegetables	Sainsbury's	61	17
Stilton cheese: *see Cheese*			
Stilton pots, blue	St Michael	405	115
Stir fry mushrooms	Safeway	80	276 per 340g pack
Stir fry rice	Waitrose	88	300 per 340g pack
Stir fry rice mix	Ross	70	20
Stir fry sweetcorn mix	Ross	70	20
Stir fry vegetables cauliflower,			
mushrooms, peas	Waitrose	39	11
continental (as sold)	Birds Eye	42	12
continental (fried)	Birds Eye	53	15
country (as sold)	Birds Eye	28	8

Product	Brand	Calories per 100g/ 100ml	Calories per oz/ pack/ portion
country (fried) courgettes, corn,	Birds Eye	35	10
mushrooms	Waitrose	36	10
mixed	Ross	50	14
rice, corn and prawns	Waitrose	101	29
Stock cubes vegetable and chicken	Bovril	190	54
vegetable and meat	Bovril	200	57
Stollen cakes	Tesco	371	105
Stork margarine	Van den Berghs	740	210
Special Blend	Van den Berghs	740	210
Stout bottled		37	10
extra		39	11
Straw mushroom: *see Mushroom*			
Strawberries fresh/frozen		26	7
canned in syrup		81	23
canned in natural juice		35	10
Strawberry and apple juice	Copella	39	12
Strawberry and cream cheesecake	Young's	240	68

Product	Brand	Calories per 100g/ 100ml	Calories per oz/ pack/ portion
Strawberry and cream ice cream, American style	Waitrose	178	53
Strawberry and cream mousse	Tesco	170	48
Strawberry and vanilla soft scoop ice cream	Tesco	167	47
Strawberry and wild herb yogurt	St Michael	117	33
Strawberry Arctic gateau	Birds Eye		105 per 1/5 gateau
Strawberry bar	Granose	374	187 per 50g bar
Strawberry blancmange	Brown and Polson	330	94
Strawberry Bon Bons	Trebor Bassett	403	27 per sweet
Strawberry cheesecake	Eden Vale	196	56
	Young's	240	68
individual	Young's	255	72
Strawberry cheesecake mix (made up)	Lyons	234	66
Strawberry conserve	Safeway	248	70
	St Michael	240	68
	Tesco	268	76
	Waitrose	250	71

Product	Brand	Calories per 100g/ 100ml	Calories per oz/ pack/ portion
Strawberry Cornetto	Wall's		205 per cone
Strawberry creams	Rowntree Mackintosh		45 per sweet
Strawberry crumble creams	Tesco	497	141
Strawberry cup	Rowntree Mackintosh		45 per sweet
Strawberry delight dessert	St Michael	116	33
Strawberry dessert	Waitrose	444	306 per 69g pack
Strawberry dessert sauce	Lyons Maid	264	75
Strawberry Devonshire cheesecake	St Ivel	250	71
Strawberry drink, semi-skimmed	St Michael	57	16
Strawberry fingers	Lyons	368	104
Strawberry flan filling	Armour	130	1034 per 795g pack
Strawberry flavour cake mix (as sold)	Green's	397	223 made up per portion
Strawberry flavour cordial, undiluted	Quosh	108	32

Product	Brand	Calories per 100g/ 100ml	Calories per oz/ pack/ portion
Strawberry flavour dessert mix	Dietade	264	75
Strawberry flavour drink	Quosh	35	10
Strawberry flavour jelly	Waitrose	272	77
crystals	Dietade	290	82
Strawberry fool	Tesco		130 each
Strawberry fromage frais slice	St Michael		365 per slice 150g jar 104
Strawberry fruit cream trifle	Safeway	132	37
Strawberry fruit filling	Morton	76	22
Strawberry fruit pie filling	Tesco	84	24
Strawberry fruit spread	Waitrose	124	35
Strawberry Fruit Whisk mix	Green's	113	124 per portion made up with whole milk
	Green's	113	104 per portion made with skimmed milk
Strawberry gateau	Co-op	268	75

Product	Brand	Calories per 100g/ 100ml	Calories per oz/ pack/ portion
	St Ivel		190 per carton
	St Michael	266	75
	Tesco	264	74
Strawberry Harlequin dessert	Wall's		110 per 1/5 pack
Strawberry ice cream	Safeway	175	52
	Waitrose	189	56
dairy	Asda	183	
	Bertorelli	167	47
	Lyons Maid Napoli	176	50
Mini Milk	Wall's		40 per portion
non-dairy	Lyons Maid	175	50
Strawberry jam	Robertson's	251	71
	Safeway	251	71
	Waitrose	248	70
diabetic	Boots	239	68
	Dietade	232	66
no added sugar	Safeway	141	40
reduced sugar	Asda	126	
	Boots	152	43
	Heinz Weight Watchers	124	35
	Waitrose	124	35
Strawberry jam sponge pudding	Heinz	286	81
Strawberry jelly	Safeway	268	76
	Tesco	57	16

Product	Brand	Calories per 100g/ 100ml	Calories per oz/ pack/ portion
diabetic crystals	Boots	365	103
table	Littlewoods	260	74
Strawberry juice, concentrated	Western Isles	325	96
Strawberry King Cone	Lyons Maid		191 per cone
Strawberry luxury cheesecake mix	Tesco	300	85
made	Tesco	245	69
Strawberry milkshake	St Michael	75	21
	Waitrose	68	20
Strawberry Mivvi	Lyons Maid		77 each
Strawberry mousse	Asda	159	
	Ross	170	48
	Safeway	150	44
	Tesco	180	51
Strawberry mousse and cream swirl	Safeway	150	43
Strawberry preserve	Baxters	240	816 per 340g jar
	Tesco	255	72
reduced sugar	Robertson's	150	43
Strawberry pure fruit spread	Robertson's	120	34
Strawberry real milk ice	Lyons Maid		49 each

Product	Brand	Calories per 100g/ 100ml	Calories per oz/ pack/ portion
Strawberry ripple ice cream	Tesco	173	49
soft scoop	Lyons Maid	181	51
Strawberry ripple mousse	Findus	171	48
	Waitrose	149	42
Strawberry sauce	Tesco	315	89
Strawberry sherbets	Trebor Bassett	359	23 per sweet
Strawberry snowballs	Littlewoods	449	127
Strawberry sorbet	St Michael	107	30
Strawberry souffle	St Michael	191	54
Strawberry Sparkles	Wall's		30 per portion
Strawberry split	Wall's		80 per portion
Strawberry supershake	Eden Vale	75	21
Strawberry Supreme Delight	Safeway	431	122
Strawberry Swiss roll	Asda	324	
	Tesco	367	104
Strawberry tartlets biscuits	St Michael	386	109
Strawberry Topsy Turvy	Ambrosia	103	29
Strawberry trifle	Eden Vale	160	45
	Littlewoods	138	39
	St Ivel	143	41

Product	Brand	Calories per 100g/ 100ml	Calories per oz/ pack/ portion
Real	Young's	150	43
Strawberry yogurt	Gold Ski	116	174 per 150g pack
	Mr Men	90	26
	Munch Bunch	100	125 per 125g pack
	Raines	80	23
	Safeway	95	27
	Ski	81	122 per 150g pack
	St Ivel Rainbow		7020
	St Ivel Real	80	23
	St Ivel Shape	40	11
	St Michael	95	27
	St Michael Lite	39	11
creamy	Waitrose	140	175 per 125g pack
French style	Littlewoods	102	153 per 150g pack
	St Michael	103	29
Funtime	Safeway	90	135 per 150g pack
low fat	Diet Ski	55	83 per 150g pack
	Littlewoods	84	126 per 150g pack
	Tesco	88	25
	Waitrose	95	143 per 150g pack

Product	Brand	Calories per 100g/ 100ml	Calories per oz/ pack/ portion
whole milk	Safeway	59	86 per 146g pack
	Waitrose	115	173 per 150g pack
Strawberryade	Corona	25	7
Strega			75 per 1/6 gill
Strike cola	Barr	30	75 per 250ml can
Strong ale		72	20
Strongbow cider	Bulmer	36	102 per half pint
1080	Bulmer	49	140 per half pint
Stuffed plaice	St Michael	109	31
Stuffed pork roll	Tyne Brand	153	43
Stuffed turkey roll	Tyne Brand	144	41
Stuffing mixes: see flavours			
Suet			
block		895	254
shredded		826	234
Suet dumpling and pudding mix (as sold)	Granny Smiths	341	1070 per 314g pack made up
Suet pudding, steamed		333	94
Sugar			
brown		394	112
caster/granulated		394	112
Demerara		394	112
icing		394	112
small cube			10 each

Product	Brand	Calories per 100g/ 100ml	Calories per oz/ pack/ portion
large cube			20 each
Sugar flakes	Tesco	367	104
Sugar free muesli	Holland and Barrett	380	108
	Prewetts	340	96
Sugar letters	Littlewoods	375	345 per 92g pack
Sugar Puffs		348	99
Sugar strands assorted	Tesco	370	105
chocolate	Tesco	423	120
Sugared almonds	Littlewoods	417	118
	St Michael	460	130
Sultana and bran biscuits, handbaked	Boots	485	137
Sultana and cherry cake	Asda	361	
	St Michael	273	77
Sultana and spice creams	Waitrose	499	141
Sultana and syrup pancakes	St Michael	280	79
	Tesco	293	83
Sultana bar	Cadbury's	450	128
Sultana Bran	Asda	318	
	Kellogg's	298	84
Sultana cake cut	Safeway	360	102
large	Safeway	360	102

Product	Brand	Calories per 100g/ 100ml	Calories per oz/ pack/ portion
whole	Waitrose	347	98
Sultana cookies	Tesco	475	135
Sultana scones	Tesco	310	88
Sultanas dried		250	71
	Holland and Barrett	240	68
	Safeway	250	71
	Tesco	256	73
	Whitworths	250	71
Australian	Waitrose	250	71
Greek	Waitrose	250	71
Summer County dairy spread	Van den Berghs	650	184
Summer fruit lattice pie	Waitrose	340	96
Summer fruit trifle	St Michael	145	41
Summer harvest mix vegetables	Findus	72	20
Summer mixed vegetables (canned)	Tesco	50	14
Summer Orchard	Kellogg's	320	91
Sundae Cups chocolate	Lyons Maid		156 each
raspberry	Lyons Maid		89 each

Product	Brand	Calories per 100g/ 100ml	Calories per oz/ pack/ portion
Sunflower fruit and nut bar	Shepherd Boy Bars		204 per bar
Sunflower margarine	Safeway	735	208
salt-free	Safeway	735	208
Sunflower oil	Asda	899	
	Boots	899	255
	Flora	900	255
	Holland and Barrett	720	213
	Safeway	900	266
	St Michael	900	255
	Sunwheel	900	255
	Tesco	875	248
	Waitrose	900	266
Sunflower seed bar, natural	Boots	464	132
Sunflower seeds	Holland and Barrett	560	159
Sunflower spread	Sunwheel	576	163
Sunfruit drink	St Michael	47	13
Sunny sauce	O.K.	85	24
Sunsnack, peanut	Sunwheel	622	176
Supa 5 chews	Trebor Bassett	364	16 per sweet
Super Fries			
salt and pepper	Hunters	441	106 per 24g pack
tomato ketchup	Hunters	441	106 per 24g pack

Product	Brand	Calories per 100g/ 100ml	Calories per oz/ pack/ portion
Super juice bar	Lyons Maid		50 each
Super Noodles, all flavours	Batchelors	465	460 per pack as sold
Super triple choc	Lyons Maid		277 each
Superfine biscuits	Rakusen	347	74 per biscuit
Supermousse tub dessert (Birds Eye): *see flavours*			
Supershake (Eden Vale): *see flavours*			
Supreme (Eden Vale): *see flavours*			
Supreme Delight (Safeway): *see flavours*			
Supreme style pot meal	Boots Shapers	328	93
Surprise vegetables (Batchelor): *see Peas, etc*			
Swedes			
boiled		18	5
raw		21	6
Sweet and savoury biscuits	Holly Mill		25 per biscuit
Sweet and sour chicken	St Michael	99	28
	Vesta	362	1018 per 281g pack for two as served
Sweet and sour Chinese stir fry vegetable dish	St Michael	25	7

Product	Brand	Calories per 100g/ 100ml	Calories per oz/ pack/ portion
Sweet and sour fried special savoury rice	Batchelors	465	665 per 143g sachet
Sweet and sour pickle	Pan Yan	139	39
Sweet and sour pork with rice	Waitrose	88	300 per 340g pack
	Birds Eye MenuMaster		670 per pack
Sweet and sour pork balls	St Michael	131	37
Sweet and sour pork vegetable mix	Ross	70	20
Sweet and sour prawns stir fry	St Michael		230 per 283g pack as sold
Sweet and sour sauce	St Michael	38	11
Cook in	Homepride	53	199 per 376g pack
Cooking-in	Baxters	94	400 per 425g can
Sweet and sour sauce mix			
Cook In	Colman's	320	100 per pack
Pour Over	Colman's	320	100 per pack
Sweet and sour savoury rice	Asda	114	
	Safeway	342	428 per 125g pack
Sweet corn			
canned kernels		76	22
on the cob, kernels only, raw		127	36
immature baby corn, canned, drained		21	6

Product	Brand	Calories per 100g/ 100ml	Calories per oz/ pack/ portion
on the cob, boiled		123	35
on the cob, raw		127	36
Sweet corn and pepper salad	Asda	175	
Sweet corn and peppers (canned)	Tesco	90	26
Sweet corn, peas and carrots	Birds Eye	53	15
Sweetcorn relish	Branston	132	37
	Crosse & Blackwell	133	38
	Tesco	109	31
Sweetcorn soup, low calorie	Knorr Quick Soup	364	103
Sweetcorn with red peppers salad	Littlewoods	159	45
Sweet military pickle	Haywards	130	37
Sweet peanuts	Trebor Bassett	406	26 per sweet
Sweet piccalilli	Waitrose	48	14
chunky	Safeway	98	28
Sweet pickle	Branston	131	37
	Littlewoods	160	45
	Safeway	91	26
	Waitrose	215	61
low calorie	Boots Shapers	66	19

Product	Brand	Calories per 100g/ 100ml	Calories per oz/ pack/ portion
Sweet pickled onions	Safeway	36	10
Sweet potatoes			
boiled		85	24
raw		91	26
Sweet red pepper with chilli soup	Sainsbury's	45	190 per 425g can
Sweetbread, lamb			
fried		230	65
raw		131	37
Sweetener, diabetic	Boots	360	102
Sweetex			
granulated	Crookes		2 per teaspoon
liquid	Crookes		1 per 4 drops
Sweetmeal biscuits, wheaten	St Michael	453	128
Swiss black cherry	Safeway	248	70
conserve	St Michael	240	68
Swiss black cherry jam			
reduced sugar	Waitrose	124	35
Swiss cup, instant	Granose	6	2 per cup
Swiss Gruyere cheese	St Michael	400	113
	Waitrose	272	77
Swiss gruyere spread	Tesco	306	87
Swiss mountain chocolate bar	St Michael	550	156
white	St Michael	562	159

Product	Brand	Calories per 100g/ 100ml	Calories per oz/ pack/ portion
Swiss muesli cereal	Waitrose	382	108
Swiss pies	St Michael	296	84
Swiss roll: *see flavours*			
Swiss style breakfast	Tesco	374	106
Swiss-style cereal	Safeway	473	134
Swiss style chocolate cake mix (as sold)	300 made up per portion Green's	401	
Swiss style muesli bar	Boots	350	99
Swiss style potato cake	Findus	80	23
Swiss style potato fry	Waitrose	135	38
Swiss white chocolate	St Michael	172	49
Sword fish fillet, raw		116	33
	Tesco	117	35
Syrup, golden		298	84
Syrup biscuits, Kennett	Huntley & Palmer	500	63 per biscuit
Syrup pancakes	Tesco	304	86
Syrup sponge pudding	Safeway	372	105
	St Michael	375	106
	Tesco	358	101
Szechuan spicy Classic Chinese sauce	Homepride	108	413 per 383g pack

T

Product	Brand	Calories per 100g/ 100ml	Calories per oz/ pack/ portion
Table crackers	Jacobs	431	33 per biscuit
	Safeway	431	8 per biscuit
Table jellies			
all flavours	Chivers	290	100 per portion
all flavours	Littlewoods	260	333 per 128g pack
Table jellies: see also flavours			
Tabouleh Salad	Waitrose	141	40
Taco filling, beef	Old El Paso	176	361 per 205g can
Taco sauce			
hot	Old El Paso	39	11
mild	Old El Paso	39	11
Taco shells	Old El Paso	490	613 per 125g pack
Tagliatelle	Buitoni	350	99
	St Michael	369	105
	Waitrose	378	107
new style	St Michael	142	40
wholewheat	Signor Rossi	275	78
Tagliatelle bianche	Signor Rossi	272	77
	Waitrose	222	63
Tagliatelle carbonara	Tesco	151	770 per pack
Tagliatelle nicoise	Waitrose	170	48
Tagliatelle vegetali	Sainsbury's	100	300 per pack
Tagliatelle verde	Buitoni	340	96
	Signor Rossi	309	88
egg, cooked	Tesco	118	33
egg, uncooked	Tesco	336	95

Product	Brand	Calories per 100g/ 100ml	Calories per oz/ pack/ portion
Tagliatelle with ham in cream sauce	Tesco	131	395 per pack
Tagliatelle with fresh vegetables	St Michael	111	315 per pack
Tagliatelle with mushrooms and ham	Sainsbury's	118	660 per pack
Tagliolini bianchi	Signor Rossi	272	77
verdi	Signor Rossi	309	88
Tahini		607	170
Tahini sesame cream	Harmony	560	159
Take-off bar	Hellas		170 per bar
Tamari sauce	Sunwheel	86	24
Tamarind leaves, raw		73	21
Tandoori bites	Asda	209	
Tandoori chicken masala	Waitrose	376	107
Tandoori chicken masala soup, dried	Waitrose	376	165 per 44g pack
Tandoori chicken sandwiches	Safeway		265 per pack
Tandoori Coat and cook sauce	Homepride	180	77 per 43g pack
Tandoori cutlet mix, vegetarian	Tomorrow Foods	318	90

Product	Brand	Calories per 100g/ 100ml	Calories per oz/ pack/ portion
Tandoori flavour chicken	St Michael	240	68
Tandoori marinade	Knorr	211	60
Tandoori paste marinade	Tesco	70	20
Tandoori style chicken breasts	Sainsbury's	221	62
Tangerine flavour jelly	Waitrose	272	386 per 142g pack
Tangerine jelly	Safeway	268	381 per 142g pack
	Tesco	57	16
Tangerine luxury cheesecake mix	Tesco	347	98
made up	Tesco	273	77
Tangerines			
raw		34	10
raw (with peel and pips)			237
Tangy lemon cheesecake mix (as sold)	Green's	429	240 made up per portion
Tangy orange and apple bubble gum	Wrigley Hubba Bubba		15/24 per chunk
Tangy pickle spread	Heinz Ploughman's	118	33

Product	Brand	Calories per 100g/ 100ml	Calories per oz/ pack/ portion
Tapioca			
raw		359	102
cooked	Tesco	121	34
Tapioca, creamed	Ambrosia	83	365 per 439g can
Tapioca pudding	Whitworths	131	37
Taramasalata		446	126
	Asda	433	
	Co-op	470	135
	Tesco	495	840 per tub
Taro tuber, raw		94	27
Tartare sauce	O.K.	255	72
	Safeway	255	72
	Tesco	279	79
	Waistline	138	39
	Waitrose	283	80
Tartare sauce dressing	Safeway	222	63
Tartex			
herb	Vessen	233	420 per 180g pack
plain	Vessen	244	440 per 180g pack
Tartlet cases biscuits	St Michael	488	138
Tastex	Granose	208	59
Tea			
black, all brands, per cup			0
Tea cakes	St Michael	270	77

Product	Brand	Calories per 100g/ 100ml	Calories per oz/ pack/ portion
	Tesco	270	77
chocolate coated	Tesco	432	122
toasted	Bassett's	441	125
Tea cakes mix	Tesco	372	105
lemon (as sold)	Tesco	422	120
lemon (made up)	Tesco	355	101
made up	Tesco	378	107
Tea crackers	Rakusen	347	17 per biscuit
Teabreak biscuits	Nabisco	420	38 per biscuit
wholewheat	Nabisco	388	38 per biscuit
Teddy bear gums, real fruit	St Michael	340	96
Ten fruits juice cocktail	Waitrose	38	11
Tendale cheese blue	Dairy Crest	252	71
Cheddar-like	Dairy Crest	253	72
Tendale cheese Cheshire-like	Dairy Crest	246	70
Tender bits	Granose	79	22
Tequila			50 per 1/6 gill
Teriyaki marinade	Tesco	207	59
Thick vegetable soup	Tesco	50	215 per 425g can
dried	Littlewoods	356	132 per pint packet

Product	Brand	Calories per 100g/ 100ml	Calories per oz/ pack/ portion
Thistle shortbread biscuits	Tesco	513	145
Thousand island dressing	Duchesse Heinz All	33	10
	Seasons	282	80
	Kraft	393	116
	Safeway	224	66
	Tesco	384	109
Thousand island dressing cream	Waitrose	194	55
Thousand island dressing fresh	St Michael	281	80
low calorie	Boots Shapers	196	56
Three bean salad	St Michael	148	42
Three fruit cocktail drink, long life	Waitrose	41	12
Three fruits marmalade	Baxters	248	70
thick-cut	Waitrose	248	70
Tigertots	Rowntree Mackintosh	380	165 per 43g bag
Tijuana dressing	Hellmanns	320	90
Tikka paste marinade	Tesco	125	35
Tilsiter cheese	Waitrose	390	111

Product	Brand	Calories per 100g/ 100ml	Calories per oz/ pack/ portion
Tinda (round gourd)			
canned, drained		12	3
fresh, raw		21	6
Tiny tots	Littlewoods	315	89
Tip Top dessert topping	Nestle	110	31
Tizer	Barr	37	122 per 330ml can
	Littlewoods	39	129 per 330ml pack
Sugar free	Barr	0	0
Toad in the hole	Findus	207	410 per pack
Toast Toppers (Heinz): *see flavours*			
Toasted bran	Meadow Farm	360	102
farmhouse	Weetabix	300	85
Toasted tea cakes	Trebor Bassett	441	125
Toffee almond ice cream, American style	St Michael	225	64
Toffee and almond ice cream	Tesco	202	57
Toffee and banana mousse	Waitrose	151	43
Toffee and mallow	Rowntree Mackintosh		45 per sweet
Toffee apple roll	Trebor Bassett	346	14 per sweet
Toffee biscuits	Littlewoods	485	76 per biscuit

Product	Brand	Calories per 100g/ 100ml	Calories per oz/ pack/ portion
Toffee bon bons	Tesco	417	118
	Trebor Bassett	403	27 per sweet
Toffee brazils	Tesco	442	125
Toffee caramello Supermousse tub dessert	Birds Eye		120 per tub
Toffee creams	Tesco	454	129
Toffee crisp	Rowntree Mackintosh	510	225 per 44g bar
Toffee crumble	Lyons Maid	303	171 each
Toffee crunch	Trebor Bassett	429	27 per sweet
Toffee cup	Rowntree Mackintosh		40 per sweet
Toffee de luxe	Rowntree Mackintosh		45 per sweet
Toffee dessert	Waitrose	444	126
Toffee finger	Rowntree Mackintosh		30 per sweet
Toffee mousse	Asda	152	
Toffee pat	Rowntree Mackintosh		30 per sweet
Toffee pecan crunch American style ice cream	St Michael	296	83

Product	Brand	Calories per 100g/ 100ml	Calories per oz/ pack/ portion
Toffee ripple ice cream, soft scoop	Lyons Maid	180	51
Toffee rolls, chocolate coated	Tesco	458	130
Toffee yogurt	St Michael	112	32
low fat	Tesco	106	30
Toffees, mixed		430	122
Toffo, plain and mint	Rowntree Mackintosh	455	25 per sweet
Tofu (soya bean curd)			
steamed		70	20
canned, fried		302	86
	Morinaga	54	160 per 297g pack
Chinese	Granose	60	17
in savoury bean sauce	Granose	120	34
in tomato sauce	Granose	90	26
Tofu dressing	Duchesse	33	10
Tofu spread			
with garlic	La Source de Vie	285	81
with paprika	La Source de Vie	285	81
Tofu with Chinese vegetables	Granose	60	260 per 435g pack

Product	Brand	Calories per 100g/ 100ml	Calories per oz/ pack/ portion
Tomato and basil soup	Sainsbury's	47	200 per 425g can
Tomato and beef soup, low calorie	Waitrose	20	59 per 295g can
Tomato and cheese pizza	Birds Eye Home Bake		270 per pizza
chilled	Safeway		850 per pizza
	St Michael		765 per pizza
frozen (4 pack)	Marietta		210 each
panbake	Tesco		935 per pizza
Tomato and chilli chutney	Sharwood	92	26
Tomato and chilli relish	Safeway	118	33
	Tesco	109	31
Tomato and green pepper soup	Heinz Spicy Soups	43	130 per 300g can
Tomato and lentil soup	Heinz Whole Soups	53	160 per 300g can
Tomato and mushroom spaghetti sauce	Campbell's	68	19
Tomato and onion Cook in Sauce	Homepride	57	214 per 376g pack
Tomato and onion spread	Heinz	218	62

Product	Brand	Calories per 100g/ 100ml	Calories per oz/ pack/ portion
Tomato and pepper relish	Crosse & Blackwell	126	36
Tomato and vegetable soup, dried instant	Tesco	355	101
instant special (made up)	Safeway	45	13
with croutons	Batchelors Cup-a-Soup Special	394	132 per 33.5g pack as sold
Tomato, cheese and onion pizza	St Michael	203	58
Tomato chutney		154	44
	Waitrose	154	44
Tomato dressing for seafoods and salads	Waistline	144	41
Tomato fruit juice	Heinz	22	7
Tomato juice canned		16	5
Tomato juice cocktail	Britvic	25	28 per 113ml pack
	Hunts	16	5
	Stchweppes	17	5
Tomato ketchup		98	28
	Asda	120	
	Crosse & Blackwell	118	33
	Heinz	97	27
	Libby	106	30

Product	Brand	Calories per 100g/ 100ml	Calories per oz/ pack/ portion
	Safeway	95	27
	Tesco	100	28
	Waistline	57	16
	Waitrose	112	32
Tomato ketchup Super Fries	Hunters	441	106 per 24g pack
Tomato Pasta Choice	Crosse & Blackwell	353	100
Tomato paste		67	19
	Tesco	68	19
Tomato pickle	Baxters	140	40
	Heinz Ploughman's	95	27
Tomato puree		67	19
	Buitoni	72	20
	Tesco	71	20
	Waitrose	86	24
with basil	Waitrose	56	16
Tomato relish	Branston	129	37
	Crosse & Blackwell	131	37
	Safeway	118	33
	Tesco	93	26
Tomato rice soup, condensed	Campbell's	96	265 per 300g can
Tomato sauce		86	24
	Signor Rossi	35	10

Product	Brand	Calories per 100g/ 100ml	Calories per oz/ pack/ portion	445
Tomato sauce crisps	Christies	520	130 per 26g bag	
	Hunters	520	130 per 26g bag	
Tomato sausage	Littlewoods	275	78	
Tomato savoury rice	Safeway	330	462 per 140g pack	
Tomato soup	Campbell's	61	180 per 295g can	
	Granny's	96	410 per 425g can	
	Littlewoods	55	234 per 425g can	
canned, low calorie	Heinz Weight Watchers	25	75 per 300g can	
	Waistline	22	6	
	Waitrose	18	53 per 29g can	
dried	Batchelors Cup-a-Soup	350	84 per 24g sachet as sold	
	Hera	364	455 per pack	
	Knorr Quick Soup	395	80 per sachet	
	Prewetts Soup in Seconds	313	70 per sachet	
	Safeway	339	96	
	Tesco	348	99	
dried, instant (as sold)	Safeway	338	96	
dried, low calorie	Batchelors Slim-a-Soup	271	38 per 14g sachet	
	Knorr Quick Soup	353	40 per sachet	

Product	Brand	Calories per 100g/ 100ml	Calories per oz/ pack/ portion
Tomato Super Noodles	Batchelors	465	460 per packet as sold
Tomato, vegetable and beef soup with croutons	Knorr Quick Soup	332	80 per sachet
Tomatoes			
canned, drained		12	3
fresh, raw		14	4
fried		69	20
canned	Tesco	21	6
crushed	Waitrose	21	6
fresh	Littlewoods	14	4
whole peeled plum	Asda	14	
	Waitrose	21	48 per 227g can
Tomme de neige cheese	Waitrose	390	111
Tomor margarine	Van den Berghs	740	210
Tongue			
canned		213	60
lamb, raw		193	55
ox, boiled		293	83
sheep, stewed		289	82
ox	Waitrose	143	41
ox, sliced	St Michael	170	48
	Tesco	280	79
pork	Waitrose	176	50
pork, pressed, sliced	St Michael	152	43

Product	Brand	Calories per 100g/ 100ml	Calories per oz/ pack/ portion
Tongue and ham paste	Littlewoods	230	81 per 35g pack
Tongue and turkey paste	Littlewoods	210	74 per 35g pack
Tonic-flavoured concentrate	Safeway	166	49
Tonic water	Safeway	28	8
	Schweppes	20	6
	Waitrose	27	8
low calorie	Safeway Diet	1	
	Schweppes Slimline	1	0.61
	Waitrose	4	1
Tonic Wine	Phosferine	137	41
Toor dahl cooked dish		109	31
Tooty Frooties	Rowntree Mackintosh	415	8 per sweet
Tooty Minties	Rowntree Mackintosh	425	9 per sweet
Top cream toffees	Trebor Bassett	439	36 per sweet
Topic	Mars	496	141
Tops cake mix (as sold)			
butterfly	Granny Smiths	432	1568 per 363g pack made up
chocolate	Granny Smiths	354	1088 per 307g pack made up

Product	Brand	Calories per 100g/ 100ml	Calories per oz/ pack/ portion
lemon	Granny Smiths	355	1104 per 311g pack made up
Tortelloni spinach, with ricotta filling	Signor Rossi	286	81
with meat filling	Signor Rossi	300	85
Tortelloni bianche	Dolmio	185	52 cooked
Tortelloni verde	Dolmio	171	48 cooked
Tortilla chips	Old El Paso	272	408 per 150g pack
	St Michael	498	141
	Tesco	502	142
chilli	Trappers	492	246 per 50g pack
Tortillas	Old El Paso	497	141
Toss 'n' serve dressing, classic	Crosse & Blackwell	219	62
herb	Crosse & Blackwell	11	3
Tostada shells	Old El Paso	459	130
Tots Bunnytots	Rowntree Mackintosh	420	180 per 43g bag
Candytots	Rowntree Mackintosh	400	175 per 44g bag
Jellytots	Rowntree Mackintosh	345	160 per 46g bag

Product	Brand	Calories per 100g/ 100ml	Calories per oz/ pack/ portion
Tigertots	Rowntree Mackintosh	380	165 per 43g bag
Traditional mixes (Colman's): *see flavours*			
Trail bar snack bar, carob coated	Sunwheel Kalibu	417	125 per 30g bar
Treacle, black		257	73
Treacle baked roll	Waitrose	379	107
Treacle cookies	Waitrose	511	145
Treacle crunch biscuits	Peek Frean	436	29 per biscuit
Treacle Granymels	Itona	400	113
Treacle roly poly	Ross	390	111
Treacle scones	Tesco	293	83
Treacle sponge pudding	Heinz	288	82
Treacle sponge puddling mix (as sold)	Green's	394	334 made up per portion
Treacle tart		371	105
	Waitrose	371	105
Treacle toffee	Littlewoods	451	128
Trebor mints	Trebor Bassett	371	6 per sweet
Treets	Mars	515	146
Trellis bramley apple tart	St Michael	223	63
Trifle		160	45

Product	Brand	Calories per 100g/ 100ml	Calories per oz/ pack/ portion
mixed fruit	Young's	150	43
Trifle: *see also flavours*			
Trifle sponge	Waitrose	309	88
Trifle sponge pack of 8	Safeway	325	24 per sponge
Trio biscuits	Jacobs	530	127 per biscuit
Tripe dressed		60	17
stewed		100	28
Triple choc	Lyons Maid		220 each
Tropical coconut cookies	Barbaras		220 per biscuit
Tropical double decker	St Michael	124	35
Tropical drink	Tesco	44	13
long life	Waitrose	43	13
Tropical 8 drink	Tesco	52	15
Tropical fruit and nuts	Waitrose	480	136
Tropical fruit cocktail	Del Monte	82	23
Tropical fruit drink	Asda	49	
	Safeway	46	14
	Waitrose	44	13
low calorie, carbonated	Boots Shapers	1	
low calorie,			

Product	Brand	Calories per 100g/ 100ml	Calories per oz/ pack/ portion
dilutable	Boots Shapers	8	2
Tropical fruit flavour cordial	Quosh	115	34
Tropical fruit flavour drink	Corona	26	8
	Quosh	34	10
Tropical fruit juice	Britvic	49	55 per 113ml pack
Tropical fruit lattice pie	Waitrose	340	96
Tropical fruit squash	Boots	167	49
Tropical fruit yoghurt	Safeway	101	152 per 150g pack
whole milk	Waitrose	115	173 per 150g pack
Tropical fruit yogurt	St Ivel Shape	41	12
Tropical muesli	Prewetts	340	96
Tropical Spring	Schweppes	30	9
Tropical supreme	Eden Vale	116	145 per 125g pack
Tropic-Ora drink, concentrated	Kia-Ora	131	39
Trout almande	Young's	160	45
Trout fillet, raw		139	39
with bones, poached/steamed		89	25
fillet, smoked		135	38

Product	Brand	Calories per 100g/ 100ml	Calories per oz/ pack/ portion
whole, poached/steamed		88	24
whole, smoked		96	26
Trout, brown			
steamed		135	38
steamed (with bones)		89	25
Trout pate	Tesco	260	74
Trout, rainbow			
whole	Waitrose	130	37
with mushrooms and onion stuffing	Waitrose	244	69
Trout veronique	Young's	130	37
Trout with savoury stuffing	Waitrose	189	54
Truffle and nougat	Rowntree Mackintosh		50 per sweet
Tuna			
canned in brine, drained		107	30
canned in oil, drained		214	60
steaks, fresh, raw		157	44
Tuna and pasta bake	Boots Shapers Ready Meals		255 per 300g pack
Tuna and pasta salad	Asda	170	
	Tesco	149	390 per pack
Tuna and prawn luxury pizza (frozen)	Safeway	198	56

Product	Brand	Calories per 100g/ 100ml	Calories per oz/ pack/ portion
Tuna and sweetcorn soup	Asda	42	
	Sainsbury's	47	200 per 425g can
Tuna and tomato quiche	St Michael	247	70
Tuna mayonnaise and tomato sandwiches	Waitrose		450 per pack
Tuna pate	Tesco	387	110
Tuna sandwiches	St Michael		370 per pack
Tunes	Mars	363	103
Turbot fillet, steamed		100	28
Turia: *see Gourd, ridge*			
Turkey			
raw, dark meat		114	32
raw, light meat		103	29
raw, meat and skin		145	41
raw, meat only		107	30
roast, dark meat		148	42
roast, light meat		132	37
roast, meat and skin		171	48
roast, meat only		140	40
breast with pork and chestnut	St Michael	328	92
breast escalope	Sainsbury's		310 each baked
escalope	St Michael		275 each

Product	Brand	Calories per 100g/ 100ml	Calories per oz/ pack/ portion
escalope in breadcrumbs	Sainsbury's		330 each baked
steak	St Michael		155 each
steaks in crispy crumb	Sainsbury's		180 each baked
Turkey and ham pie	Waitrose	221	63
plate	St Michael	220	62
Turkey and ham Toast Topper	Heinz	85	24
Turkey and vegetable broth, condensed	Campbell's	76	235 per 300g can
Turkey, asparagus and ham pie	Sainsbury's	273	77
Turkey breast oak smoked	Asda	140	
Turkey breast roll	Asda	146	
Waitrose	136	39	
Turkey burgers (4 pack)	Co-op		185 each
	Tesco		185 each
Turkey, cheese and tuna brioche	Waitrose	311	88
Turkey crunchies pie	Tesco	293	83
Turkey ham, cooked	Waitrose	130	37
Turkey in mushroom sauce	Findus Lean Cuisine		195 per pack
Turkey paupiettes	St Michael	74	21

Product	Brand	Calories per 100g/ 100ml	Calories per oz/ pack/ portion
Turkey pie, rich pastry	St Michael	318	90
Turkey recipe sausages	Wall's Light and Lean	199	99 per sausage
Turkey roll, stuffed	Tyne Brand	144	41
Turkish delight without nuts		295	84
	Cadbury's	360	185 per 51g bar
Turmeric powder		354	100
Turnip tops, boiled		11	3
Turnips boiled		14	4
raw		20	6
Tuscany Prego sauce	Campbell's	106	30
Tutti frutti chews	Trebor Bassett	379	36 per sweet
Tutti frutti Cornetto	Wall's		240 per super cone
Tutti Frutti ice cream dairy	Lyons Maid Napoli	199	56
Tutti frutti ice cream	Wall's Gino Ginelli Sliceable	189	53
TVP beef	Itona	250	282 per 113g pack

Product	Brand	Calories per 100g/ 100ml	Calories per oz/ pack/ portion
chunks	Itona	250	71
minced	Itona	250	282 per 113g pack
strips (vegetarian)	Boots	329	93
TVP mince			
vegetarian	Boots	329	93
Twiglets			
large	Peek Frean	400	6 per biscuit
small	Peek Frean	400	2 per biscuit
Twix	Mars	499	141
Tzatziki	Co-op	125	35
	Sainsbury's		200 per tub
	Tesco	107	180 per tub

U

Product	Brand	Calories per 100g/ 100ml	Calories per oz/ pack/ portion
Ugli, fresh	Tesco	50	14
Umbongo fruit drink	Libby	41	12
Urad dahl, duhli (cooked dish)		88	25
Urad gram, whole (cooked dish)		85	24

Product	Brand	Calories per 100g/ 100ml	Calories per oz/ pack/ portion
V8 Juice	Campbell's	20	6
Valor beans: *see Balor beans*			
Vanilla and caramel choc ices	Safeway	259	77
Vanilla and chocolate ice cream	Tesco	180	51
Vanilla and mint choc ices	Safeway		130 each
Vanilla arctic circles	Birds Eye		155 per piece
Vanilla blancmange (dry)	Brown and Polson	328	93
Vanilla choc crunch ice cream	Lyons Maid Napoli	219	62
Vanilla choc flake ice cream	Lyons Maid Gold Seal	219	62
Vanilla choc ices	Safeway	259	77
Vanilla cup	Lyons Maid		84 each
Vanilla dessert	Waitrose	444	126
Vanilla ice cream	Lyons Maid	182	52
	Safeway	182	883 per family brick
	Tesco	182	52
	Waitrose	171	51
	Wall's		65 per slice
	Wall's Alpine		125 per 1/10 pack

Product	Brand	Calories per 100g/ 100ml	Calories per oz/ pack/ portion
	Wall's Blue Ribbon		105 per tub; 1/5 pack 85
Cornish	Tesco	181	51
cream of Cornish	Wall's		95 per 1/5 pack
dairy	Bertorelli	202	57
	Lyons Maid Napoli	183	52
	Safeway	230	68
economy	Safeway	182	51
mini milk	Wall's		35 per portion
non-dairy	Tesco	179	51
soft	Waitrose	155	46
soft scoop	Lyons Maid	181	51
	Safeway	169	50
	St Michael	183	52
	Wall's Blue Ribbon	90	90 per 1/40 4-litre pack
Vanilla King Cone	Lyons Maid		203 per cone
Vanilla real milk ice	Lyons Maid		50 each
Vanilla sandwich mix (as sold)	Tesco	417	118
Vanilla yogurt, French style	Littlewoods	102	153 per 150g pack
Veal			
cutlet, fried		215	61
fillet, raw		109	31
fillet, roast		230	65

Product	Brand	Calories per 100g/ 100ml	Calories per oz/ pack/ portion
jellied, canned		125	35
Veal, ham and egg slicing pie	Waitrose	221	63
Vegebanger			
herb	Real Eats	828	235
spicy	Real Eats	828	235
Vegeburger			
chilli	Real Eats	200	140 per 70g burger
herb and vegetable	Real Eats	200	140 per 70g burger
no salt	Real Eats	200	140 per 70g burger
Vegetable and beef soup			
dried	Batchelors	273	142 per 52g pint pack as sold
	Batchelors Cup-a-Soup	379	91 per 24g sachet as sold
dried, low calorie	Batchelors Slim-a-Soup	300	39 per 13g sachet
dried, with croutons	Batchelors Cup-a-Soup Special	373	97 per 26g pack as sold
low calorie	Heinz Weight Watchers	23	70 per 304g can
Vegetable and chicken stock cubes	Bovril	190	54
Vegetable and leek soup	Knorr	313	89

Product	Brand	Calories per 100g/ 100ml	Calories per oz/ pack/ portion
Vegetable and meat stock cubes	Bovril	200	57
Vegetable and pasta bake	St Michael	160	455 per pack
Vegetable and spicy sausage pizza	Tesco	225	64
Vegetable and steak pie	Fray Bentos	185	52
Vegetable and steak pie filling	Fray Bentos	115	33
Vegetable and steak pudding	Fray Bentos	215	61
Vegetable au gratin	Granose	100	350 per pack
	Heinz	70	211 per pack
Vegetable bake	St Michael	90	255 per pack
Vegetable Bolognese	Hera	333	94
Vegetable broth with beef	Granny's	35	23 as served
Vegetable burger mix	Boots	281	80
Vegetable chilli	Asda	92	
	Heinz		195 per pack
	St Michael	84	210 per pack
	Tesco	47	215 per pack
Vegetable chilli mix	Hera	350	99
Vegetable cubes	Knorr	308	87
Vegetable curry	Asda	155	

Product	Brand	Calories per 100g/ 100ml	Calories per oz/ pack/ portion
	Hera		695 per pack
	St Michael		265 per pack
	Tesco		290 per pack
with rice	Birds Eye		
	Menu Master		410 per pack
	Heinz		285 per pack
with basmati rice	Sainsbury's		550 per pack
Vegetable curry mix	Prewetts	297	84
Vegetable cutlet	St Michael	119	33 fried
Vegetable dhansak	Sainsbury's	130	390 per pack
Vegetable dip, fresh	St Michael	718	204
Vegetable drink	Knorr	248	70
Vegetable flan, fresh	St Michael	228	65
Vegetable goulash mix	Hera	352	100
	Prewetts Ready Meals	57	16
Vegetable juice	Prewetts	25	7
Vegetable lasagne	Birds Eye MenuMaster		365 per pack
	Prewetts Ready Meals		295 per pack
	Safeway trimrite Meals		260 per pack
	St Michael		215 per pack
	Waitrose	106	30

Product	Brand	Calories per 100g/ 100ml	Calories per oz/ pack/ portion
Vegetable mix traditional	Asda	60	
Vegetable moussaka	Heinz		157 per pack
	Sainsbury's		360 per pack
	Tesco		145 per pack
Vegetable oil		899	255
	Asda	899	
	Safeway	900	255
	Spry Crisp 'n' Dry	900	255
	Waitrose	900	266
pure solid	Waitrose	900	255
Vegetable pate	Granose	296	84
Vegetable pear: *see Cho cho*			
Vegetable Provencal mix	Prewetts	301	85
Vegetable salad	Eden Vale	141	40
	Heinz	152	43
	Littlewoods	146	41
	Safeway	208	59
	Tesco	122	35
in reduced calorie dressing	Tesco	76	22
mild	Eden Vale	208	59
other recipes	Tesco	98	28
Vegetable samosa	St Michael	186	53
	Waitrose	226	64

Product	Brand	Calories per 100g/ 100ml	Calories per oz/ pack/ portion
Vegetable sausage mix	Boots	468	133
Vegetable soup			
canned, ready to serve		37	10
	Campbell's Bumper Harvest	40	170 per 425g can
	Crosse & Blackwell	41	180 per 432g can
	Granny's	37	160 per 425g can
	Heinz Big Soups	39	170 per 435g can
	Heinz Weight Watchers	22	65 per 295g can
	Littlewoods	37	157 per 425g can
	Safeway	39	166 per 425g can
	Waitrose	44	187 per 425g can
condensed	Campbell's	67	205 per 300g can
low calorie	Waistline	22	6
	Waitrose	22	65 per 295g can
Vegetable stock cubes	Safeway	295	34 per 11.5g cube
Vegetable tikka masala	St Michael		220 per pack
Vegetable, yogurt, cheese and onion dip	Waitrose	311	88
Vegetarian Burgamix	Ranch House Meals	538	153
Vegetarian canelloni	Prewetts Ready Meals	103	29

Product	Brand	Calories per 100g/ 100ml	Calories per oz/ pack/ portion
Vegetarian casserole mix	Hera	351	100
Vegetarian cheese	Tesco	405	115
Vegetarian jumbo grills	Protoveg Menu	251	71
Vegetarian mince beef flavour	Direct Foods	273	77
natural flavour	Direct Foods	250	71
Vegetarian sizzles	Protoveg Menu	587	166
Vegetarian Tandoori cutlet mix	Tomorrow Foods	318	90
Velvet black cherry yoghurt	Safeway	98	147 per 150g pack
Velvet strawberry yoghurt	Safeway	99	149 per 150g pack
Velvet tropical yoghurt	Safeway	104	156 per 150g pack
Venison, roast		198	56
Vermicelli raw		355	101
	Buitoni	350	99
	Tesco	348	99
cooked	Tesco	104	29
Vermouth dry		118	33
sweet		151	43

Product	Brand	Calories per 100g/ 100ml	Calories per oz/ pack/ portion
Vesta meals (Batchelors): *see flavours*			
Vichyssoise	Baxters	53	230 per 425g can
	Tesco		185 per can
fresh	Sainsbury's		430 per tub
specialty soup	Crosse &		
	Blackwell	47	220 per 425g can
Victoria plum yoghurt			
low fat	Waitrose	85	128 per 150g pack
Victoria plums	Waitrose	80	23
in syrup	Asda	77	
Victoria sponge mix,			179 made up per
classic (as sold)	Green's	430	portion
Viennese chocolate			
sandwich biscuit	St Michael	510	145
Viennese whirls	Lyons	516	146
Viennetta			
mint	Wall's	232	65
original	Wall's	232	65
strawberry	Wall's	232	65
Vimto	Barr	26	85 per 330ml can
	Littlewoods	24	79 per 330ml can
Vinaigrette, reduced			
calorie	Kraft	88	26
Vinaigrette salad, diet	Eden Vale	33	9

Product	Brand	Calories per 100g/ 100ml	Calories per oz/ pack/ portion
Vindaloo Classic curry sauce	Homepride	118	452 per 383g pack
Vine leaves		15	4
Vinegar		4	1
all varieties	Boots	4	1
cider	Safeway	3	1
distilled	Safeway	4	1
malt	Safeway	4	1
	Waitrose	4	1
red wine	Safeway	7	2
white wine	Safeway	6	2
	St Michael	6	2
Vinegar and oil dressing, low calorie	Safeway	155	44
	Waistline	150	43
Vino bianco Prego sauce	Campbell's	43	12
Vintage orange marmalade	Baxters	248	70
Virginia sweetcorn soup	Knorr	368	104
Vitafood	Boots	445	126
Vodka			50 per 1/6 gill
Vol au vent pastry	Jus-Rol	393	111
Vol au vent pastry cases	Birds Eye		70 per case

W

Product	Brand	Calories per 100g/ 100ml	Calories per oz/ pack/ portion
Wafer Club biscuits	Jacobs	517	100 per biscuit
Wafers			
filled		535	152
	Safeway	505	143
milk chocolate	Littlewoods	530	104 per wafer
Waffles	Safeway	216	61
potato	Ross	190	54
Waldorf salad	Tesco	180	51
other recipes	Tesco	126	36
Walnut and apple salad	Safeway	114	32
Walnut and maple ice cream	Asda	206	
Walnut cheese spread, processed	St Michael	310	88
Walnut flavour cake mix (as sold)	Green's	399	259 made up per portion
Walnut halves	Whitworths	525	149
Walnut layer cake	Littlewoods	424	120
	Waitrose	372	105
Walnut sandwich	Sainsbury's	393	110
Walnut supreme ice cream	St Michael	239	68
Walnut thins	St Michael	504	143

Product	Brand	Calories per 100g/ 100ml	Calories per oz/ pack/ portion
Walnut Whip, milk chocolate			
coffee flavour	Rowntree Mackintosh	480	170 per whip
vanilla flavour	Rowntree Mackintosh	480	170 per whip
Walnut Whip, plain chocolate			
vanilla flavour	Rowntree Mackintosh	465	165 per whip
Walnut whips	St Michael	474	134
Walnuts		525	149
(with shells)		336	95
	Haywards	80	23
	Holland and Barrett	520	147
	Tesco	542	154
kernels	Littlewoods	525	149
shelled	Whitworths	525	149
Water biscuits		440	125
	Jacobs	394	31 per biscuit
	Safeway	394	8 per biscuit
	St Michael	395	112
	Tesco	412	117
high bake	Jacobs	394	31 per biscuit
	Safeway	390	111
high baked	Tesco	402	114
rich table	Jacobs	411	30 per biscuit
small	Safeway	394	5 per biscuit
thinner	Jacobs	387	27 per biscuit

Product	Brand	Calories per 100g/ 100ml	Calories per oz/ pack/ portion
Water chestnuts, canned, drained		49	14
Watercress			
raw		14	4
	Tesco	14	4
Water ice			
lemon	Bertorelli	109	31
orange	Bertorelli	110	31
raspberry	Bertorelli	101	29
Watermelon: *see Melon*			
Weetabix		340	96
	Weetabix	335	95
Weetaflakes	Weetabix	335	95
Weetaflakes 'n' raisin	Weetabix	345	98
Weight Watchers ice cream	Lyons Maid	97	27
Welsh rarebit		365	103
Wensleydale cheese: *see Cheese*			
West Countryman cheese	Dairy Crest	286	81
West Indian bread		284	81
Wheat			
bulgur	Holland and Barrett	370	105
cracked	Holland and Barrett	311	88

Product	Brand	Calories per 100g/ 100ml	Calories per oz/ pack/ portion
Wheat bran	Holland and Barrett	210	60
	Waitrose	248	70
Wheat crackers	Safeway	490	139
	Tesco	466	132
	Waitrose	454	129
with bran	Tesco	418	119
Wheat crispbread	Tesco	390	111
Wheat crunchies	Sooner	483	145 per 30g pack
	Waitrose	482	137
Wheat flakes	Holland and Barrett	343	97
	Waitrose	335	95
whole	Safeway	312	88
Wheatears	St Michael	432	122
Wheateats	Allinson	429	90 per 21g pack
Wheaten sweetmeal biscuits	St Michael	453	128
Wheatgerm	Holland and Barrett	230	65
natural	Jordans	325	92
stabilized	Boots Second Nature	379	107
Wheatgerm bread, sliced	Vitbe	230	65 per slice

Product	Brand	Calories per 100g/ 100ml	Calories per oz/ pack/ portion
Whelks			
boiled		91	26
boiled (with shells)		14	4
Whipped dairy cream tub dessert	Birds Eye	203	60
Whisky			50 per 1/6 gill
Whisky and American ginger ale	Britvic Drivers	31	57 per 180ml pack
White bread mix (as sold)	Granny Smiths	248	1190 per 480g pack made up
White Cap cooking fat	Van den Berghs	900	255
White chocolate	St Michael	172	49
White chocolate and croquant sticks	St Michael	565	160
White currants			
raw		26	7
stewed without sugar		22	6
stewed with sugar		57	16
White fish, dried, assorted, raw		148	42
White grape juice	Schloer	48	14
	Waitrose	59	17
sparkling	Schloer	49	15
White marzipan	Waitrose	408	116
White pudding		450	128

Product	Brand	Calories per 100g/ 100ml	Calories per oz/ pack/ portion
White rum and cola	Britvic Driver's		65 per 180ml bottle
White sauce			
savoury		151	43
sweet		172	49
White sauce, dessert	Ambrosia	97	27
White sauce mix	Safeway	366	104
Pour Over	Colman's	380	108
savoury	Knorr	360	102
White Stilton cheese: *see Cheese*			
White wine			
dry		66	19
medium		75	21
sparkling		76	22
sweet		94	27
White wine Cook in Sauce	Homepride	83	312 per 376g pack
White wine Cooking-in Sauce	Baxters	91	387 per 425g can
White wine sauce mix	Knorr	426	121
White wine vinegar	St Michael	6	2
Whitebait, fried		525	149
Whiting			
fried		191	54
fried (with bones)		173	49

Product	Brand	Calories per 100g/ 100ml	Calories per oz/. pack/ portion
steamed		92	26
steamed (with bones)		63	18
	Tesco	105	30
fillets	Ross	80	23
fillets	Young's	73	21
fillets, breaded	St Michael	118	33
ovencrisp	St Michael	238	67
smoked fillets	Ross	80	23
Whole grain mustard	Colman's	145	41
powder	Colman's	505	143
Whole green chillies in brine	Old El Paso	25	28 per 113g can
Whole milk yogurt			
natural, French	St Michael	68	19
set with mango	St Michael	103	29
Whole nut chocolates	Nestle	557	158
Wholegrain fruit muesli	Granose	408	116
Wholemeal/wholewheat bread: *see Bread*			
Wholemeal bran biscuits	Littlewoods	431	62 per biscuit
	Safeway		65 per biscuit
	St Michael		60 per biscuit
	Tesco		60 per biscuit
Wholemeal flour: *see Flour, wholemeal*			
Wholemeal food	Boots Second Nature	306	87

Product	Brand	Calories per 100g/ 100ml	Calories per oz/ pack/ portion
Wholemeal fruit and nut loaf mix (as sold)	Green's	370	150 made up per portion
Wholemeal mince pies	Waitrose	401	114
Wholemeal muffins	Sunblest Muffin Man	214	154 per muffin
Wholemeal scone mix, classic (as sold)	Green's	434	134 made up per portion
Wholemeal shortbread fingers	Tesco	505	143
	Waitrose	500	142
Wholemeal slab cake	Tesco	294	83
Wholemeal spaghetti	Holland and Barrett	350	99
Wholemeal toasties	Granose	407	115
Wholenut bar	Cadbury's	555	305 per 55g bar
Wholewheat breakfast biscuit cereal	Safeway	344	98
Wholewheat breakfast cereal	St Michael	333	94
Wholewheat cereal	Asda	335	
	Tesco	360	102
Wholewheat cereal biscuits	Waitrose	335	60 per biscuit
Wholewheat cheese crisps	Nature's Snack	550	110 per 20g pack

Product	Brand	Calories per 100g/ 100ml	Calories per oz/ pack/ portion
Wholewheat crispbread	Allinson		90 per biscuit
Wholewheat crisps	Nature's Snack	550	110 per 20g pack
Wholewheat flakes	Tesco	360	102
Wholewheat fruit munch biscuits	Moorlands		60 per biscuit
Wholewheat macaroni: *see Macaroni*			
Wholewheat muesli	Tesco	346	98
Wholewheat pasta shells in spicy tomato sauce	Heinz	65	18
Wholewheat pasta spirals	Signor Rossi	275	78
Wholewheat ravioli: *see Ravioli*			
Wholewheat spaghetti: *see Spaghetti*			
Wholewheat teabreak biscuits	Nabisco	388	30 per biscuit
Wholewheat with raisins	Kellogg's Nutrigrain	326	92
Wieners	Soyapro	210	60
Wild berry crumble ice cream	Safeway	233	69
Wild bramble jelly preserve	Baxters	255	72
Wine gums	Trebor Bassett	324	92

Product	Brand	Calories per 100g/ 100ml	Calories per oz/ pack/ portion
	Littlewoods	311	88
	St Michael	342	97
	Tesco	372	105
	Waitrose	342	97
mini	Tesco	381	108
Wine, red		68	19
Wine, white			
dry		66	19
sparkling		76	22
sweet		94	27
medium		75	21
Winkles			
boiled		74	21
boiled (with shell)		14	4
Wispa	Cadbury's	565	200 per 35g bar
Woodpecker cider	Bulmer	29	82 per half pint
dry	Bulmer	30	84 per half pint
Worcester apples	Tesco	46	13
Worcester sauce crisps	Christies	520	130 per 26g bag
	Hunters	520	130 per 26g bag
Worcestershire sauce			13 per tablespoon

Y

Product	Brand	Calories per 100g/ 100ml	Calories per oz/ pack/ portion
Yam			
boiled		119	34
raw		131	37
Yeast			
fresh		53	15
dried		169	48
Yeast extract	Waitrose	224	64
Yellow pepper, fresh	Tesco	35	10
Yellow Quick-Set Jel	Tesco	365	103
Yoga biscuits	St Michael	518	147
Yogurt: see also flavours			
Yoghurt, natural	Safeway	47	71 per 150g pack
Greek style		118	33
Whole milk, natural		78	22
Yogurt, French style all varieties	Eden Vale	87	25
Yogurt, natural set whole milk	Waitrose	75	113 per 150g pack
Yogurt, whole milk set with mango	St Michael	103	29
Yogurt and chive dressing	Heinz All Seasons	291	82
Yogurt and cucumber crisps, natural	Hedgehog	407	110 per 27g pack
Yogurt and gram flour raita		94	27

Product	Brand	Calories per 100g/ 100ml	Calories per oz/ pack/ portion
Yogurt coated nuts and fruit	Waitrose	570	162
Yogurt coated peanuts and raisins, no added sugar	Sunwheel	477	135
Yogurt coated peanuts, no added sugar	Sunwheel	559	158
Yogurt coated raisins	Tesco	451	128
no added sugar	Sunwheel	396	112
Yogurt coated snack bar			
banana	Sunwheel Kalibu	323	97 per 30g bar
raisin	Sunwheel Kalibu	340	102 per 30g bar
Yorkie			
almond	Rowntree Mackintosh	530	350 per 66g bar
milk chocolate	Rowntree Mackintosh	525	320 per 61g standard bar
raisin and biscuit	Rowntree Mackintosh	470	260 per 55g bar
Yorkshire pudding		215	61
Yorkshire pudding and pancake mix (as sold)	Granny Smiths	267	648 per 243g pack made up
	Whitworths	348	99
Yule log cake	Tesco	448	127
giant	Safeway	428	121

Product	Brand	Calories per 100g/ 100ml	Calories per oz/ pack/ portion
Zakuski	Phileas Fogg	487	136
Zucchini: *see Courgettes*			
Zucchini lasagne	Findus Lean Cuisine		250 per pack
Zywiecka	Waitrose	358	101